THE THEORY AND METHOD OF POLITICAL ANALYSIS

THE DORSEY SERIES IN POLITICAL SCIENCE

EDITOR NORTON E. LONG *Brandeis University*

MACRIDIS & BROWN *The De Gaulle Republic*

MACRIDIS & BROWN (eds.) *Comparative Politics: Notes and Readings* rev. ed.

DRAGNICH *Major European Governments*

ROBINSON *Congress and Foreign Policy-Making: A Study in Legislative Influence and Initiative*

JACOBINI *International Law: A Text*

MANGONE *The Elements of International Law: A Casebook*

GRIPP *Patterns of Soviet Politics*

MINAR *Ideas and Politics: The American Experience*

MEEHAN *The Theory and Method of Political Analysis*

THE THEORY AND METHOD OF POLITICAL ANALYSIS

EUGENE J. MEEHAN · RUTGERS UNIVERSITY

1965 · **THE DORSEY PRESS** · HOMEWOOD, ILLINOIS

First Printing, June, 1965

Library of Congress Catalog Card No. 65–22418

PRINTED IN THE UNITED STATES OF AMERICA

PREFACE

This volume is a by-product of a study of the influence of science on contemporary social and political thought, begun some years ago and not yet completed. As the study progressed, it became increasingly clear that the work being done in theory of inquiry, particularly by logicians and philosophers of science, was of enormous significance for political science, and indeed for all of the social sciences. That is, some knowledge of the nature and form of scientific explanation, of the meaning and use of scientific methods, techniques, and constructions, and of the various other aspects of scientific inquiry, is already an essential part of the intellectual equipment of any adequately trained political scientist and the need for this training seems very likely to increase rapidly in the near future. The political scientist has as much, if not more, need to be self-conscious about his methodology as the scientist. I do not mean that the political scientist must become a physical scientist; that is manifestly impossible. But every empirical inquiry, every effort to formulate explanations of empirical phenomena, every effort to construct empirical political or social theory, necessarily involves reference to the existing body of scientific knowledge or to the logic of scientific inquiry. Furthermore, even normative criticism of social policy is involved, indirectly, with questions on which science can in some degree pronounce. Science, methodology, or theory of inquiry is a matter of concern to everyone engaged in social or political inquiry.

Despite the importance of the topic, there is at present no source to which the political scientist can turn for information about those aspects of scientific inquiry that are germane to his own work. Even in the wider field of social science, no single work is completely satisfactory as an introduction to the subject matter. The aim here is to fill this gap in the literature by providing in a single volume a reasonably comprehensive discussion of the basic questions that arise in political inquiry and analysis. The book is intended primarily for advanced students in political science and for those who teach the subject, but it should also prove useful for other social scientists. Hopefully, the reader can obtain from the book some appreciation of the nature of contemporary science, some knowledge of the formal properties of scientific inquiry and of the reasons why scientific knowledge is preeminent in our time, and some appreciation of the desirability, and indeed necessity, of reproducing these same qualities in his own discipline. In the penultimate chapter, I have tried to indicate in a preliminary way some of the points at which modern science will impinge upon normative political or social philosophy, though it must immediately be said that the discussion is only partial and much remains to be done in this area. In every case, the value and usefulness of scientific standards have been tempered by reference to the limits of their applicability in the social sciences and particularly in the study of politics, and to the conditions that must be satisfied before scientific inquiry can be adapted to the study of human society. Methodological self-consciousness is a necessary tool, but it is not a panacea and it would be tragic if anyone sought to elevate it into a dogma through misunderstanding.

In any sustained inquiry, one accumulates enormous obligations, personal and intellectual, and prefaces provide a suitable opportunity for acknowledging them. My students have for a number of years borne with my excursions into methodology with grace and even with lively interest and for that I am grateful for I have learned much trying to answer their questions. My wife, who has endured with dignity and fortitude the endless hours of silence that necessarily accompany book production, can never be suitably recompensed. Various publishers have kindly allowed me to quote from their publications and these debits are suitably acknowledged in the body of the text. A number of persons read various drafts of the manuscript and offered invaluable suggestions and critcisms, notably professors Robert Bierstedt of New York University and Joseph Murphy of Brandeis University. The editor of this series, Professor Norton E. Long of Brandeis University, made a number of very useful suggestions for expanding the manuscript into its present form. None of these persons bears any responsibility for the content of the book, of course, nor do they necessarily endorse or approve what I have said. Responsibility for the book is mine alone.

Finally, there is the pleasant duty of recording the extent of my obligations to a former colleague—Edward McNall Burns. His careful reading of the manuscript uncovered a number of errors and suggested various revisions. More important, he provided that continuous support and encouragement from a respected source that is so necessary for the consummation of a prolonged and at times dreary investigation. To him this book is gratefully dedicated.

EUGENE J. MEEHAN

New Brunswick, New Jersey
May, 1965

TABLE OF CONTENTS

CHAPTER ONE

INTRODUCTION

EVERY form of human inquiry, whether it is directed toward the properties of living organisms or the structure and function of the inanimate portions of the natural universe, or to the individual and social life of man himself, depends ultimately upon a substructure of assumptions relating to the criteria of evidence employed in the enterprise, the validity of the techniques and methods applied in the inquiry (judged according to the criteria of evidence that have been adopted), and the modes of reasoning by which the conclusions are affirmed or supported. Systematic human thought quite literally and necessarily implies a methodological foundation, and every attempt at intellectual criticism that moves beyond the bare confutation of data necessarily involves some reference to the terms of this substructure. Thought may proceed unaware of the methodological assumptions on which it rests; it cannot proceed without the assumptions themselves.

So much granted, it would appear that a careful examination of the methodological assumptions of any given discipline is an essential part of its development. Yet the problem has been ignored, for the most part, by political scientists; there is, at the time of writing, no book on the methodology of political science, though various volumes touch upon the subject peripherally. Further, the role of methodology in the teaching of political science is slight. Students enter and leave graduate school without even the most primitive kind of training in this area, even without any conscious realization of its importance.

Scope and methods courses which offer a general introduction to the principal subfields in political science, and perhaps to major recent writings in such fields, are no substitute for a rigorous examination of the fundamental assumptions of the discipline and the problems arising therefrom. In many cases, techniques, methods, and assumptions have been borrowed from other disciplines, notably sociology, without sufficient regard for the conditions required to validate the transfer. And finally, it must be said that the understandable tendency for subject matter specialists to concern themselves with the operational results of research and study that bear most directly upon the subject matter often leads to a minimization of concern with formal and logical aspects of the discipline, and even to disdain for those who devote their time to such questions. In a society like the United States, where concern for results is deeply ingrained into the value structure of society, it is only too easy to succumb to vulgar pragmatism.

The position taken by many of the physical scientists on methodological questions tends to bolster this negative attitude to some degree. It is reasonably clear that the social sciences will, in the near future, tend to develop  along the lines that have already been laid down by the physical sciences—indeed, it is one of the purposes of this book to urge political scientists to do precisely that. But the physical scientist is not, as a rule, overly concerned with methodological questions. The extensive development of the methodology of science in this century has been the work of philosophers of science and not working scientists. Many scientists are openly hostile and even contemptuous in their attitude toward philosophy of science. Ought the working political scientist to follow his colleague in physics and simply continue his research unencumbered by a lot of logical limitations whose relevance he does not see?

To put the question in this guise is to mistake the problem. The physical scientist *has,* whether he realizes it or not, a well-developed methodology which he acquires along with his other training. The function of the philosopher of science is simply to make explicit what is already implicit in the scientist's working practices. He discovers, and clarifies; he does not produce. For the political scientist, who does not have a methodology clearly implied in his work and training, it would be foolish indeed to ignore the valuable fund of knowledge that the philosophers of science have accumulated. The task is to translate this information into a form that is useful for the political scientist.

PURPOSE OF THE TEXT

The aim of the book, in these terms, is to determine what is valuable and useful for political science in the methods of investigation and explanation employed in science, and to inquire into the extent to which it is possible, desirable, or even necessary to cast the study of politics in the same mold. We are concerned with the nature of science only to the extent that it helps us define the qualities that political science ought to possess. The book does not pretend to be a contribution to science or to philosophy of science, though the extent of its indebtedness to the latter will be apparent on every page. It is not exhaustive, but seeks to deal only with a few of the prime areas of methodology, selected for their importance to political science and not to philosophy of science. It is assumed, without argument, that political science is a distinct and worthwhile enterprise in its own right, with significant and attainable goals, hence that the integrity and autonomy of the discipline should be maintained. Nothing would be gained, so far as I can determine,

and much would be lost if political science were dissolved and its practitioners converted into biologists or physiologists, or even into sociologists and psychologists. There are political problems, and phenomena that are clearly political; these problems and phenomena require explanation and justification on their own accounts.

The book should not be construed as either an attack on or a defense of what is called "behavioralism" in political science. In general, I am inclined to believe that political science has gained a great deal from the work of those who call themselves by this label. The active search for new modes of inquiry, new theoretical structures for handling the available data, new explanatory systems, new facets of the ancient phenomena of political activity to explore, and new techniques and methods for exploring them has been at least partly successful; it would be unwise to discard and inhibit so salutary an influence.

The attack on "traditional" political science, carried out chiefly in the name of "behavioralism," has forced a long overdue examination of first principles. True, the gains must at times be balanced against excesses of enthusiasm for particular methods and techniques that have led to extremism, for example, unjustified and uncritical claims for particular techniques like the mathematical theory of games or the "systems theory approach." But the modern propensity for intellectual fads has been scolded often enough, and it is in any case not limited to political science. Even a perfectly legitimate methodological requirement like empiricism has, at times, been abused through the failure of those urging its adoption to realize its limitations when applied to human society. And, occasionally, the clash with tradition has seemingly generated an attitude of mind that assumed it was somehow more important to discover new techniques or invent new terms than to produce significant and meaningful assertions about real political problems. All this can be granted to the enemies of "behavioralism" without in the least impugning the value of its contribution. Extremism is, after all, a commonplace in most new enterprises, and perhaps most especially in those which attack the old order. The war on tradition calls forth the "pioneering spirit," foments intense loyalties and hatreds, and opens the door to martyrdom. It also generates a smugness among the initiates that is extremely irritating to those who do not share its principles. Doubtless, these features of "behavioralism" account—in some measure—for the vigor with which it has been attacked in recent years. But all this is beside the point, and too much of the attack has been *ad hominem*. It is the principle, and not the manner of its expression, that matters here.

The point is that political science does not have an implicit methodology waiting discovery; the methodology must be created *de novo*. The claim that political science, as an academic discipline, had, and has, faults in urgent need of correction must be granted at once; they are obvious, numerous, and irritating. Very often, too often perhaps, the student of politics begins his studies with a set of assumptions and a *modus operandi* that differ only in detail from those employed by Hobbes and Locke, or even Plato and Aristotle. For some political scientists, at least, and for most textbook authors, modern science—and modern philosophy—might just as well not exist. This is tragic, for the tools that science and philosophy have developed in this century have made mincemeat of many of the older presuppositions of political science, and produced standards and techniques of very high quality that can be employed in their stead.

A bare beginning has been made in the use of this armory against the problems of politics, but much remains to be done. The terminology of politics, to give an illustration, teems with ambiguities and imprecisely defined categories, with mystique, with religious overtones, all august remnants of an age when philosophy and religion were one and philosophy was everything—the mother of sciences. Modern analytic techniques, though they cannot offer "final" solutions to our problems, can most certainly provide the tools needed to clarify the nature of the enterprise, and stabilize the search for reliable knowledge; they have not been used to full advantage within the discipline. The failure of political scientists to conform to even the more elementary rules of logic is notorious, except among political scientists, and the "classic" political writings are spattered generously with unverified assumptions, unwarranted inferences, untenable data, and plain bad argument, often couched in language that is most sententious. Robert A. Dahl has shown how much can be done in this area by closely reasoned analysis.[1] Further, there are still powerful fragments remaining of the rather sterile historicism that dominated political philosophy for many centuries, despite the work of rigorous analysts like Karl Popper.[2] To put the complaint succinctly, the output of political science has been unsystematic, of indifferent quality, often trivial, and sometimes diletantish. Generations of scholars have seemingly failed to produce the kind of solid foundation on which the scholar of the present day could build with confidence. The edifice we now teach is, in part, beyond repair and worthy only of destruction. These conditions, among others, have made it difficult to attract first-rate minds to the field; it has been a very long time, for example, since a really good mathematician turned his attention to political problems. In sum, political science can quite reasonably be held to lie in a shocking state of disrepair. This implies only a program of rebuilding, without any commitment to a particular approach to the problem, and indeed without any necessary assumption that the goal can be fulfilled.

[1] Robert A. Dahl, *A Preface to Democratic Theory* (Chicago: University of Chicago Press, 1956).

[2] Karl R. Popper, *The Poverty of Historicism* (London: Routledge and Kegan Paul, 1957).

THE APPEAL TO SCIENCE

It is hardly surprising to find that those who attacked traditional political science did so in the name of science, and borrowed from the sciences many of the weapons used in the attack. Science is commonly held, not always with complete justification, to possess those attributes that political science so clearly lacks—clarity, precision, predictability, etc. American culture in particular tends to accept the qualitative superiority of the physical sciences over the social sciences and the humanities almost as a matter of course; this is one of the Baconian "Idols of the Theatre" inherited with the language and strongly reinforced by the educational system. Further, the physical sciences were, in fact, very closely associated with the intellectual upheaval—early in this century—that played so large a part in the extension of emphasis upon methodological considerations in general. And, of course, science has enormous achievements to its credit and it seems only reasonable to suppose that other disciplines could share in these accomplishments by suitable emulation and borrowing. Finally, the very nature of academia in the United States has pressed the social scientist in the direction of the sciences, ostensibly, if not in terms of genuine performance. Showers of gold have rained down on the scientists from both public and private sources since the "Age of Research Teams" and the "Era of the Giant Foundation" began in the 1940's. The key to research funds, all too often, has been the degree of "scientism" embodied in the description of the proposed research program, and the practical results envisioned by the author of that program. Since funds imply prestige, time for independent study, more graduate assistants, and hence more freedom, the poverty-stricken social scientists quite reasonably sought to exploit this great natural resource with means calculated by a cool appraisal of the road to success that others employed. Acting in the name of "sci-

ence," whatever the meaning attached to the term, became almost an act of self-preservation.

Under the circumstances, we could expect to find that the term "science" has been appropriated to all manner of uses for which it is in fact ill suited, and that has certainly been the case. By and large, social scientists have used the term chiefly as an honorific, as a means of assigning status or ascribing worth and not as a carefully defined set of qualities that identify a particular mode of intellectual activity. The first task, then, is to arrive at a reasonably adequate definition of "science" which can be taken as a point of departure for the study. Here, fortunately, the philosophers of science have charted a course through the maze for others to follow. In fact, the meaning of "science" is perhaps more fully and formally defined in philosophy of science than among scientists themselves—a condition that is not without its dangers. For the most part, we will follow the philosophers of science in their construction of the meaning of the term "science," but with some due regard for the pronouncements of working scientists where these are available.

Can political science be confined within bounds set by the physical sciences? To the extent that the aims of political scientists go beyond the functions of science, the answer is "No!" But a large part of political science is directed toward goals that are common to all forms of inquiry. The essence of "science," according to philosophy of science, is the explanation of empirically defined phenomena by relating them in ordered patterns. Political scientists may perform other tasks, normative criticism of political actions, for example, which require different methods and criteria of argument, but to the extent that they seek explanations of empirical phenomena they can, and should, follow the scientists. It is one thing to demand autonomy of inquiry and quite another matter to argue for autonomy of method.[3]

[3] This point is treated beautifully by Abraham Kaplan, *The Conduct of Inquiry: Methodology for Behavioral Science* (San Francisco: Chandler Publishing Co., 1964), chap. 1.

The logic of explanation holds good whatever the subject matter under investigation, and the mode of explanation used in science is valid for any discipline. Although the standards of evidence accepted by physical science may have to be weakened in political science, and political scientists may feel that they are responsible for the exercise of critical functions that physical science need not employ, the canons of logic employed in science are quite appropriate for political science, and in fact cannot be faulted without invalidating the inquiry.[4]

THE REVOLUTION IN METHODOLOGY

The present agitation over methodology in political science is chiefly, if not entirely, an outgrowth of developments in science, mathematics, and philosophy that can be traced to the early part of this century. Since this very broad intellectual movement supplies the perspective in which an adequate appraisal of the relationship between the methodological needs of physical and social science, respectively, can be made, a brief survey of the salient features of that development may help to clarify the aims and purposes of the book, and place the problem of comparative methodology in its proper light.

It is not too much to say that an intellectual "revolution" took place around the beginning of the twentieth century, brought about mainly through certain massive and fundamental developments in physical science, mathematics, and logic. The full consequences of the revolution are still being explored, and in fact "lived out," for it is far from having run its full course. One of its more profound effects has been a drastic revision of the standards used to judge the validity of intellectual activity or the results of intellectual inquiry—of the content of methodology. New techniques for acquir-

[4] Cf. Ernest Nagel, *The Structure of Science* (New York: Harcourt Brace and World, 1961), chaps. xiii-xv. Nagel does not point out that *what can be accomplished* depends greatly on the subject matter.

ing knowledge, new criteria for judging the validity of claims to the possession of knowledge, and new analytic tools for refining the meaning of terms and raising the level of precision of logical inference were introduced more or less concurrently. Most of the early work was carried out by men intimately connected with science, logic, and mathematics: Bertrand Russell, Ernest Mach, Pierre Duhem, C. S. Peirce, Moritz Schlick, for example; or, somewhat later, Ludwig Wittgenstein, Rudolph Carnap, Morris Cohen, Ernest Nagel, A. J. Ayer, and C. G. Hempel. They were also, for the most part, interested in philosophy, either professionally or as a corollary to their professional interests. The training and interests of this early group tended to set the pattern of work in the 1920's and 1930's; it led, directly or indirectly, to both the philosophy of science and to the various branches of empirical or analytic philosophy. In fact, the dominant philosophic trend in both the United States and Britain, as well as Scandinavia, is still supplied from this same initial impetus. It is marked by concern for precise meaning and syntactical analysis, for logical analysis of terms and relationships and, above all, for the foundations of the claim to knowledge.

It would be inappropriate to undertake here a detailed discussion of the nature and significance of the actual changes in science, logic, and mathematics that constitute the "revolution" to which I have been referring; that is best left to the historians and philosophers of science. Suffice it to say that in science the rigid construction of the universe implied in Newtonian mechanics was abandoned under the impact of quantum theory and relativity theory. The deterministic, mechanistic world view of men like LaPlace (who believed that, given the position and velocity of every particle in the universe, it was theoretically possible to predict the future of the entire system) was replaced by a probabilistic interpretation of natural phenomena, and there was a growing recognition of the part played by the human observer in the ordering of the universe and its parts.

Both science and philosophy benefited enormously from a series of major developments in mathematics and logic. The powerful intellectual tools developed by mathematicians like Russell and Whitehead made possible the growth of modern philosophy of science and provided the foundation for modern analytic or empirical philosophy. The methodology of the sciences was subjected to a searching investigation, largely because a somewhat rigid positivistic outlook tended to construe philosophy as the handmaiden of science rather than a normative activity. And a sustained attack on traditional philosophy, particularly ontology and metaphysics, reduced a surprising number of problems hitherto considered of the first order to piles of meaningless semantic rubble.

This twentieth century attempt to place human knowledge on a sound logical–empirical base marked a fundamental swing of the philosophic pendulum away from the great metaphysical system builders of the nineteenth century. Obviously, it had roots in the past, particularly in the writings of Comte and his followers, in the works of Darwin and his interpreters, and above all in the work of David Hume. Positively, it was an effort to keep philosophy within the bounds of science; negatively, it was a revolt against the influence of the Romantics, the Idealists, the neo-Platonists, and the Marxists. Traditional metaphysics became the special bête noire of the "new" philosophers, particularly the rigid logical positivists in the so-called Vienna Circle. Indeed, it appeared at times that some members of that group were more concerned to exclude metaphysics from philosophy than to accomplish anything positive by philosophic activity.

The new philosophy offered its followers a rather Spartan diet for the mind, an ascetic philosophic ideal. The search for massive intellectual constructions of the Kantian sort was replaced by a search for particular answers to specific, limited questions; the approach was piecemeal, and heavily laced with strict logical analysis. Actually, a number of disparate strands were combined in a single movement—empiricism, mathematical logic, linguistic analysis, skepticism, naturalism, and even "scientism." No single characterization provides an adequate summation for every member of the new school and no person can really be considered "typical." Bertrand Russell, who provided much of the initial impetus for the new philosophy, soon parted company with the continental positivists. Ludwig Wittgenstein, whose *Tractatus* was a "bible" for continental positivism in the 1930's, never took an active part in the meetings of local philosophic circles like the Vienna group. Some of the "new" philosophers remained consistent; others changed position from time to time. There were fierce quarrels and considerable differences in emphasis. Some relied heavily on severe formal analysis and the development of logical languages, others relied on everyday language seeking to eliminate ambiguities and explore meanings. There were "radicals" and "conservatives," and they fought at times with that bitterness and rancour that often invests academic quarrels.

Despite their differences, what was agreed among the new philosophers was fundamental and decisive. Traditional conceptions of philosophy were abandoned. Philosophy was conceived as an exercise in the clarification of meaning, carried out by rigorous logical analysis. Empiricism was firmly enforced as the only possible epistemic base for human knowledge. Kant's conception of a priori knowledge was demolished. A close alliance between philosophy and physics was established. Moral philosophers of the logical–empirical school left off discussing concrete proposals for ameliorating the life of man or relating it to any spiritual absolute and concentrated on the analysis of the terms used in moral propositions. It is quite impossible to do justice to so rich and fruitful a movement in a few short sentences; we must concentrate on those aspects of the development of the new philosophy most relevant to the task in hand.

The immediate consequences of the application of this new conception of philosophizing were most gratifying. Immense piles of philosophic rubbish, accumulated from over two millenia of speculation, were speedily dissolved by its cauterizing touch. Traditional philosophy was subjected to a ruthless attack and forced to defend its own first principles for perhaps the first time since the speculative genius of the Greeks ran dry. All this was to the good, but there were also excesses and irregularities. The desire to be free of metaphysics sometimes led to extreme scientism on the order of John B. Watson's futile and disastrous effort to force psychology into the Procrustean bed of strict empiricism.

The sharp decline in moral philosophy in the twentieth century was, at least partly, an outcome of the influence of logical–empirical philosophic standards, as was the serious decline in speculation in the social sciences and the humanities. The enterprise became the victim of the methodology. This does not mean to imply that the exponents of logical empiricism were or are cold and inhuman monsters without the slightest trace of warmth and human sympathy, nor even that they sought to reduce philosophy to the mechanical calculation of logical consequences, ignoring the fact of human emotions. Logical empiricism was concerned to change the point of emphasis in philosophy from concern with the nature and destiny of man to concern with the nature of philosophy, and succeeded in shifting that emphasis from content to method and methodology.

For once philosophy is defined as the explanation and clarification of propositions, the kind of activity in which philosophers will engage, the types of questions that philosophers will seek to answer, is largely determined. The prime task becomes the making of distinctions between knowledge and nonsense, which in turn involves making precise distinctions in meaning and establishing in highly formal terms the validity of particular inferences based on these distinctions. The redeeming feature of what appears as essentially a Neo–Scholastic outlook was a firm insistence on the need to reason from an empirical base. It was asserted, often quite dogmatically, that propositions which could not be verified by reference to empirical observation, defined with varying degrees of severity, were either meaningless or empty. A predilection for empirical fact led reasonably enough to a concern with physical science, and to the use of physics as virtually a paradigm for the accumulation of human knowledge. Indeed, one branch of European empiricism for a time proclaimed that the sole function of philosophy was to analyze and explain scientific propositions, though that position ultimately proved untenable. The belief that philosophy should retain very intimate connections with science and logic remains, however, a powerful influence in most branches of empirical philosophy even today, and of course dominates philosophy of science. Science, as it were, provides the criteria by which modes of inquiry and claims to knowledge are judged. This can be a salutory influence, provided that it is coupled with a willingness to grant the essential autonomy of all disciplines. In fact, that is the attitude strongly urged throughout this book. If, however, one insists that every inquiry must achieve the precision of physics or chemistry or abdicate intellectual status, then the requirement is stultifying and cannot be enforced.

SCIENTIFIC PHILOSOPHY AND POLITICAL SCIENCE

The point that commands our attention here is the significance of these standards of inquiry for political science. It is almost unthinkable that future generations of political scientists will not be profoundly influenced in their work by what has already been accomplished in philosophy, philosophy of science, and physical science. In the near future, if the signs of the present can be interpreted correctly, we can expect the political scientist to frame his goals, conduct his inquiries, and evaluate his findings using the framework molded by analytic philosophy and philosophy of science, at least in those cases where the goal is explanation of empirical phenomena. In fact, it is a major criticism of contemporary political science that it has thus far failed to absorb the intellectual standards available in philosophy of science as rapidly as it might. It is commonplace today that assertions made by social science that contravene scientific data must give way to the latter, and rightly so. The major argument against Freud's theory of the influence of inherited archaic memory traces on human behavior, for example, is that it does not agree with accepted theories in genetics, and that failure seems to me to be fatal. Similarly, when the quality of the reasoning employed in social inquiry fails to meet the standards of reasoning established in science and philosophy it cannot hope to command the unqualified assent of the intellectual community. In many cases, too many for comfort really, it is quite impossible for the political scientist to approach the qualitative standards of science or empirical philosophy, and in such cases it would be foolish to reproach him for not doing so. But that political scientists ought to *try* to achieve these standards, without elevating them into a dogma, seems beyond dispute.

It is worth emphasizing, in this context, that the reason why political scientists ought to make a serious effort to learn from the physical scientists and philosophers of science is not that political science would in some mysterious fashion become "more scientific," but that the quality of political science could thereby be improved. The intellectual tools developed in philosophy and science are immensely more powerful than the common-sense reasoning employed in everyday life. Logic, after all, is not limited to the formulation of axiomatic systems patterned on Euclidian geometry. As Ernest Nagel has pointed out, there is a wider meaning of the term "logic" that has significance for every academic discipline, whatever its subject matter:

In this wider meaning, the task of logic is to make explicit the structures of methods and assumptions employed in the search for reliable knowledge in all fields of inquiry. Logic so construed seeks to evaluate the connecting links by whose means the flying moments of thought may become essential elements in the achievement of trustworthy beliefs. So understood, logic articulates the principles implicit in responsible critiques of cognitive claims; but it also assesses the authority of such principles, and weighs the merits even of special postulates and intellectual tools that may be used in quests for knowledge.[5]

Construed in this manner, logic is essential in every inquiry, and without logic there is no way in which the propositions asserted by a discipline can be related, tested, or made more meaningful. Every academic discipline must conduct its own investigations, develop its own explanatory principles, and evolve patterns of explanation appropriate to the subject matter, but the logic of explanation employed in the inquiry does not change with the subject matter.

Having agreed that political science will be influenced in a vital way by the impact of the standards of inquiry that philosophy and science have developed, and concurred in the view that this influence should be healthy, it remains to emphasize once again the fact that there are limits to the extent of that influence which must be respected. I am not prepared to eliminate the study of politics in the interests of science, to paraphrase Churchill's famous statement about the British Empire. The goal must be a program of action for political science that will take advantage of the refinements in methodology and method that science has produced and still carry out the tasks that define political science as an academic discipline. If legitimate inquiries in political science would be stultified by the imposition of rigid methodological standards, then those standards must be eased and the work allowed, indeed encouraged, to continue. After all, if the standards were defined rigidly enough, the political scientist could do nothing whatever.

[5] Ernest Nagel, *Logic Without Metaphysics* (Glencoe, Ill.: The Free Press, 1956), p. ix.

However, the limits must be established knowingly, and not simply as a matter of convenience; exceptions must have reasons, and the consequences of the exception need to be kept in mind. It is the aim of the book to demonstrate some of the possibilities that inhere in the use of scientific standards of inquiry in political science and at the same time to indicate where some of the major limits lie. For that reason, an historical description of the changes that have taken place in political science in recent decades, as a consequence of the effort to borrow from the sciences, would be inadequate.[6] What is needed at the present time is a clear statement of the principles on which legitimate scientific activity rests, and an evaluation of the applicability of specific features of scientific method and methodology to inquiry in the field of political science. The statement that follows is, therefore, both prescriptive and critical and not simply descriptive—and it contains a substantial polemic. This can cause little harm so long as we realize that there can be no "final word" in such matters, for terms of that sort are out of place in this context; the book is meant as an aid and stimulant to discussion and not as an historical summation.

In general, I have avoided reference to specific political problems or research efforts, hoping, by framing the study in broad and abstract terms, to avoid the bottomless pit of *ad hominem* argument and academic provincialism. The reader can compensate easily for the absence of concrete illustrations by referring to specific studies in his own particular field. Even examples and illustrations are used sparingly, for there is always the danger that the principle will be argued in terms of the illustration and not the converse. I have tried particularly to avoid the "behavioralist"—"nonbehavioralist" controversy wherever possible. Discussion couched in these terms can only lead to polemic until such time as "behavioralism" can be defined with sufficient precision to make discussion of principles a real possibility. That

[6] Those interested in this question should consult Bernard Crick, *The New Science of Politics* (Berkeley: University of California Press, 1959).

is not presently the case. Some of those who use the term identify "behavioralism" with particular techniques like quantification, or the use of statistics. In other cases, "behavioralism" is equated with empiricism, vaguely and crudely defined. And in many cases the term is simply a synonym for "being scientific," without assigning any specific meaning to the process, or for some particular "approach" to the study of political phenomena. There is no consensus. It may be that the conception of political science that emerges here will prove acceptable, in whole or in part, to many of those who count themselves members of the "behavioral" school, and it may be that opponents of "behavioralism" will find points to their liking. In either case, that is totally irrelevant. The task is to examine the viability of a particular set of standards when applied to a particular kind of enterprise.

Finally, the reader who is seeking an answer to the question, "How can political science be made into a science?" will be disappointed. Although this book is concerned with the influence of a development occurring mainly within science or philosophy of science, no attempt will be made to deal with the question as it is here framed. Social science texts, and even professional monographs, usually pay lip service to the current prestige and status of the sciences in their introductory discussions, most frequently by alluding to the necessity for, or merits of, some alleged "scientific method"—crudely defined. For the most part, such discussions have as their chief purpose the assignment of honorific status to particular topics, particular methods, or even particular persons, not infrequently related to the authorship of the text in question. The fact is that there is no "scientific method," except, perhaps, in a sense so broad that it could not be the possession of the natural or physical sciences alone; the scientific method is a chimera pure and simple. The inquiry undertaken here can be construed as an answer to a question, certainly, but the question takes quite a different form, to wit, "Considering what has occurred in science and philosophy in the past half century, what sort of discipline ought political science to be and what sorts of things can and should political scientists do, or abstain from doing, without regard to what is current practice in the discipline?"

In this context, it is worth noting that the inability of political scientists to employ the standards and criteria that science applies, which appears frequently in the pages that follow, is not necessarily a tragedy. Science is no godhead, and the term alone confers no particular sanction on objects, methods, epistemology, or practitioners. To know that "X is a scientist," and to know nothing else is to know very little indeed. One may study witchcraft employing the criteria that are considered necessary to establish science, though we may doubt that the enterprise will produce any substantial findings. It is also possible to make use of the most precise of scientific instruments in a very sloppy manner, thereby invalidating any results that may be achieved. The fact that X performs his work in a laboratory is certainly no guarantee of results, as my own recollection of undergraduate days assures me. One may be an empiricist and yet not be a scientist, though in professional life, at least, the converse is not true. And the fact that X is a working scientist confers no special status on either the man or his output. In particular, the fact of being a scientist has no implications whatever regarding the individual's competence in politics. Some scientists are stupid, bigoted, and dogmatic; many are not. Some men are good scientists, some are poor scientists, doubtless some are hopelessly incompetent, and, hopefully, some are superb. In an age when the opinions of well-proportioned females who perform in motion pictures or on television are actively sought on all manner of topics, it may seem heresy to assert that no physical scientist has anything to say about politics that is worth hearing merely by virtue of his occupational status, yet there is no reason whatever to suppose otherwise. Indeed, the writings of some of the scientists who have ventured into the political arena attest all too clearly to this simple but easily forgotten fact, and it bears repetition. The extent to which political science can and should be guided by the precepts of the scientists depends always on the needs of political science and not on the needs of science. The use that can be made of these principles must be established independently of the sciences. We begin, in the chapter that follows, with an attempt to define the salient characteristics of the kind of activity that is designated science. The choice of starting point is at least partly determined by the manner in which the point is phrased in contemporary discussion. We could begin quite easily with the question, "Given the present state of human knowledge, what is the best way for political scientists to conduct their inquiries into political phenomena?" The result would be the same in either case.

BIBLIOGRAPHICAL NOTE

A fairly substantial body of literature dealing with political science as a discipline has appeared in recent years, much of it directed toward the "scope and methods" of political science or the special problems raised by "behavioralism." Those particularly concerned with methodology include Abraham Kaplan's *The Conduct of Enquiry* (Chandler, 1964), Quentin Gibson's *The Logic of Social Enquiry* (Routledge and Kegan Paul, 1960), and W. G. Runciman's *Social Science and Political Theory* (Cambridge University Press, 1963)—the former two being the more useful. Herbert J. Storing's (ed.) *Essays on the Scientific Study of Politics* (Holt, Rinehart, and Winston, 1962) is an attempt to deal critically with current use of scientific techniques in political science; it was rather roughly handled by the critics. Bernard Berelson's (ed.) *The Behavioral Sciences Today* (Harper Torchbooks, 1963) contains some interesting essays, and Heinz Eulau's *The Behavioral Persuasion in Politics* (Random House, 1963) suggests both the strength and the weaknesses of the behavioral commitment. Maurice Duverger's *An Introduction to the Social Sciences: With Special Reference to Their Methods* (Praeger, 1964), a reprint of the 1959 edition, is worth consulting, as is Arnold Brecht's massive *Political Theory: The Foundations of Twentieth Century Thought* (Princeton University Press, 1959).

Less formal, but more directly concerned with political science, are David Easton's *The Political System* (Alfred Knopf, 1953); Bernard Crick's *The American Science of Politics* (University of California Press, 1959); Charles S. Hyneman's *The Study of Politics* (University of Illinois Press, 1959); Vernon Van Dyke's *Political Science: A Philosophical Analysis* (Stanford University Press, 1960), which most closely resembles the present work; Roland Young (ed.), *Approaches to the Study of Politics* (Northwestern University Press, 1958); James C. Charlesworth (ed.), *The Limits of Behavioralism in Political Science* (American Academy of Political and Social Science, 1962), and *Mathematics and the Social Sciences* (American Academy of Political and Social Science, 1963); and Harold Lasswell, *The Future of Political Science* (Atherton Press, 1963).

For an interesting comparison between the British and American outlooks on political science, see David Butler, *The Study of Political Behavior* (Hutchinson University Library, 1958); Peter Winch, *The Idea of a Social Science* (Routledge and Kegan Paul, 1958); Maurice Cowling, *The Nature and Limits of Political Science* (Cambridge University Press, 1963), and Bernard Crick, *In Defense of Politics,* or Michael Oakeshott, *Rationalism in Politics and Other Essays* (Methuen, 1962). Compare, for example, with Robert A. Dahl, *Modern Political Analysis* (Prentice–Hall, 1963); but see Andrew Hacker, *The Study of Politics* (McGraw–Hill, 1963), for yet another point of view.

Among the relatively rare attempts to apply linguistic analysis to the problems of political science, T. D. Weldon's *Vocabulary of Politics* (Penguin, 1953), Thomas L. Thorsen's *Logic of Democracy* (Holt, Rinehart, and Winston, 1962), and Robert A. Dahl's *Preface to Democratic Theory* (University of Chicago Press, 1956) are outstanding.

On the "new" philosophy, see in particular A. J. Ayer's *Logical Positivism* (The Free Press, 1951), J. O. Urmson's *Philosophical Analysis: Its Development between the Two World Wars* (Oxford University Press, 1956), Gilbert Ryle's (ed.) *The Revolution in Philosophy* (Macmillan, 1957), and Joergen Joergensen's *The Development of Logical Empiricism* (University of Chicago Press, 1959). Joergensen's book is Volume II, Number 9 of the International Encyclopedia for a Unified Science, published by the University of Chicago Press, hereafter abbreviated as IEUS with appropriate volume and number citations. Richard von Mises' *Positivism* (Harvard University Press, 1951) is an interesting personal interpretation of modern trends in empirical philosophy, and Victor Kraft's *The Vienna Circle* (Philosophical Library, 1953) deals specifically with the continental version of logical empiricism in the period between the two wars. Edgar Zilsel's *The Development of Rationalism and Empiricism,* IEUS, Vol. II, No. 8 (University of Chicago Press, 1941) is also useful, as is Ernest Nagel's *Logic Without Metaphysics* (The Free Press, 1956).

Bertrand Russell's *My Philosophic Development* (Allen and Unwin, 1959) offers a mild criticism of the direction taken by logical empiricism under the influence of continental philosophers. Ernest Gellner's *Words and Things* (Gollancz, 1959) is a savage and scorching attack on the whole linguistic movement. C. E. M. Joad's *A Critique of Logical Positivism* and Julius R. Weinberg's *An Examination of Logical Positivism* (Harcourt, Brace, 1936) are milder and more reasonable critiques.

Since so much of contemporary philosophy is to be found in the journals, rather than in book-length publications, it follows that anyone concerned with the details of the new philosophy must consult the various indices for appropriate citations.

More general works that proved valuable by virtue of the background they provided, or their discussion of particular issues involved in the inquiry undertaken here, include:

A. J. Ayer, *Language, Truth, and Logic* (Dover Publications, no date). The original edition of 1935 is a fine example of extreme positivism and its consequences, particularly in the field of value theory; the introduction to the second edition, written in 1946, offers a useful index to the kinds of changes in attitude that were enforced by the findings of the next decade of philosophic inquiry.

Bernard Barber's *Science and the Social Order* (Collier Books, 1962) is particularly concerned with the relation of science and sociology and offers some useful insights to the political scientist as well.

G. Bergmann's *Philosophy of Science* (University of Wisconsin Press, 1957) is an interesting, but somewhat idiosyncratic approach to philosophy of science.

R. B. Braithwaite's *Scientific Explanation* (Cambridge University Press, 1956) is one of the pioneer books in logic of science, still very useful, though somewhat difficult.

P. W. Bridgmann's *The Logic of Modern Physics* (Macmillan, 1927) and *The Nature of Physical Theory* (Princeton University Press, 1936) provide an introduction to Bridgmann's "operationalism."

J. B. Conant's *Modern Science and Modern Man* (Doubleday, 1952) and *Science and Common Sense* (Yale University Press, 1951) are both extremely readable and intelligent nonformal examinations of modern science.

J. Bronowski's *Science and Human Values* (Harper, 1956) and *The Common Sense of Science* (Vintage Books, no date) are both interesting and valuable statements on science by a working scientist.

E. Durkheim's *Rules of the Sociological Method* (The Free Press, 1950) offers an interesting comparison with the methodology of an older sociological tradition.

H. Feigl and W. Sellars' (eds.) *Readings in Philosophical Analysis* and H. Feigl and B. Brodbeck's *Readings in Philosophy of Science* each contain some excellent and pertinent articles. Feigl has also been joint editor of the Minnesota Studies in the Philosophy of Science, of which three volumes are available. Again, particular articles in these collections are well worth careful study.

Philip Frank's *Philosophy of Science* (Prentice–Hall, 1957) and the collection edited by Frank entitled *Validation of Scientific Theories* (Collier Books, 1961) are both excellent.

L. Gross's (ed.) *Symposium on Sociological Theory* (Harper, 1959) is excellent, particularly articles by Robert Bierstedt on real and nominal definitions, by C. G. Hempel on the logic of functional analysis, and by May Brodbeck on models, meaning, and theories.

N. R. Hanson's *Patterns of Discovery* (Cambridge University Press, 1958) is difficult but suggestive. Hanson remains one of the few philosophers of science still seeking a logic of discovery that will go beyond Carnap's work with inductive logic.

C. G. Hempel, though he has published no books to my knowledge, has produced a number of excellent articles on scientific explanation, particularly "The Logic of Explanation" in *Philosophy of Science,* (1948) (with P. Oppenheim), and *Fundamentals of Concept Formation in Empirical Science,* IEUS, Vol. II (University of Chicago Press, 1952).

Abraham Kaplan's *The New World of Philosophy* (Vintage Books, 1963) contains excellent articles on pragmatism and analytic philosophy.

F. Kaufmann's *Methodology in the Social Sciences* (Oxford University Press, 1944) is dated but still worth reading.

Paul Lazarsfeld's (ed.) *Mathematical Thinking in the Social Sciences* (The Free Press, 1954) is excellent in many respects and must be read.

E. H. Madden (ed.) *The Structure of Scientific Thought* (Houghton Mifflin, 1960).

Ernest Nagel's *The Structure of Science* (Harcourt, Brace, and World, 1961) is mandatory. See also his "Concepts and Theory in the Social Sciences" in *Language, Science, and Human Rights* (with C. G. Hempel) (American Philosophical Association, 1952).

Maurice Natanson's (ed.) *Philosophy of the Social Sciences: A Reader* (Random House, 1963) is valuable, especially articles by E. Nagel, C. G. Hempel, and Alfred Schutz.

Karl Popper, *The Logic of Scientific Discovery* (Science Editions, 1961), *The Open Society and Its Enemies,* 2 vols. (Princeton University Press, 1963), *The Poverty of Historicism* (Harper, 1964), and *Conjectures and Refutations* (Routledge and Kegan Paul, 1963) are all excellent and very useful. Compare with F. Hayek, *The Counterrevolution of Science* (The Free Press, 1955).

H. Reichenbach, *Experience and Prediction* (University of Chicago Press, 1938).

Stephen Toulmin's *Philosophy of Science* (Harper, 1960) is still the best brief introduction to the subject, though I am inclined to disagree with his analogy of theories and maps.

Max Weber's *The Methodology of the Social Sciences* (The Free Press, 1949) along with various other works available now in translation is still very valuable.

A. N. Whitehead's *Science and the Modern World* (Macmillan, 1925) offers an interesting contrast to empirical philosophy by one of the founders—with Russell—of analytic philosophy.

Finally, some mention should be made of the delightful and informative article entitled "Onward and Upward with the Arts," published in the *New Yorker* for December 9, 1961. Ved Mehta's peregrinations through contemporary British philosophy rightly deserve to become a classic.

CHAPTER TWO

SCIENCE

THE body of knowledge that has been accumulated by the physical sciences is widely acknowledged to be qualitatively superior to any other body of information available to man. Indeed, extreme proponents of logical empiricism have asserted that it is the only kind of information entitled to be called "knowledge." The grounds on which the qualitative superiority of scientific knowledge are affirmed obviously have nothing to do with any intrinsic superiority of scientists over nonscientists as human beings, nor is it a consequence of some kind of superiority of the subject matter of science. The real basis of the claim to superior worth on the part of scientific knowledge must lie in the properties of the activities and procedures by which that information is produced; hence, in the last analysis, in its logical properties. We must seek the defining qualities of scientific inquiry if we are to obtain the criteria that account for the value and worth of science. And it is important to note that these qualities cannot be defined formally or nominally; they must be derived from the actual performance of the scientific enterprise. This accounts for the great value of philosophy of science for the political scientist concerned with the methodology of his own discipline; the defining properties of science have been clearly identified in that discipline, and their logical interrelationships have been developed very fully.

Because our aim is to identify the qualities that make scientific activity a superior source of knowledge, we are more concerned with logical properties than with empirical description. For that reason, the construction of science that is advanced in this chapter bears little resemblance to the mental image of crowded laboratory and white-smocked scientist that figures so largely in the popular conception of science. The key points in the discussion are matters of logic and not questions of descriptive activity. We are concerned with the epistemic requirements of the sciences, with the manner in which scientists explain the phenomena they investigate, with the role and function of theories and models in science, with the methods and techniques that scientists employ, and with the role of values in scientific endeavor. We must also examine the relationship between the objects that science studies and the phenomena of politics if we are to have a firm base for discussing the feasibility and usefulness of transfers between the two sets of disciplines. Each of these major problems occupies a chapter of its own.

MISLEADING TRAILS

The first point to be made clear is that it is quite pointless to appeal to common usage for assistance in defining the necessary and/or sufficient properties of science. In fact, common usage is so hopelessly vague and imprecise about science that it is more of a hindrance than a help. It is true that "sciences" have proliferated in recent decades, but the uses to which the term has been put seldom indicate the presence of any clearly defined set of properties. When, for example, a single term in common usage is applied to activities so diverse as physics and chemistry, dry cleaning, dishwashing, and floor polishing, to mention but a few of the cases in which "science" has been employed, it is hard to believe that the activities in question share common qualities. The confusion is compounded by the tendency for common usage to identify systematically the kind of activity that is science with the quiet different kind of activity that is technology. Science is, in essence, a systematic search for knowledge of the universe and its contents; technology is the use of that information for human purposes. Usually, though not always, scientific activity leads to technology, though the converse may occasionally occur. The chief distinction between the two concepts lies in the "putting to use" that technology implies.

Properly speaking, science is no more concerned with the application of its findings to human needs than is the logician or the mathematician; its task is the explanation of phenomena in a particular way according to definite criteria, and, of course, the discovery of new phenomena that want explanation. This should not be taken to imply that science is in some manner more lofty and admirable than technology; each has its own virtues and uses and individual preference for one or the other is a matter of taste. But the problems arising out of science and technology, respectively, are of quite different orders. In general, science has its impact on the intellectual or the philosophical life of man, though indirectly (through technology) it will influence other aspects of human life as well. The influence of technology will usually be felt most directly in the everyday affairs of man. That is, a significant advance in theoretical physics, say quantum theory or relativity theory, will have an enormous impact on human thought, but very little direct influence on the way men live. A technological advance, such as the discovery of a new drug or a new medium of communication, will influence daily life directly and immediately, for technology provides all of the products and services that are available in society. Obviously, technology will produce social problems, and help to solve them as well; its intellectual influence seems slight by comparison. People will perhaps be influenced in what they think by changes in technology, particularly in terms of an expansion of wants and desires. But their *way of thinking* seems unlikely to be influenced so much by technology as by science.

The difficulties associated with common usage cannot be solved by an appeal to the lexicons, for dictionaries only reflect common usage, and they have the additional disadvantage of being somewhat "behind the times." The reader will be offered a number of separate and qualitatively distinct definitions of science and invited to choose among them, but the lexicons have no way of determining the proper choice, and different editions of dictionaries offer quite different definitions, both qualitatively and logically. For example, in the Second Edition of *Webster's New International Dictionary*, science receives quite a different treatment than that accorded the term by the Oxford series of dictionaries. In the latter, a sharp distinction is made between an *exact* science (quantitative treatment of data), a *pure* science (deductive operations from self-evident principles), and a *natural* science (observation and experimentation with natural phenomena). American usage, as reflected in Webster, seems to combine the British conception of exact science with the conception of a natural science and to treat pure science as a means of distinguishing between science and technology. It may seem picayune to quibble over international usage in a volume intended for an American audience, but the fact remains that appeals to dictionary definitions simply cannot provide the kind of precise basic distinctions that are needed for any meaningful examination of the defining properties of science.

It is also worth pointing out that disputes over the definition of *a* science, or questions whether this or that particular discipline is or is not a science, are usually rather pointless. It is far better, and more accurate, to seek a definition of the properties of scientific activity and leave the question of

assigning status to particular disciplines in other hands. The various disciplines that claim membership, or are accorded membership, in the family of sciences, or in even the more limited family of physical sciences, are so different that any distinction introduced on the basis of subject matter would be arbitrary and unjustifiable. Further, the classification would entail a prior set of criteria and its application would necessarily involve circularity—science being defined simply as a discipline that satisfied the arbitrary criteria chosen as defining terms. It follows that no science is "typical," or representative, and the fact that physics is commonly used as a model does not justify the assertion that it is indeed a prototype of all scientific activity.

Finally, if we can be grateful to philosophy of science for the task it has accomplished, that does not mean that there are no unresolved questions, or that science has been reduced to a formal and mechanical procedure. Nothing of the sort is the case, and we cannot really do more than sketch out the fundamentals that have been fairly well established, indicating, when necessary, questions remaining to be solved and areas of serious disagreement. Furthermore, philosophers of science are not, in the last analysis, scientists; they are more commonly logicians and philosophers, and there is always a danger of exaggerating the significance of a formal property of scientific activity at the expense of practical considerations. Philosophers of science are parasitic upon the sciences, standing behind the working scientist and examining his explicit and implicit assumptions, his epistemology, his methods and techniques, and the nature of his conclusions. The scientist himself may place quite a different construction on what he does and often is quite unaware of the logic of his efforts. Methodological self-consciousness is usually the result of consistent and systematic effort and not an accidental acquisition. If, therefore, we accept what philosophy of science has to offer, it should be tempered with due consideration for the practical and informal aspects of science. Our prime concern is with a dynamic and on-going process, and not with a static phenomenon. The results of the study ought to indicate not only the logic of scientific inquiry but also some of the more practical problems involved. It is one thing to idealize science as a process for formulating deductive systems, for example, and another thing to realize that scientists seldom achieve the ideal in practice—in some branches of science, at least. Similarly, the "idealized" experiment is rarely if ever produced in a working laboratory. The general point here is that working concepts can seldom achieve the precision and clarity of abstract concepts and we do not wish to attribute to science what in fact science does not achieve.

CHARACTERISTICS OF SCIENCE

The essential function of scientific activity is the explanation of sets of natural phenomena *(ϕ)*. This involves a number of activities, ranging from the selection of data for explanation (which cannot be formalized) to the validation of high-level theories. To begin with, the phenomena to be explained must be described accurately and classified as definitely as possible. This presupposes the existence of some grounds for selecting phenomena and including or discounting evidence (an epistemic requirement). The phenomenon to be explained must be related in a logical fashion to other data—and other theories—and this too presumes the existence of a body of theory that can be used as a base. In brief, science comprises all of the activities required for the discovery, classification, and relating of empirical data. As we shall have reason to state again in another context, scientific activities make up an integrated or interrelated whole; no single part of the scientific process is alone sufficient to establish the quality of the inquiry. For the political scientist, the crucial points in scientific inquiry are the criteria of evidence, the explanatory process (which includes the process of generalization, theorizing, and the use of models), and the concrete body of facts and theories that are the end product of science.

In theory, the political scientist might—with profit—borrow from science at any one of three basic points: he could adopt the scientist's epistemology for his own; he could make use of scientific techniques and methods, or scientific modes of explanation; finally, he could utilize the body of information about the universe and its contents that science has accumulated. The third possibility is logically independent of the others, hence there can be no restriction on the use of scientific information by political scientists. The scientist's epistemology, techniques and methods, and modes of explanation, however, are interrelated, and the use of one is in some degree contingent on the use of the others. This is particularly true at the practical level, for if the logic of explanation is the same whatever the subject matter, successful application of that logic may depend in very large measure on the kind of data that the epistemology permits. The dependence of technique and method on epistemology is even more obvious.

Although our main discussion of the influence of subject matter on scientific inquiry is reserved for the following chapter, certain preliminary observations can be made about the role it plays in science. It is a common error to suppose that the qualities of the phenomena under investigation in some way *define* science. This is not the case. But scientific activity must be appropriate to the kind of phenomena under investigation and this raises some interesting practical problems for the political scientist who is trying to achieve scientific rigor in his work. If the nature of scientific activity (A) is the crucial factor in determining the quality of the results of inquiry, whatever the nature of the phenomena (ϕ), then $A\phi =$ Quality. Yet if the definition of science has the effect of making A a constant, then the political scientist may be faced with a choice between lowering Q, for example, accepting work of lower quality as an end result of his labors, or maintaining Q but achieving no significant results because ϕ is not compatible with substantial results when combined with A. On the other hand, the consequences of lowering Q may be very serious for the totality of the enterprise. The unfortunate political scientist is then caught on the horns of a genuine dilemma: if he maintains qualitative standards, he may produce nothing; if he lowers his qualitative standards, what he produces may prove worthless. We return to this question in Chapters 3 and 5.

Turning now to the formal properties of science, we find that the various authorities, if they do not always agree on the details, are in broad agreement on the properties that are necessary for scientific activity. We shall examine these basic properties first, seeking to define with maximum rigor the necessary conditions for science. We shall then consider certain subordinate properties of science that seem peculiarly important for the political scientist, though they are not usually emphasized by philosophers of science. Their importance for political science derives from their mitigating influence; they soften the rigor of the formal conception of science, and perhaps open the way for a wider range of inquiries by the political scientist who is unable to meet the full, formal standards of strict scientific inquiry.

Science as explanation

Perhaps the most important single point about science that the nonscientist needs to grasp is that the aim of science is explanation, and that explanation has a fairly definite meaning, at least at its lower reaches. Faced with a set of phenomena, the task of science is to explain them, by which is meant defining them strictly, ordering and classifying them, and then relating them logically to other data and other logical explanatory structures in science. All of this activity must be carried out according to certain

fairly well-defined rules and limitations. To borrow from Professor Ernest Nagel:

> It is the desire for explanations which are at once systematic and controllable by factual evidence that generates science; and it is the organization and classification of knowledge on the basis of explanatory principles that is the distinctive goal of the sciences. More specifically, the sciences seek to discover and formulate in general terms the conditions under which events of various sorts occur, the statements of such determining conditions being the explanations of corresponding happenings. This goal can only be achieved by distinguishing and isolating certain properties in the subject matter studied and by ascertaining the repeatable patterns of dependence in which these properties stand to one another.[1]

Nagel has here stated the formal properties of scientific activity very compactly. Essentially, science is the production of systematic explanations, based upon empirical data joined logically to form regular patterns.

Of course, not every scientist on every occasion is concerned directly with the total explanatory process. Explanation is a final goal, and though it conditions the intermediate steps in an inquiry we do find some scientists actively engaged in the search for new data, others seeking classifications of increasing accuracy, others still concerned with the confirmation of current theories or the formulation of new theories to supersede those in existence. The details of the explanatory process can be left to Chapter 4; certain general features of scientific explanation need to be noted briefly because of the influence they exert on other aspects of science.

In essence, a scientific explanation asserts that, on the basis of the knowledge already in our possession, certain phenomena (those to be explained) are to be expected. This is not the same as the process by which the unfamiliar is reduced to familiar terms, though that is sometimes assumed

[1] Ernest Nagel, *The Structure of Science* (Harcourt, Brace, and World, 1961), p. 4.

to be the meaning of explanation. Nor does it require any assertion about the nature of "reality." Science frames its explanations purely in terms of human experience and the rules of logic—where it can. The point is sometimes confused because science quite commonly makes use of terms like "atoms" or "genes" which may readily be taken as "real" entities in the natural universe if scientific discourse is taken literally and the logical structure of terms is ignored. An atom, or a gene, is a theoretical construction; it has no "real" counterpart in nature, so far as man can tell.

Science seeks to establish relationships. It does not seek "understanding" if that term implies some peculiar or undefinable relationship between observer and object—if it goes beyond the ordering and classification of empirical or observable properties. The gradual decay of strict logical positivism has somewhat weakened the fear and distrust of terms like Max Weber's *verstehen* conception of understanding once so powerful in empirical philosophy, but science continues to reject, or at least ignore, claims to knowledge based on supernatural intuitions, or indeed on any grounds other than the operation of the human sensory apparatus. That does not mean that men with long experience in a field do not "intuit" conceptions or conclusions whose genesis they cannot trace, for such unsystematic mental operations are common, and valuable, even in science. But if "understanding" implies some "higher" form of knowledge, some "getting inside things" in search of their "essence" after the manner of Henri Bergson and others, science does not accept the validity of the suggestion. In science there are no essences to be comprehended by inquiry into the Platonic categories. There are only human perceptions to be ordered and arranged as best we can. The human perceptions of the natural universe *are* the things that scientific knowledge relates; science is unconcerned with something "out there." And scientific constructions are human creations and not discoveries. It is

pointless to demand more by way of explanation, for science has no more to give. This position is sometimes attacked as "only a description," but that is only a consequence of misunderstanding. It may be said, of course, that a complete descriptive account of the empirical aspects of human behavior would be inadequate as a summation of the totality of what is involved in a conscious human action, and that position can be defended strongly by reference to subjective experience. But science is limited by its epistemology to information that is public, that is open to a plurality of observers, and though this has certain consequences for explanation, it does not mean that scientific explanation is inadequate. To make this assertion is simply to misconstrue the meaning of the term "explanation."

A scientific explanation is always partial and particular; science does not have a total and final structure, like a jigsaw puzzle, in which every piece has its place. Each stage in an explanation can always be construed to have a successor. Explanations are conditional, approximate, and valid only so long as they serve their purposes; when a better explanation appears, the old explanation is absorbed or superseded. Explanations are relative to the here and now, and not final solutions to scientific problems. Certainly the scientist would be delighted to have an all-encompassing logical structure in which every observation would fit nicely, but science has no way of knowing that such a structure is possible, and even if it were achieved, science would have no grounds for asserting the achievement.

Finally, it should be noted that explanation is not the same as prediction, and although some philosophers hold that predictive capacity is an essential part of any good explanation, others assert both that prediction is possible without explanation and that an explanation may be possible even though prediction lies beyond the power of the explanation. As Abraham Kaplan points out, knowledge is always limited and partial and this alone is sufficient to interfere with prediction. For example, if the conditions necessary for a particular phenomenon are known but the sufficient conditions are not, prediction might be impossible although the explanation would still be considered satisfactory. The political scientist, for example, may be able to predict the outcome of a particular election without being able to give good reasons for his prediction. Similarly, political scientists can assert many of the conditions necessary for the phenomena we call wars, and thus be able to give at least a partial explanation of wars without being able to predict the outbreak of any particular instance. Since most explanations of political phenomena are partial and not complete, and since it is peculiarly difficult to establish both the necessary and the sufficient conditions for particular political events, it seems likely that partial explanations will appear frequently in the discipline, and that explanation without predictive capacity will be the rule and not the exceptional case.

The empirical base

Turning to the properties that distinguish a scientific explanation, we begin with the epistemological foundation, for this determines the pattern of every inquiry in some measure. Science, as everyone knows, is empirical. Although empiricism alone is not sufficient to establish the validity of scientific inquiry, science necessarily demands that every explanation must rest on a foundation of empirical facts and that the phenomena that science investigates be defined empirically, directly or indirectly. Science deals with facts, but facts are not self-evident; the function of an epistemology is to supply the criterion of factual information. Empiricism, while it serves as a general definition of scientific epistemology, is in fact enforceable in varying degrees of rigidity, and it will be argued below that much of the power of scientific explanation flows from the application of a rigorous construction of empiricism that can be used in

only a limited area of political science. Empirical standards can range from the extreme case in which only measurable phenomena are acceptable as evidence in argument to the very loose case in which any subjective "feeling" is considered a datum. As the rigor of the criterion is increased, the body of available data decreases and it is a nice question of judgment what level ought to be adopted in order to maximize the effectiveness of any given inquiry.

Formally, an empirical fact is contained in a synthetic proposition, a nonlogical proposition in which the predicate is not contained in the subject; to be defined as empirical, the proposition must be verifiable through observation—the term "observation" remaining for the moment undefined, since, as we have already noted, the strictness with which "observe" is defined tends to determine the usefulness or limits of inquiry. An empirical fact is a claim to knowledge which is independent of and not a derivative from existing knowledge. There are various ways of stating the same point, and it is important to differentiate them. In one sense, an empirical fact is a symbolization of perceptive experience; in another sense, an empirical fact is a law relating to the behavior of a carefully specified entity under stipulated conditions; in yet another sense, a fact is a prediction about the experience that any trained observer would have under stipulated conditions; finally, a fact can be construed as a prediction about the behavior of specified objects under stipulated conditions. The defining condition is verification by observation. And brute facts, like traces on a photographic plate that can be measured accurately, must be distinguished from logical constructions (theories) relating such facts, like atomic "particles." In science, there may be many layers of conceptualization between a particular theory and the brute facts on which it is based and this can lead to confusion if the theory is verbalized in forms usually considered to imply that "real" entities are being discussed. It is easy to see that the law of gravity is not a fact but a theory, a human construction; it is perhaps less easy to see that a gene or a neutrino falls into the same class, though statements *about* genes or neutrinos may be facts.

The whole enormous superstructure of modern science rests on a foundation of brute facts. The singular importance of explanation derives from its role as a relater of facts into meaningful propositions that are general in form—explanations provide the classifications, laws, and theories that link brute data in patterns of increasing power and complexity. Whatever the flights of theoretical fancy that the scientist indulges, however rarified the mathematical atmosphere in which he functions, in the last analysis his conclusions must be subjected to the test of correlation with brute fact, and in practice he must seek out and deliberately challenge any and all brute facts that might dispute his conclusions. The hard core of science is an enormous edifice compounded of brute fact and logical inference. Of course, there is more to it than simple mechanical operations directed to the ordering of facts, but the factual–logical core is largely responsible for the immense stability of the fundamental body of scientific knowledge.

Corollary to scientific empiricism we find a form of philosophic naturalism, implicitly or explicitly stated, that plays a significant role in scientific activity, particularly at the practical level. That is, the scientist assumes, usually implicitly, that the phenomena that men perceive, though not necessarily a picture of "reality," are nevertheless a consequence of the organization and structure of the natural universe and of nothing else. This being the case, man can hope to acquire, through suitable modes of investigation, the kinds and amount of information that he needs to cope with and comprehend the universe. Of course, this must be done within the limits of human capacity, for if someone could "really" explain the universe, no human being would be capable of understanding the explanation in any case. Im-

plied here is a further assumption that rational inquiry affords the means by which natural phenomena can be explained successfully and adequately, that man is able, through his own efforts and within the limits of his own capacities, to satisfy his needs without referring to non-natural agencies. The universe, on this view, is not a great mystery but understandable. The limiting factor in human understanding is man himself, but that limit is built into the system and cannot be eliminated. This naturalistic attitude is very annoying to those who believe that there is "something beyond the brute facts of the universe," and that the search for that "something" is a worthwhile enterprise. But for the scientist there can be no real problem since the criteria that science requires precludes the search for explanations couched in terms that cannot be specified, for explanations beyond all possibility of verification, for theories whose meaning or significance cannot be assessed. Metaphysically, scientific naturalism is doubtless an unsatisfactory point of view, and in metaphysical terms, it cannot be defended. But that is only an indication of the immense gap between two philosophic outlooks, not a scientific problem to be solved by scientific means.

Structure and order

Science is systematic and logical. At the very lowest level of generality, scientific explanation requires the systematic ordering and classification of empirical data. Indeed, some of the physical sciences have not moved very far beyond this kind of taxonomic activity, and in political science even an agreed taxonomy has yet to appear. The differences in the degree to which the preliminary task of sorting and classifying data has been carried out led F. S. C. Northrup and others to assert that the sciences actually develop in orderly and regular stages.[2] According to Northrup, the

[2] F. S. C. Northrup, *The Logic of the Sciences and the Humanities* (New York: Macmillan, 1947), esp. pp. 35–77.

early or "natural history" stage of scientific development is characterized by the accumulation, classification, and simple linking of raw data. Only in the "higher" stages of development do scientists seek, and find, deductive theoretical systems like those presently available in physics. Primitive science, in other words, consists mainly in direct observation and simple classification; only after this has been done can science become logical and mathematical, seeking theories of greater power.

There is some merit in Northrup's distinction, for it rightly suggests that disciplines like political science, which are poorly developed, need to produce a systematic classification structure for their data. C. W. Mills has echoed the same attitude in his protest against the formulation of "grand theory," and those like Robert K. Merton or David Easton who suggest that sociology and political science, respectively, ought to seek theories of the "middle range" rather than "grand" theories in view of their present stage of development, are in effect suggesting the same point. We must learn to walk before we can learn to run.

However, this question is by no means closed, and I believe that Northrup's suggestion may be highly misleading. There is no reason to suppose that scientific development *must* follow any particular pattern, nor that scientists ought to follow some orderly sequence of personal development which is determined by the state of the discipline and not by the capabilities of the individual scientist. Technological inadequacy may preclude the application or verification of theories, as the lack of an adequate source of power prevented Leonardo da Vinci from producing an operating aircraft. But Leonardo's accomplishments suggest that theories may very well transcend the limits of available technology. It *may* be a waste of time to look for broad general theories but no one can say in advance that this will be the case and there are no grounds on which it can be argued that the best strategy is necessarily the search for

less commodious conceptual structures. Moderation is not always or necessarily a wise and fruitful policy.

The point here is that we simply do not know how theories are produced; therefore, we are in no position to assert confidently that certain roads to theory ought to be closed. The Baconian conception of scientific development has haunted social science long enough. The fact is that one scientist may collect data until his files burst their seams yet produce nothing, while another may glean significant generalizations from scanty evidence. Tycho Brahe, the sixteenth century Danish astronomer, spent a lifetime collecting data about the solar system—yet left behind a meaningless pile of facts. It was Johannes Kepler who produced from that data, and rather quickly too, the now-famous laws of planetary motion that link and explain these observations. Furthermore, a theory may be self-validating, in the sense that it stimulates and directs research which justifies or validates the theory. In many cases, a theory borrowed from another field has produced fruitful results when suitably adapted to new data; a powerful development in theory may stimulate research and generalization in disciplines only vaguely related to the area in which the theory appears. Careless application of borrowed theories is, of course, to be avoided. The uses to which organic theories have been put in social science, or Brooks Adams' attempt to transpose the Second Law of Thermodynamics to social systems, are adequate evidence of the need for care. But the end result of any scientific inquiry is explanation and explanation requires both generalizations and theories; the strategy of research and inquiry should be directed accordingly.

Systematic inquiry depends upon, and has as one of its goals, an accurate, precise, and unambiguous classification structure—the higher the standards of precision that classification can achieve, the greater the power of the generalizations derived from it. As taxonomies increase in sophistication, they tend to become increasingly abstract; simple classifications, which make use of concrete observed properties, are less useful. Obviously, where data can be quantified, greater accuracy can be achieved and the use of mathematics is facilitated.

Formal logic and mathematics, properly employed, serve to limit unwarranted inferences and facilitate the exploration of relationships among the data. They also serve as devices which simplify the problem of verification or validation. In the final analysis, logic is the guarantor of the quality of scientific constructions, and if it can be demonstrated that a given explanation violates the rules of logic, that is usually sufficient to invalidate the conclusions of the inquiry.

Generalizations

Science is a generalizing activity. Without generalizations —statements which link together a number of separate observations—no explanation is possible. Even a simple classification system is, in effect, a generalized structure linking together, according to similarities and differences in observed properties, a range of phenomena. And a single generalization is in effect a simple explanation, often, as in the case of a nomic or lawlike generalization, an explanation of considerable power. The extent to which a discipline has managed to generalize its findings is a good index to the degree of development of the discipline. A well-developed science, in Northrup's terms, will possess a number of generalizations of considerable power, that is, they will subsume a wide range of factual data. A poorly developed discipline, on the other hand, will have at its disposal only a weak set of general statements, applicable only in certain limited cases, and with little or no predictive capacity. The concept of "power," applied to a general statement, is perhaps best seen in the Law of Gravity, which relates an enormous number of simple facts into a coherent system and explains them. Theories, which are special

forms of generalizations that relate other generalizations, have the peculiar property of facilitating and stimulating the production of additional laws and generalizations, and disciplines which are rich in theories have a decided advantage in every phase of inquiry over those which possess a very weak theoretical framework. In science, as in other areas of human endeavor, "Them as has, gets!"

Facts alone have no meaning—a point too often overlooked by those enamored with the accumulation of facts or absorbed in the "pack-rat" conception of research. A fact must be part of some relational structure before it has any meaning; for example, it must be in some way related or subsumed by a more general proposition. The procedure by which a fact is subsumed within a generalization remains a mystery, for there is no set of formal rules which can be applied to a body of facts in some mechanical fashion to produce general statements. General rules, like those enumerated by John Stuart Mill in his *System of Logic,* may prove useful, but they cannot guarantee results. Most philosophers of science assert that there can be no logic of discovery, though a few sturdy souls continue to examine the problem in hopes of finding a solution. In essence, we are dealing here with the nasty problem of induction. Some authorities like Reichenbach assert that scientific generalizations are produced by inductive operations from a given body of data; others like Karl Popper assert with equal emphasis that generalization cannot be formalized, hence, that science can only concern itself with the means available for testing generalizations once they have been produced. I find Popper most persuasive in this matter, for most discussions of "induction" seem to me to be rationalizations made after the fact, but anyone concerned with the problem ought to consult the specialized literature on the subject —some of which is listed in the bibliographical note at the end of the chapter.

We cannot settle the question of induction here, of course,

but a brief examination of the point may clarify the nature of the problem and the reason for its importance in inquiry. That a given object falls to the ground when thrown into the air may be established as an empirical fact by suitable observation. With refined controls and techniques, the speed, time, and distance of the trajectory can be determined with fair accuracy. A very large number of such facts, relating to a large number of different kinds of objects, can be collected quite easily by anyone with sufficient interest and energy and a modicum of equipment. Obviously, however, we cannot examine *every* object capable of being thrown into the air, and we now know with certainty that if certain objects like rockets are thrown into the air with sufficient velocity, they do not return to the earth but continue out into space. The generalization that links all of these data together is the Law of Gravity, and the Law of Gravity in turn is explained by Einstein's Relativity Theory. The question we are concerned with is, "How does the scientist arrive at the Law of Gravity?" Is it "induced" by an examination of the facts of falling objects? Could it be produced without any knowledge of the facts about falling objects? That seems unlikely. Yet the nature of the relationship between facts and the production of generalization remains beyond our specification. If we did know how to produce generalizations, presumably that process could be taught, and a very valuable adjunct to learning it would be. If, on the other hand, generalizations are always "accidental" results of some concatenation of facts within a particular human mind, then it would be pointless to continue the search for an inductive procedure. More speculatively, the mind is considered by many to be a logical instrument; for example, it operates logically as a computer does, and this raises the possibilities that computers could, in some manner, be programmed to produce generalizations if we could find the key to the process in the human mind.

Karl Popper's treatment of the inductive problem has the

great merit of concentrating attention on the *quality* of scientific generalizations rather than on the manner by which they are produced. The validity of a generalization is, in any case, independent of the means used to produce it, and it is far more useful to know that a generalization is universal or probabilistic in form, for example, takes the form "All *X* is *Y*" or the form "Some *X* is *Y*," than to argue about the presently undecidable question whether or not it was produced "inductively." Validation depends ultimately on the relationship, logical or nonlogical, between a generalization and the data to which it applies, and not on the relationship between the generalization and the data with which it originates. We will return to this question again in the chapters on explanation.

As generalizations accumulate, science seeks further generalizations and systems of generalizations that can link increasingly wider ranges of information into a single logical network. One goal is axiomatization, the reduction of all of the postulates in a given field to a single set of very broad theories from which all other generalizations in the field can be deduced. A second goal is the reduction of one field to another; for example, a procedure by which the axioms in two or more fields are reduced to a single set from which all of the generalizations in both fields can be deduced. The physical sciences have been moderately successful with reduction, though efforts to encompass sciences dealing with inanimates and sciences dealing with living organisms in a single axiomatic structure have thus far failed. Can the whole of science be reduced to a single set of axioms? There is no way of answering a question of this sort, for science would not, in any case, be able to state that it had reached a final stage in axiomatization—however successful its structure might appear. Can the social sciences be integrated with or reduced to the physical sciences? On practical grounds, this is unlikely for the immediate future, though we shall consider the question more fully in the chapter that follows.

Ethical neutrality

Science is "value free," by which is meant that if science can treat observed expressions of value as data it cannot, qua science, express a preference for one set of values in preference to another. This is not an absolute limit, of course, for any point of view involves certain value assumptions, and science, which has a point of view, is no exception to the rule. Thus scientists must assume that empirically defined facts are qualitatively superior to all other data available to man, that truth is "better" than falsehood or fiction, and that common-sense propositions can be denied only by being absurd (though there is no formal reason why complete skepticism should not be adopted as a philosophic position). The position of the scientist rests on the logical distinction between propositions that assert empirical facts and propositions that assert values. It is a commonplace that normative propositions cannot be deduced from premises that contain only factual statements, and the scientist limits his initial premises very strictly to empirical facts. There is no room in the intellectual structure for normative propositions. That does not mean that the scientist is inherently unconcerned with human values; it only asserts that human values have no place in the frame of reference that defines the scientist's functions and activities.

The reason why this is the case seems obvious. Values are human creations and not Platonic categories or qualities of the universe, to be discovered by suitable research. To state that "Human life is valuable and should therefore be maintained," for example, is to make a statement that has no literal meaning because "valuable" implies a "valuer," and that can only be a human being. Values arise only in the discussion of human affairs because they are assertions about the emotional attitudes, preferences, and beliefs of men, individually or as groups. Clearly, the fact that men make value judgments is a phenomenon requiring explanation, and it poses some peculiar problems for the political scientist. The extent to which this distinction will influence the nature of inquiry in political science and physical science, respectively, is a matter that requires detailed exploration and we return to the question in Chapter 8.

Analytic method

To the extent that it can do so within the limits imposed by subject matter, science is analytic, that is, its general method is to specify structure and process by careful observation, isolating wherever possible the different elements and processes in a system and specifying them uniquely and in terms of relationships. In practical terms, science is concerned with the accurate specification of the structure and functions or processes of the various energy aggregates that make up the sum of the observed universe (including what can be observed through the use of suitable instruments). These aggregates seem to be organized in definite patterns according to definite rules and both organization and behavior patterns are related in a uniform manner. That is, the behavior of any particular aggregate is predictable on the grounds of knowledge of structure and the relationship between structure and past behavior. And when the physical structure of the system changes, the changes themselves appear to be orderly and regular. Given these assumptions (and science could not proceed very far without them, practically if not theoretically), an event can be explained by specifying the conditions under which it occurs invariably in terms of the presence or absence of particular factors. This is not so formidable as it sounds; given the assumption that human behavior is the outcome of the interaction of genetic inheritance and accumulated experience functioning in a specified external environment, precisely the same kind of explanation is called for. The difficulty arises when we examine the stupendous number of particulars that could be involved in any given act of human behavior. Interestingly enough, there seems to be an absolute limit on the extent to which science can proceed analytically, for Werner Heisenberg has shown that, below a certain level of magnitude, it is no longer possible to specify antecedent conditions accurately because the act of measuring these conditions affects the conditions them-  selves—it is not possible to specify the consequences of measurement, or to separate the effect of the phenomenon observed from the effect of the observation. In such areas, science must make use of statistical data relating to the behavior of the whole system and not seek to define the elements or factors contributing to that behavior or specify their relative importance. Obviously, the same conditions obtain very frequently in political science; for example, we are able to specify the behavior of an organized group but quite unable to specify the particular factors that "cause" the behavior by their interaction. In general, social phenomena seem less amenable to analytic techniques than  physical phenomena, if only because of the presumed stability of the latter, and their observability.

NONLOGICAL CHARACTERISTICS OF SCIENCE

Thus far we have identified six prime characteristics of scientific activity; whether or not they are sufficient to define scientific activity, most experts agree that they are a necessary prerequisite to it. In the remainder of the book, we will examine the question how far these characteristics can be obtained in political science. However, before doing so, it is well worth pointing out that even after the logical properties of scientific activity have been enumerated exhaustively, that is still not the whole story of science; science is not logic, however important the part that logic plays 

in scientific work. For science is inquiry, and inquiry must go beyond logical manipulation if it is to be fruitful. Furthermore, there is a great deal of difference between science conceived from the point of view of the logician and science construed from the viewpoint of the working scientist. What appears in logic to be clear and precise may appear in practice to be blurred and hard to discriminate. These nonlogical qualities of science deserve as much emphasis as logic, and perhaps even more, in a study designed to winnow out of scientific practices what the political scientist can use. It is too easy to become discouraged by the logical precision of the philosopher of science's treatment of science and despair of ever converting political science into a reasonably respectable academic discipline. And it is cheering to note that the working scientist often encounters the same stubborn problems that plague the political scientist, and that he ends by treating them in a very cavalier fashion indeed if he must.

First of all, it is surprising to find the extent that science makes use of nonfactual and nonlogical criteria, particularly in its theoretical work. The scientist, in other words, is called upon—and quite often—to render judgment in areas where the criteria of judgment have not even been formulated, let alone standardized. It is not uncommon, for example, to meet terms like "elegant," "simple," or "beautiful," in scientific evaluations of theoretical constructions, and when theories conflict, or more accurately when the scientist must choose among a number of possible theoretical formulations, the grounds on which his choice is justified sound suspiciously esthetic. It is true that some writers, usually logicians, disdain the use of such terms and seek to eliminate them, but it is also the case that others believe they are likely to remain and to perform a useful function in scientific explanation. The use of esthetic terms suggests, at least, that the scientist, like the mathematician, arrives eventually at a level of abstraction wherein the only real criterion of criticism is the subjective response of the expert to the propositions stated in a theory, and that he reacts as much to the form in which the propositions are stated as to their content.

Although the experts disagree over the value of such "esthetic" judgments, there is no reason to assume that they are necessarily invalid, and some reason to suppose that they are a valuable and even irreplaceable part of scientific development. Long experience with a given subject matter amounts to a complex conditioning process that is far too detailed for complete specification. "Esthetic" judgments are consequences of the application of that conditioning to particular situations and it is not difficult to accept the view that failure to stipulate the chain of reasoning leading to a particular judgment is not a good reason for rejecting the judgment out of hand. Furthermore, if it is true, as I myself believe that all explanations are part of an endless regression or could be extended into an endless regression, then the question when we ought to be satisfied with a given explanation will always depend, in some measure, upon a subjective psychological condition which is a consequence of the previous experience of the organism. That is, men learn through experience and training to be satisfied with explanations that carry to a given depth in the regression; indeed, that seems to me one of the major features of an academic education. There is nothing alarming in this state of affairs, for it implies only that the logic of science is incomplete (which we already know to be the case), and that the human intellectual apparatus is capable of a degree of subtlety and complexity that cannot yet be matched, and may perhaps never be matched, by formal or electronic apparatus. It is in fact tempting to postulate that the existence of this condition in science, and elsewhere, is simply a verification of the most ancient adage that there is no substitute for the concentration of intelligence and experience upon a given problem, whether that problem is scientific or political.

In this connection, the uncertainty and tentativeness of the scientific outlook is worth special emphasis. In common usage, and even in academic discussions, there is an unfortunate tendency to assume that science is a court of final appeal or an absolute base to be cited as a final solution to argument. In some few areas, this is a reasonable attitude; but in very large areas of science there is no final word and none is likely to be forthcoming in the near future. More generally, science really accepts *no* final word: the scientist is taught to remain skeptical about even his most cherished beliefs and he has what amounts to a moral obligation to question all of the facts and theories that he employs each time he employs them. This is the principal device by which science corrects and refines its own content. That is an attractive goal, particularly in an age when absolutism in politics is so common, and it could be imported into political science with a positive gain for everyone and, so far as I can see, no loss whatever.

Finally, it would be a very serious error to ignore the importance of boldness, imagination, originality, iconoclasm, and a general willingness to abandon theory or tradition when it has served its purpose in scientific enterprise. The scientist, to repeat, is not merely a logician, nor is he a simple gatherer of facts. In fact, the scientist who generates endless streams of facts is performing only one small part of the task of science and, in many respects, an unimportant part. So is the scientist with highly developed analytic skills. For in the last analysis, it is the synthesizer, the producer of generalizations and theories, who performs the greatest service for science, who makes possible the growth and development of particular branches of science. Doubtless, the synthesizer could not perform his functions without the others, but it is also true that without the syntheses the activity of the others would not be very meaningful. And it is here, above all other areas in scientific activity, that the need for vision, courage, and boldness is most easily seen. Many of the truly striking gains in science have required a repudiation of what had hitherto been accepted by the scientific community. Quantum theory required science to abandon the notion of continuous flow of energy; relativity theory put an end to the Newtonian conception of absolute space and time. To attack such fundamental concepts and constructs requires flexibility of mind, a willingness to examine propositions on their merits alone and not on the basis of their pedigree, and a willingness to experiment freely, not to say wildly. To accept the results of such great theoretical leaps requires the same attitude of mind. Science is committed to the search for truth, but it is always spelled with a small "t" and never taken as absolute and infallible. Doubtless, this is a value judgment, but in common-sense terms it is an admirable value judgment, particularly for those who deal in the products of the human intellect.

This concludes an all-too-brief summation of the essentials of scientific inquiry. In combination, these are the prime factors that account for the qualitative superiority of scientific knowledge over all others available to man. It remains now to examine their usefulness in the field of political science. In the interests of completeness, possibilities and limitations will be included in the discussion that follows which may appear as commonplaces. In self-defense, it may be said that commonplaces are perhaps more frequently breached than are rare and unique limitations, hence they bear repetition. In other cases, it may appear that the limits have little practical significance, or that the possibilities are too remote for practical consideration. Here I can only plead for tolerance on the ground that we are not in a position to say what is remote and what is near, and that what seems to have significance, present or future, deserves our consideration. The aim is to explore, as fully

as possible, the extent to which political scientists can gain by borrowing from scientific practice in certain selected areas and not to explore the manner in which these considerations have been employed or ignored by political scientists in the past.

BIBLIOGRAPHICAL NOTE

Most of the general works used in this chapter have been listed in the Bibliographical note to Chapter 1. Those that remain fall into two categories: first, books which look at science from the standpoint of the philosopher of science; second, those which advance the viewpoint of the working scientist.

The best works available in philosophy of science include: Ernest Nagel's *The Structure of Science* (Harcourt, Brace, and World, 1961), perhaps the best general introduction to the subject; Stephen Toulmin's *The Philosophy of Science: An Introduction* (Hutchinson University Library, 1953); R. B. Braithwaite's *Scientific Explanation* (Harper, 1960); Karl Popper's *The Logic of Scientific Discovery* (Science Editions, 1961); and the simpler work by R. Harré, *An Introduction to the Logic of the Sciences,* (Macmillan, 1960). Norman Campbell, *What Is Science?* (Dover, 1952) is also excellent.

Norwood R. Hanson's *Patterns of Scientific Discovery* (Cambridge University Press, 1958) is interesting for its insights into the development of scientific insights and comprehension. Karl Popper's *Conjectures and Refutations* (Routledge and Kegan Paul, 1963) contains some fascinating speculations, particularly in chap. x. Victor F. Lenzen's *Procedures of Empirical Science* IEUS, Vol. I, No. 5 (University of Chicago Press, 1938) and *Causality in Natural Science* (Charles C. Thomas, 1954) are worth careful study. Henry Madden's *The Structure of Scientific Thought* (Houghton Mifflin, 1960) is solid but harder to read than some of the others. Henry Margenau's *Open Vistas* (Yale University Press) is very readable, though considered somewhat idiosyncratic by those more concerned with the formal properties of science. Hans Reichenbach has produced two useful books, *The Rise of Scientific Philosophy* (University of California Press, 1954) and *Modern Philosophy of Science* (Routledge and

Kegan Paul, 1959), both worth reading. R. Taton's *Reason and Chance in Scientific Discovery,* trans. by A. J. Pomerans (Hutchinson Scientific and Technical Library, 1957) can be compared with N. R. Hanson. Philip Frank's *Modern Science and Its Philosophy* (Harvard University Press, 1949) is excellent, though now somewhat dated. Finally, Sir Edmund Whittaker's *From Euclid to Eddington: A Study of Conceptions of the External World* (Dover, 1958) helps enormously to clarify the nature and function of modern or contemporary scientific activity.

The scientists themselves have not been prolific, but a few published works of a general, nontechnical nature are available. David Bohm's *Causality and Chance in Modern Physics* (Van Nostrand, 1957) deals with the inferences to be drawn from the discovery of the indeterminacy principle from the point of view of a convinced proponent of causality. Percy W. Bridgman's *The Nature of Physical Theory* (Princeton University Press, 1936) is an older work expounding the "operationalist" concept of physical science and physical theory. Werner Heisenberg's *The Physicist's Concept of Nature* is extremely interesting and easy to read as Edwin Schrodinger's two little volumes, *Science, Theory and Man* (Dover, 1957) and *Mind and Matter* (Cambridge University Press, 1956). Schrodinger's *What Is Life?* and *Other Scientific Essays* (Doubleday, 1956) proved less useful but still quite interesting. A great deal can be gleaned from a steady diet of *Scientific American, Science,* and other nontechnical publications, as well as from the *Journal of the Philosophy of Science* and other academic media.

The reader may also wish to examine C. P. Snow's thesis about the relationship between the scientist and nonscientific worlds (which I believe to seriously misconstrue the problem). The original Rede Lectures were published by Cambridge University Press in 1961 as *The Two Cultures and the Scientific Revolution.* F. R. Leavis' bitter attack on Snow, chiefly as a novelist, was made in the Richmond Lectures for 1962, and published as *Two Cultures? The Significance of C. P. Snow.* Michael Yudin has examined Snow's position in more reasonable fashion in his *Essay on Sir C. Snow's Rede Lecture* (Chatto and Windus, 1962).

CHAPTER THREE

SUBJECT MATTER

THE properties of the phenomena under investigation—the nature of the subject matter of a discipline—are obviously prime factors in determining the direction that the discipline will take as it develops. In very strict terms, it is somewhat improper to speak of the "objects" of a strict empirical science that deals with direct perceptions, for "objects" like atoms and molecules are theoretical constructions rather than observable entities. However, the constructions and conceptions employed by political science and physical science, respectively, to describe their phenomena can be compared on common-sense grounds and it is useful—and even essential—to do so. The properties of the subject matter, taken in conjunction with the rules for the acquisition of data accepted by the investigator, serve to define both the theoretical and practical limits of the mode of investigation. It follows that the extent to which political science can be guided in its aims, methods, techniques, and epistemic requirements by the standards current in physical science is contingent, in some degree, on the extent to which the phenomena that political science investigates are amenable to the criteria that science employs. Both theoretical and practical distinctions are worth our consideration, for what is theoretically possible may be quite impracticable, and a limit that is theoretically sur-

...act, act as a complete inhibition on ...nvestigation of particular phenomena.
...eing is something more than an aggregate ...eems obvious; that human society differs ...om a colony of bees or a crystal lattice is ...o one seriously disputes the fact that animate ...ate objects differ in quite significant ways. The ...that needs to be raised, however, is whether these ...ions are sufficiently important to enjoin fundamental ...ences in epistemology, method and technique, or mode ...xplanation. It will be argued in this chapter that there ...e certain basic differences between animate and inanimate ...bjects that serve to separate the biologist and the physicist or chemist and maintain the autonomy of the former. Further, I hope to demonstrate that human associations differ from social aggregates of lower animals to a degree that removes the political scientist further away from the biologist than the latter is removed from the physicist or chemist. Some of these distinctions are formal, but the practical differences are of far greater importance for the methodology of political science. That there is no logical distinction between the objects of physical science and the objects of political science is important, if true; but operations that are theoretically possible in political science in practice involve difficulties of such magnitude that it is little more than a verbal quibble to assert that they are not theoretical limits on the development of the discipline. The autonomy of political science from the physical and biological sciences is assured, on practical grounds, for the immediate future. It remains to specify the precise grounds on which this autonomy is founded.

ANIMATES AND INANIMATES

The natural universe, which includes everything that man perceives, may be conceived as a vast and perhaps infinite field of energy, ordered and structured in a variety of ways. Energy itself remains undefined, for it is pointless to ask what energy *really is*. Science can only identify energy as a range of perceptions or observations that follow upon the movement of energy. In these broad terms, man can study nothing but energy in its various forms as they appear to human perception, suitably augmented by instruments. This point of view is a useful frame of reference for demonstrating both the similarities and the differences among animate and inanimate entities. It also provides a means for illustrating some of the special difficulties that arise in the study of living organisms and creates some measure of separation between the physical and the biological sciences.

A part of the energy that makes up our universe is in free motion; the remainder, though still in motion, has been locked or stabilized into dynamic equilibria, which are organized systems of varying degrees of complexity and duration. The distinction is not a matter of energy moving randomly in one case and energy organized to some purpose in another. It lies, rather, in the relationships that obtain among the elementary units of energy. Some energy, presumably once in motion, has been "captured" and stabilized in orderly patterns; hence the Second Law of Thermodynamics, which asserts the tendency for the observed universe to increase its entropy, decreasing the amount of free energy available for change. Energy at rest, if that has any meaning, cannot be perceived by man, for all human perceptions—whether direct or aided by instruments—derive from the movement of energy.

The aim of science, as we have already noted, is the organization and explanation of the energy systems open to human perception. Viewed naturalistically, human perceptions indicate energy systems ordered in regular patterns according to definite rules; further, when energy systems change their structure, the pattern of change is also orderly and regular. The elements of the universe seem bound together in an orderly and regulated fashion that is related directly to structure. Is this a consequence of the nature of the human perceptive apparatus? Or does science depend upon an assumption about the Principle of the Uniformity of Nature? The subject has been much disputed. But for our purposes it does not appear to be a vital point. That human perception is a limit on man's ability to gather information about the universe we can take for granted; it is a constant limit at any given point in time and will extend to any human calculation based on perception. And if there is no formal reason why a particular organization of energy should behave in a particular way under specified conditions, this is at least a working assumption in science, and it is rarely if ever faulted. Philosophers of science aside, it is difficult to see how science could proceed without some assumption about the regularity and orderliness of identical objects (structurally and behaviorally defined) just as human thought seems impossible if a "causal" relationship between successive events is denied. The concept may be given another title, but the essentials of the concept seem needed for human thought, just as "private property" in some form is absolutely imperative for the existence of organized human relationships.

BIOLOGY AND PHYSICS

The classification of energy systems into those that are living and those that are not is one of the most fundamental distinctions made by man. The task is not simple, for if it is unlikely that living things consist of anything more than inanimate structures ordered in a peculiarly complex manner, that organization has thus far defied precise specification or reproduction in the laboratory. Ignoring the special problems raised by the viruses, science differentiates between animates and inanimates by referring to the capacity of the former to absorb energy from the surrounding environment and use that energy to grow and reproduce. The question, then, is whether organized systems that have the capacity to grow and reproduce by internalizing free energy from the environment differ so fundamentally from those energy systems that do not have that capacity, that the study of living organisms must proceed in a manner fundamentally different from the study of inanimate entities. Is biology, in other words, an autonomous subject, radically distinct from physics and chemistry? The question has both practical and theoretical importance for the political scientist. If the philosophy of physical science differs fundamentally from the philosophy of organism, then we can expect the methodology of political science to be significantly different from the methodology of science to the degree that the latter is patterned upon the activities of physicists and chemists.

That biologists make use of different methods and techniques than physicists, and even that they must explain kinds of phenomena that do not appear in physics, is beyond dispute; the methodological significance of these distinctions, on the other hand, is argued with great heat. Even the biologists are not agreed among themselves on the status of their own discipline. One school contends that living organisms can be defined, in the last analysis, in the same physicochemical terms used in physics and chemistry; another claims that the methods and concepts of physics and chemistry will not suffice to explain the behavior of living organisms. This is not simply a matter of deciding the best research strategy for the field of biology; that is a matter best left to biologists in any case. The opponents of physicalism in biology are willing to agree that biologists quite commonly employ concepts, tools, techniques, and even physicochemical laws borrowed from physics and chemistry, but they hasten to point out that the laws of biology cannot presently be deduced from the laws of physics and chemistry. Some rest content with the assertion that the reduction of biology to physicochemical laws is impracticable; others go further and assert that it is impossible in principle. Both points are examined below, but it is worth noting that even if the theoretical possibility is granted, the argument from practicality may still uphold the autonomy of biology in the foreseeable future.

The qualities of living organisms that act to set them off from inanimate objects are fairly well agreed upon by all observers; differences arise when we begin to draw inferences from the agreed base. They go well beyond the obvious, and perhaps trivial, fact that biologists must use concepts and terms not found in physical science. A brief review of the major points involved in the argument will help clarify the position of the two sides.

The argument from complexity

Modern proponents of an autonomous biology argue on practical grounds that living organisms are far too complex to yield to the kind of physicochemical analysis that "mechanistic" biologists seek to accomplish. While they are prepared to grant the principle that living organisms and inanimate systems differ primarily in structure and organization and not in fundamental components, hence both are in theory open to the same kind of physicochemical specification, they assert that it is very unlikely that biologists will reach this goal in the immediate future. It follows, the argument goes, that biologists would be mistaken if they were to rely solely upon the physicochemical approach to the study of living things.

There is much to be said for the argument, at least on practical grounds. The special quality that marks the living cell is destroyed when a physical analysis of the structure is undertaken. Once the cell wall is broken, the organism ceases to be a living structure and becomes an aggregate of inanimate particles and fluids. An essential element or

property of the living organism is thereby destroyed and cannot be captured in the analysis. In practice, and perhaps in principle as well, this inhibits a complete mechanistic explanation of living organisms well into the foreseeable future.

Further, the complexity of even the tiniest one-celled plant or animal is staggering, and analysis is made even more difficult by the very tiny dimensions involved. The constituent elements of the living cell have been identified in gross terms, and many of the mechanisms employed within the cell have been identified. Thus we find conceptual models of the basic building blocks of the living system—the DNA molecule, the chromosome, the gene, and so on. Yet it is clear that the precise organization and operation of the system defies the biologist's attempts to specify fully. A single cell, perhaps a thousandth of an inch in diameter, contains enough information to direct and control the development of a complete human body, given time and a favorable environment. The data are carried in the form of structural and chemical variations occurring in some two dozen pairs of tiny, hairlike chromosomes. Together, they occupy only a tiny fraction of the volume of the cell. The chromosomes themselves are very complex, and are presently envisaged as very complex spirals constructed of complex building blocks arranged in orderly patterns. The practical difficulties encountered in any attempt to specify the organization and interrelationships that are found within this very small space are almost unimaginable. And behind the whole endeavor there lurks the possibility that the deciding features of the structure may occur at such very small magnitudes that efforts to measure will begin to influence the measurement—this is already known to occur in physics at the subnuclear level.

The argument against the "mechanistic" approach to the study of living things seems, on this basis, well founded in practical difficulties. And there is at least a possibility that the task may be impossible in principle to complete. It can be argued, to the converse, that there is no reason to suppose that living organisms are more complex than some of the inanimate systems that physicists and chemists investigate, but that seems beside the point. The complexity of living structures is known, and the analogous position in physics, where extreme complexity is combined with small magnitudes that are very difficult to investigate, has indeed led to an impasse of sorts and the use of statistical as against analytic techniques in microphysical investigations.

The holistic argument

The more radical argument against "mechanistic" biology asserts that even if biologists were able to produce a complete physicochemical specification of a living organism, the task of explaining the organism and its behavior would still be incomplete. It is very important to note that this position is taken on scientific grounds by many eminently respectable biologists. That is, the argument does not depend upon some mystique or metaphysical proposition, nor does it require the introduction of divine will and purpose or some prime vitalistic principle for its validity. The grounds on which the claim is put forward are generally admitted and agreed; again, it is the inference to be drawn from acknowledged properties of living organisms that is at issue. Three fundamental properties of living things are usually cited as evidence for the antimechanistic or "organismic" position.

Dynamism. A living organism is a dynamic structure and not a static system; it has a basic function or purpose that does not occur in any inanimate structure—it must remain alive. Any adequate explanation of the behavior and processes of an organism, so it is claimed, must take this purposefulness into account, for example, the goal-directedness of the organism is an important element in any explanation of its behavior. At the simplest level of life, the goal may be no more than remaining alive by carrying out automatic and limited operations in search for free energy and suitable internal procedures for converting the energy into living substance. In complex organisms, the relationship between goals and behavior is less easily defined in detail. In both cases, so the organismic biologists assert, adequate explanation demands some attention to the relation between behavior and goal.

Now it is certainly true that the biologist has, historically, found it both natural and convenient to explain the functions of living organisms in terms of goals or purposes. Further, the practice of explaining parts of organisms in terms of their contribution to the fulfillment of the life-goals of the total organism, so-called functional explanation, has been widespread and very useful. For example, we "explain" the behavior of the total organism as a "search for food," and we "explain" the liver by studying its performance and the role it plays in maintaining body functions. Moreover, we are very often puzzled by organs like the appendix which have no apparent function, although we are likely to explain that, as it appears presently in man, it is a vestigal remnant of herbivorous ancestors. Biologists find such functional and purposeful (or teleological) explanations readily comprehensible and psychologically satisfying. Physicists, on the other hand, tend to be suspicious of functional and teleological explanations and avoid them if it is at all possible.

The principal drawback to an argument for the autonomy of biology based on this position is that logicians argue that teleological or functional explanations are logically equivalent to other nonfunctional or nonteleological explanations. Thus, Ernest Nagel claims that "every statement about the subject matter of a teleological explanation can in principle be rendered in non-teleological language. . . ."[1]

[1] Ernest Nagel, *The Structure of Science* (Harcourt, Brace, and World, 1961), p. 421; chap. xii deals generally with the problems involved, and though Nagel's references seem badly dated, the logic is not affected by the sources he employs.

If true, this equivalence would seem to be fatal to the argument. But those who assert the contrary insist that equivalence "in principle" and equivalence in practice are two quite different matters. Nonteleological explanations, they claim, do not convey the same meaning and inference as teleological or functional explanations. Logical equivalence in principle, in other words, does not necessarily imply equivalent meaning in practice. This objection doubtless has some force, though it is not conclusive. If an explanation of the behavior of living organisms framed in terms of purpose or function, goals or motivation, conveys meaning  more clearly and precisely than other explanatory forms this is a not unreasonable justification for preferring it. And when we come to the explanation of human behavior, with its complex interaction of motivations and purposes, the subjective evidence available to each of us individually is some reason for supposing that an adequate explanation of that behavior will include reference to such motives. And it is no reply to the argument to maintain that it is very difficult to do so. That is, it is not a justification for nonteleological explanations to assert that teleological explanations are too difficult.

Hierarchy. Living organisms are organized hierarchically in ascending scales of complexity. They are not merely additive systems like a lump of coal. Indeed, there is no  living equivalent to homogeneous substances like iron. A living organism, particularly in its higher forms, is an elaborate structure of integrated and interrelated levels. This does not rule out the possibility that the operation of the complete structure can be explained in physicochemical terms, but it does make the task immeasurably more difficult. For one thing, the higher levels of the structure cannot be inferred from the lower levels any more than the  function of telling time can be derived logically from an explanation of the individual parts of a watch. Each level must be examined on its own terms, and the relationships among the various levels in the hierarchy must be explored independently. For example, the various sets of organs in a higher animal (digestive tract, glandular system, circulatory system, and so on) are each suitable objects for study, but we learn very little about the behavior of the total animal from a study of these independent lower systems, individually or completely.

This hierarchical property of living organisms has led some biologists to assert that all living organisms must be studied and explained holistically rather than analytically because any mechanistic explanation based on an explanation of the parts of the organism will be partial and incomplete. If this has at times led to something very close to mysticism it must, nevertheless, be granted that concern for the integrity of the whole organism seems well founded. A living organism *is* an entity, a complete operating unit, and in a sense something more than the sum of its parts, for example, properties of the whole are logically independent of the properties of the parts and must be established by observation of the whole. We do not determine all of the properties of a crowd by observing the behavior of individuals, and there are propositions that can be made about a crowd as a collective that cannot be made about the individual members of the crowd. Is this different than the situation in physical science? On the face of it, the distinction seems to hold, for the scientist dealing with inanimates deals with no parallel situation. But it would seem to imply a difference in research strategy rather than a fundamental difference in mode of explanation. This has considerable practical significance but is not methodologically decisive.

Continuity. Finally, living organisms, particularly in their higher forms, introduce a factor into explanation that is not found in the study of inanimates simply by virtue of being alive. For there is a sense in which the present state of any organism is a consequence of the genetic inheritance and past history of that organism, and the future of any organism is in some degree contingent on both the past and the present. The student of living things attends to an "ongoing" process in which the future is not completely determined by the past in a way not true of nonliving substances. Acquired physical traits are not transmitted genetically, but environmental influences act to condition the survival value of different traits, hence "select out" certain members of a class of organisms for survival. This is quite unlike the relationship that obtains between an inanimate object and its physical environment. The chain of life, to use a hackneyed simile, stretches back unbroken to the very beginning of life, but the present organism is not necessarily identical to the organism of the past and the future organism may differ from that of the present. There is, in brief, an element of uncertainty in the development of living things that arises out of their potential for change—and in man that potential is exaggerated beyond all measure in comparison with the simpler forms of life.

Here, it would appear, is an irreducible distinction between the living and the inanimate; the former can alter its structure in time in a way that the latter cannot. It can adapt to the environment, in varying degree, and need not merely change or alter in accordance with fixed rules. Iron placed in a particular environment will rust, and we can predict the rust if we know the environmental conditions. With the living organism, and particularly with man, this is not the case. Arnold Toynbee elevated the interaction of man and environment into a theory of social change, but its predictive capacity is nil. The more complex the life form, the wider the margin of error introduced into our explanations by the influence of this factor of adaptability and there seems no means by which man can eliminate its influence from his calculations.

These various objections to the equivalence of biology and physical science are not exhaustive or final; they may not even be binding in principle, though the theoretical dependence of biology on physics and chemistry remains to be demonstrated. Nevertheless, they seem adequate to support the belief that the two disciplines differ significantly in kind, and that such differences will influence both research strategy and mode of explanation. Though our prime concern is the study of human society, it is, nonetheless, suggestive to find that the two major branches of science can dispute among themselves on these matters and even if the dispute proves to hinge upon practicality, rather than principle, that does not vitiate the importance of the distinctions.

THE SOCIAL AND THE PHYSICAL

The gap that separates biology from physics and chemistry seems trivial when it is compared with the gulf that separates both natural sciences from political science. Peculiarities that appear in embryo, as it were, in the biologist's study of simple organisms are magnified beyond measure in the study of political society. And whatever the case for the autonomy of biology from physics and chemistry, the autonomy of political science from the physical sciences, or more accurately, from the tyrannous influence of those who seek to impose strict scientific standards on political science, seems guaranteed in the foreseeable future. In the remainder of the chapter, the various arguments on which this position depends will be set forth as clearly as possible. We can then undertake a more detailed examination of the consequences of these differences for political inquiry.

To begin, consider the respective attitudes of biologist and political scientist toward their common object—man. The biologist sees a living organism, a complex structure of systems and subsystems, organs and tissues, bound together and coordinated by an intricate network of nerve fibers and a massive central nervous system. In his work, the biologist seeks an accurate analytic description of the component parts of the organism and the various processes that maintain the system alive and intact. His data are strictly empirical, and his conclusions, if they differ in form from physics and chemistry are, nonetheless, usually specified in physicochemical terms. His explanatory structures and theories are subjected to the same verification procedures that chemists and physicists employ. Many of his terms and concepts are taken directly from chemistry and physics, as are some of his generalizations and laws. Today, the biologist tends to attach more importance to the interaction of organism and environment and to the influence of physical factors on the physical characteristics of the organism than was true a few decades ago, but the basic orientation in biology is toward the physical and not the social sciences. In practice, the borderline between biology and psychology tends to break down, but that seems mainly due to the psychologist's tendency to concentrate on the biological aspects of human behavior, particularly in the United States. In fact, however, psychology seems to be shaking off some of the effect of three decades of rigid behavioralism and concerning itself more with the whole animal and with psychic as well as physical properties of the human organism.

The political scientist, on the other hand, whatever his special field of interest, is concerned with the behavior of a creature that is construed in terms of an inseparable interaction of physical endowment, psychic development, and social interaction. Man is a living organism, a creature that can think, that abstracts from the concrete, possesses a language, and communicates more or less successfully with others of his kind. Further, man seeks information, stores it systematically, engages in logical and other rational introspection about his data, interacts with others of his kind in various ways, and constructs societies of considerable complexity. Man has the unique capacity to associate himself with the objects and organisms that share the earth with him in a way that we refer to as making value judgments.

Here is a creature that can learn and forget, and can alter his behavior by learning and forgetting. The plasticity of human behavior is unmatched in the animal world. Driven by a whole host of factors, in part genetic and in part environmentally determined; to some degree, at least, beyond the reach of empirical observation or even subjective specification; incapable, in many respects, of conveying accurately to others the objects of subjective consciousness; unconscious, in many cases, of the urges or drives that impel him to particular efforts—man is truly an awesome object of study and an inspiring challenge to the intellect. The list of human properties is virtually endless, yet few of the definitive properties of man are shared even with the lower forms of animal life, let alone the inanimate objects of the natural universe. The traits that distinguish the phenomena that political science investigates are distinctly *human;* they separate man from all other entities known to man.

Whereas the biologist shares with other natural scientists a wide range of terms, standards, and procedures, he shares very little indeed with the political scientist. His epistemic standards, his techniques and methods, his standards of measurement, his experimental procedures, and many of his explanatory structures are taken directly from physical science. How very little, by comparison, the biologist shares with the political scientist. We need only reflect on the degree to which the biologist or physiologist would have to alter his mode of inquiry if he turned to the study of politics, and how much the political scientist would have to change in order to become a biologist to realize the degree of separation of the two disciplines. Further, it is very unlikely indeed that the political scientist could function as a biologist and still fulfill the needs of political science. The reasons why the transposition could not be made derive from the specific qualities of political phenomena that set them apart from the phenomena of the natural sciences.

POLITICAL PHENOMENA

Every political phenomenon is a complex event. It occurs in a social environment, at least partly structured in regular patterns of norms and statuses. It involves an act of behavior —a physical performance—by a particular individual. Behind the act of behavior lies human subjective consciousness, usually, but not always, related directly to the physical performance. Beyond consciousness, if Freud and his followers are correct, lurks the unconscious element of the mind and it too appears as overt behavior, but undiscerned by consciousness. The physical structure of man has only a very limited meaning for the political scientist, though it may be related to behavior indirectly through the mediating influence of psychology.

Political phenomena are further complicated by the fact that human consciousness has content as well as form. In general terms, an act of human behavior is the outcome of an interaction between the external environment and the internal state of the organism. The internal state of the organism is in turn a consequence of the genetic inheritance of the individual as modified by the sum of its past experiences. This internal state is in some degree unique for each person. Further, it includes an assessment of the external situation at any given moment in time, and that assessment, rather than any objective properties of the situation, determines the nature of human behavior and, of course, signifies the meaning of that behavior.

Presumably, every political phenomenon is analyzable in these terms. In practice, this is only rarely achieved, and that is one of the principal reasons why political science has failed to develop an adequate classification system for its phenomena. If the classification includes statements about each separate element in a political event, it is difficult—if not impossible—to assign a classification to a particular

action because the constituent elements in the action are not open to observation. If the classification system depends solely on observable properties of human behavior, the danger of error is serious, for example, it is always possible that factors which cannot be observed are, in fact, the true determinants of the act of behavior. Because the individual's assessment of the environment, and not some observer's assessment of the environment, is the determining factor in behavior, it is not always possible to infer from observed behavior to private subjective consciousness with any degree of certainty; logically, it is indefensible. Personal reports by individual actors are available, of course, but they too can be misleading, either because of deliberate deception or unconscious deception.

Political science, then, faces a genuine dilemma, though it is not inescapable. To the extent that we try to deal with political phenomena in all their richness and complexity, giving due weight to every factor involved in the human behavior that makes up the political event, we complicate the task of explanation by multiplying influences, and at the same time we weaken our epistemic standards if we are to obtain any evidence at all about subjective aspects of the behavioral act. On the other hand, when explanations are predicated on only one phase of political action, perhaps by limiting evidence to empirical data strictly defined, the explanation is always and necessarily partial and incomplete, hence likely to be mistaken. To make matters worse, there is no way in which the likelihood of such partial explanations being correct can be stipulated without a rule for determining the relative significance of all of the factors interacting in a given case, except in the rather rare case where a sequence of actions permits comparison and allows us to attribute a degree of influence of all of the factors omitted from the explanation by the method of residues. This does not rule out all possibility of political explanations, of course, for it is always possible to explore limited political phenomena in depth or macrophenomena in broad terms and seek to correlate the findings in such manner that a multidimensional picture will emerge. But political scientists do need to be aware of the precise nature of these limitations, if only to avoid asserting claims on behalf of given explanations that are not warranted by the scope or accuracy of the inquiry. A more detailed examination of the prime factors involved in political phenomena should therefore prove useful.

The "social" factor in human behavior is entirely absent from physical science and qualitatively distinct from the social life of the lower animals. The "social" life of a bee colony can be inferred from the behavior of individual bees, indeed it can be nothing more than the sum of the behavior of individual bees, because the behavior of bees is fixed inexorably by the genetic inheritance and the structure changes little if at all. If the environment alters to a degree that the conditions needed for the survival of the "social" structure are no longer present, the colony will simply perish —it cannot adapt. Human society, by way of contrast, is open to very substantial, though not total, variation; men quite literally help create their own environment, and by doing so they have been able to adapt to a wide range of physical conditions and, of course, adapt physical circumstances to their own wishes and desires. The political philosopher, and more particularly the utopian theorist, has always been very much aware of the volatility of social institutions. They have sought, since Plato's time at least, the causes of social change (and this still remains a major problem in social theory) and the "perfect" social organization.

Overall social organization is, on the surface, the most readily available aspect of politics and it is hardly surprising to find that political explanations were, for the most part, framed in terms of social institutions rather than individual actions. In this sense, the recent "behavioral movement" performed a genuine service to the discipline by calling

attention to the individual and noninstitutional factors at work in politics. There is some danger, however, of behavioral influences forcing political science to the other extreme in which all political explanations are presumably to be couched in individual terms (methodological individualism). Universals are a very useful class of terms for the explanation of social phenomena, and they cannot be wholly replaced by individual terms—at the very least it would be very inconvenient to do so. Consider, as an example, how very difficult it would be to express a simple statement like "The crowd was noisy and colorful" in terms of statements about individuals, or to make statements about collectives like "The tennis club decided to construct another tennis court during the coming year." Moreover, groups have attributes that cannot be deduced from the attributes of members of the group; and social institutions, which play an obvious role in human behavior, must be studied as entities. Certain group phenomena may well be expressed in terms of individuals or individual actions, but others are *sui generis* and must be explained in group terms.[2]

The designations of collective terms in political science, then, appear much wider than their counterparts in science, if only because of our awareness of the complex individual relationships—of the potential for change—implied in human social groups. That is not to say, of course, that it is not sometimes very good strategy for the political scientist to follow the physical scientist and treat collections of human beings as statistical aggregates, ignoring individual motivations and other similar factors. The theory of gases relies

[2] Quentin Gibson, *The Logic of Social Enquiry* (Routledge and Kegan Paul, 1960), chap. ix, contains a good statement of the case for methodological individualism. However, compare with Ernest Nagel, *op. cit.*, pp. 535–46. Nagel's argument seems to me to be superior and his conclusion (p. 540) just: ". . . although it is a sound methodological assumption to interpret collective terms in social science as designations for groups of human beings or their modes of behavior, these terms are not in fact invariably *defined* by way of individual terms, nor does the assumption necessitate that collective terms must in principle be so definable."

upon statistics because it would be an impossible task to attempt to specify the behavior of a given volume of gas in terms of the behavior of individual gas molecules. Happily, statistical generalizations about the behavior of collections of individual molecules of gas have been verified empirically and perform their explanatory functions very well. A similar situation may obtain in political science, say with relation to voting behavior or other large-scale phenomena. However, in the latter case there is always the uneasy realization that the generalization may not hold because the *ceteris paribus* is violated. When this occurs, it is always a consequence of changes in individual behavior, hence is not explicable in group terms.

Finally, we need to point out that human groups are, or can be, organized in a sense that does not occur in the natural universe. The point is best illustrated by an analogy taken from biology, so long as it is clearly realized that it is only an analogy and not meant to be taken literally. Consider the consequences of increasing the complexity of organic systems. Clearly, specialization appears as a necessary prerequisite, or consequence, of complexity of structure; as living systems become increasingly large and complex, specialization must occur. In simple life forms, size is limited, for the maximum size is determined by the relationship between cell volume (area to be fed) and cell surface (feeding area). Since the former increases much more rapidly than the latter, a cell cannot grow beyond a given size without losing its capacity to feed itself. The answer, in growth terms, is combination of cells. In some structures, like Algae, the cells remain independent and self-sufficient but group together; units like sponges are also made up of self-sufficient cells, but the rudiments of intercellular organization appear. In a highly developed organism like man, individual cells have lost their capacity to remain alive by their own efforts; they have become specialized—and dependent—and they can only exist within the complex that supplies the missing functions through the activity of other equally specialized cells. Large organic units, and particularly complex organic units, have an absolute need for an integrating mechanism that can maintain the system and regulate the operation of its parts. Human society has the same requirement. There is no parallel to this need in the physical sciences. The function of government, the fact that aggregates of human beings living in close proximity is only possible when there is specialization and interdependence and, therefore, a coordinating and controlling mechanism, creates a problem for political science that physical scientists do not face. Further, the coordination and control of social behavior can be performed by various institutions according to quite different norms. The selection of institutions and norms, which is the continuing function of politics, is an evaluating and not a descriptive process.

THE HUMAN INDIVIDUAL

When political phenomena are explained in terms of individuals mankind can no longer be treated as a single class. Generalizations must deal with the variety of factors that can influence human behavior, selecting some and eliminating others in the search for a worthwhile explanation. Here, too, political science must deal with problems that physical science does not encounter. Two are central: first, the uniqueness of each member of humanity sets behavioral phenomena off from "natural" phenomena; second, the peculiar "open" quality of the human endowment generates some unique and distressing hazards in generalization.

The uniqueness of each man is a biological fact. Even uniovular twins, who are genetically identical, differ both physically and experientially in significant ways. The state of a human organism at any given time is the outcome of a very complex interaction of genetic endowment, physical and social environment, and the totality of past experience.

In each case, this combination is unique. Men differ in size and shape, in glandular activity, capacity of the nervous system, susceptibility to disease, efficiency of body functioning, and in almost every other conceivable physical and psychic property. Countless different factors can be involved in any act of behavior. The influence of the social environment alone (education, family training, etc.) defies specification. Yet explanation of political phenomena depends upon similarities, as we shall see in the following chapter, and not on differences. That need not be a source of alarm, actually, for men are also similar in many respects and for the same reasons (influence of social and physical environment, genetic inheritance) and the similarities may be of greater importance than the differences in any particular case. However, the uniqueness of individuals does underline the dangers of generalizing about men as a class, for the defining properties of the class may not be the factors that are important in accounting for the kind of behavior to which the generalization refers. Moreover, the uniqueness of men tends to support the view that universal generalizations, which are applicable to the class of men without exception, are likely to be trivial and not significant influences on behavior. Classical economic theory rests on the axiom that all men seek to maximize their money gains in business dealings, yet that would not necessarily account for the behavior of parents toward their children. The generalization must be hedged with a few restrictions, which weakens its application and usefulness but relates it more precisely to the empirical evidence at our disposal. In sum, to state that "X is a man" is to know both a great deal and very little about him; the question is how important that knowledge is for the explanation of political phenomena.

Far more important, however, is the "openness" of the human genetic endowment; there is no parallel to this quality of subject matter in the physical sciences. Man, above all other creatures, determines his own patterns of

behavior, collectively if not individually, for the genetic inheritance seemingly has only a slight influence on the way men behave. Men inherit capacity or potential rather than fulfillment, and from a strictly anthropocentric point of view, this seems a highly desirable state of affairs. For the political scientist, concerned with the explanation of a particular kind of social behavior, it creates headaches. Von Frisch could, by a careful study of bee colonies, produce the rules of behavior that guide the activities of hive members, and the generalizations he produced are applicable to any hive, and presumably will continue to be applicable to bee hives in the future. But no amount of study of existing society can produce rules of behavior of this necessary quality. Indeed, Karl Popper argues with great force that no scientific predictor (society) can predict its own future results by scientific methods so long as human knowledge is expanding.[3] Since human behavior depends upon the state of knowledge at any given point in time, the conditions on which human behavior in the future would have to be predicated cannot be assumed to hold indefinitely. That does not mean that useful short-range predictions cannot be made; it does mean that any prediction must add a caveat to the effect that it rests upon the continuation of a state of knowledge that is, in fact, open to change.

In effect, man is endowed at birth with a neural system that is in most essentials unfinished; certain parts of the autonomic nervous system needed to maintain essential body functions are "wired in place," but the remainder of the system is open, waiting to be filled by experience. It is analogous to a gigantic electronic computer that has been programmed only very partially. Since the computer can generate its own rules of response, and neither information nor operating rules have been fed into the structure, it

[3] Karl R. Popper, *The Poverty of Historicism* (New York: Harper, 1964). See especially the Preface to the First Edition, pp. vi–viii.

begins almost, though not quite, like the *tabula rasa* in Locke. The system operates according to definite rules, of course, for, like the computer, the construction of the nervous system determines its mode of operation. The central nervous system, for example, has been shown to be a logical machine, capable of a very wide range of activities but performing each activity in a definite manner determined by its construction. All human nervous systems are roughly alike in structure and operation, though they differ greatly in capacity, and in the use that is made of them.

The evidence seems to support the generalization that all human behavior is a consequence of the operation of the nervous system and of nothing else; until the nerves fire, neither mental nor physical activity occurs and there can be no consciousness. Behavior is the outcome, in some complex sense, of the movement of impulses through the system; the movement of impulses apparently alters the actual physical structure of the system and thus facilitates or inhibits the further passage of impulses of the same type through given channels. The nervous system is in a dynamic state, constantly building and erasing, connecting and disconnecting channels. We do not know exactly the precise nature of the channels, but what we think and do is presumably determined by their configuration. The system can do no more than what it has "learned" to do, using the term in very broad sense, just as a giant computer can do no more than its program demands. Of course, a computer programmed to do simple arithmetic is only an adding machine—and a very expensive one at that—a terrible waste of potential. A human brain that has been "programmed" to do no more than handle trivia is a trivial machine, and a much more serious waste of potential in most, if not all, cases. Men must be fed information, and principles for handling that information, before they can perform adequately—however "adequately" is defined; the output of the system can be modified by internal stimulation or rumina-

tion. The type of performance produced will depend upon its substantive rules of operation, its past experience, and the present situation.

To use a slightly different analogy, the human nervous system is built to follow rules of operation analogous to the rules of a game like baseball. These rules cannot determine the outcome of any particular nervous action, for that depends on the content of the system at the time that action is taken, just as the rules of baseball determine in general the kind of actions that occur on the field but do not determine the outcome of any particular game. Everything depends on the nature of the inputs to the system, and on the manner in which the system handles that information internally. Thus a computer can be programmed to produce unintelligible gibberish, though the gibberish will follow logically from the rules of operation that have been programmed into the machine. Human beings, too, can produce gibberish or nonsense by applying principles of operation that are common to all men to a body of content that has been modified by the particular experience of one person.

Two computers that have been constructed in an identical fashion (make use of the same principles of operation) and fed identical programs could be expected to produce identical responses to a given situation. So, theoretically, would two human beings with the same genetic endowment and the same experience behave identically. It is probably impossible for two persons to have exactly the same genetic inheritance and the same body of experience; even identical twins include at least one different person in their external environment. But it is certainly possible to produce behavior that is isomorphic in many respects by suitable training and indoctrination—that is why skilled propaganda is so detestable. I have tried to show, in another work, that when men agree on basic political principles they tend to interpret all political phenomena in terms of that set of principles and the result is a surprising degree of uniformity in behavior and opinion. Critics of contemporary society point to "conformity" in individual behavior, usually with alarm, and historians usually point with pride to the manner by which the vast territory of the United States has been unified and drawn together into a single national unit by centralized communication networks, common educational principles, and so on. The identification of similarities in the social environment, and a linking of these similarities to patterns of political behavior, is at least theoretically possible, and in all likelihood could be carried to a considerable degree even today. The future, if the portents are correctly read, is increasingly likely to produce similarities that are both broader and more intense.

It is interesting to note that what is denounced as conformity by one segment of society is eagerly sought by another, and that the first is quite likely to applaud the second. The whole purpose of scientific training, for example, is to produce a particular kind of conformity in the scientific community. It happens that society tends to approve in this particular case but the procedure is instructive. Responses are sought to formalized, abstract symbols, devoid of cultural overtones if that is at all possible, and the procedure used to obtain this conformity is an extensive indoctrination period—to a certain point in his development, the scientist is "conditioned" in the Pavlovian sense to respond "correctly" to a given stimulus. It is a relatively simple matter to train two persons to read a dial or meter accurately; it may take quite a period of time to teach two men to "read" an astronomer's photograph in the same way. This type of training is only valid to a certain point, of course, but within its limits it is useful and perhaps essential. The scientists manage very well with it simply because there is general agreement on the type of "program" that needs to be fed into the budding young scientist, and one is tempted to say that some of the most important developments in science relate to changes that are made in the original indoctrination program on which they rest.

In political science, as is well known, there is often real disagreement on the meaning of a given experience, even when the data are public and verifiable. Doubtless, this is in some measure due to the absence of an agreed basic training program in the discipline. There is, in short, need for some agreed approach to the classification of political phenomena, a theoretical structure that would serve as a guide to research and a plan for the accumulation of more knowledge about politics.

To return to the explanation of political phenomena in terms of individual behavior, the peculiar capacity of the individual human to learn, to acquire new knowledge, and to do so both through direct experience and vicariously through the experiences of others, marks the real line of demarcation between the study of human behavior and all other subjects. Learning is irregular, and unending, and it differs in one sense from the accumulation of habits. Habits, which keep us from the tedium of dealing with recurring events, are learned; as the content of the nervous system is filled with experience, if that content is not confined to trivia, men alter their beliefs, their conceptions of the existent, the desirable, and the possible. But there is more, for intellectual manipulations of past experience make possible the production of new ideas, new goals, and new means of attaining them; man has the capacity to produce new knowledge and to act upon it. Herein lies the real importance of Popper's strictures against historicism. When men are actively learning, we cannot, paraphrasing Heraclitus, gaze on the same man on two successive occasions. Of course, some men, perhaps most men, never have the opportunity to undergo the experience of creation, in the sense of creating knowledge new to mankind, though everyone has the experience of learning things new to him. Men react quite differently to new ideas and new information. The stimulation that some men derive from the search for new ideas moves others to retreat into rigid reliance upon past experience. But some men do learn, and some do produce new ideas and concepts, and so long as they continue to do so, the study of human phenomena will remain in some degree logically distinct from the study of physical phenomena. Brute physical necessity requires that men must eat, but learning and ingenuity determine what they will eat, and this is often the important part of the behavior pattern.

Finally, the human being as an object of study differs from the subject matter of science by virtue of the fact that man must choose among alternative modes of behavior and his choice involves more than a rational or logical exercise in formal inference. In this context, the issue of "determinism versus free will" is irrelevant, for if even human choices are forced or determined by the past experience of the individual, some human decision (by parents, educators, etc.) is involved in the selection of experience for training the person. Human beings must make decisions that are evaluative or normative, and if the principles on which such choices are made are simply absorbed from the surrounding society, it is, nevertheless, the case that choice was at some point involved in the process of determining those social mores; no particular set of values is a necessary corollary to the existence of human society.

Where evaluative principles are a necessary prerequisite to an act of human behavior, whether consciously applied or not, an adequate explanation of the behavior will clearly involve some reference to those principles. No similar problem exists for the scientist, yet for political scientists it is peculiarly important. Those concerned with the formulation of "empirical political theory," for example, often assume that because a theory is intended as an explanation of concrete human actions its terms must necessarily be ethically neutral. Yet in politics, which is evaluative behavior par excellence, references to motivation, goals, purposes, etc., will almost invariably designate evaluative principles held by the individual actor. An adequate theory of politics, "empirical" or not (and all theory refers to empirical data in the end), will certainly contain terms which refer to political values; for example, "Most men prefer X to Y," along with statements about the conditions under which such propositions or principles are applied. The influence of this factor on political science will be considered in detail in Chapter 8.

We turn now to consider the influence of these distinctions in subject matter upon the mode of inquiry in physical science and political science, respectively. In the chapter that follows, we examine their influence on modes of explanation; in Chapter 5, we compare the use of models and theories in the two sets of disciplines. Successive chapters deal with the influence of subject matter on epistemology, on techniques and methods employed in inquiry, including the use of formal logic. The aim is to clarify, to establish limits, and to point out permissive and proscriptive limits where they can be found.

BIBLIOGRAPHICAL NOTE

Scientific writings on the physiological, genetic, and neural structures in man are extremely important for political science, and indeed for anyone concerned with the study of human behavior. Much of the writing available is surprisingly readable and not so technical that the general reader is hopelessly lost from the outset. Needless to say, it makes fascinating reading.

Among the best and most useful things I have found are two wonderful books by C. H. Waddington: *The Strategy of the Genes: A Discussion of Some Aspects of Theoretical Biology* (Allen and Unwin, 1957) and *The Ethical Animal* (Allen and Unwin, 1960); the former is a classic and the latter is quite likely to join it. The last two chapters of Charles E. Raven's *Science, Medicine, and Morals* (Harper, 1959) are extremely well done. J. H. Woodger's *Physics, Psychology, and Medicine*

(Cambridge University Press, 1956) is also excellent. For methodological discussions, chap. xii of Ernest Nagel's *Structure of Science* is essential, as is chap. x of R. B. Braithwaite's *Scientific Explanation.*

On philosophy of organism, see W. E. Agar, *A Contribution to the Theory of Living Organism* (rev. ed.; Melbourne University Press, 1951); C. Judson Herrick, *The Evolution of Human Nature* (University of Texas Press, 1956); H. S. Jennings, *The Universe and Life* (Yale University Press, 1933); Ralph S. Lillie, *General Biology and Philosophy of Organism* (University of Chicago Press, 1945); Felix Mainx, *Foundations of Biology,* IEUS, Vol. I, No. 9 (University of Chicago Press, 1955); and J. H. Woodger's older *Biological Principles* (Cambridge University Press, 1929). The writings of Ludwig von Bertalanffy or E. S. Russell, though dated, are good illustrations of earlier "organismic" biology.

Scientific knowledge about the operation of the human nervous system, and particularly the brain, has grown in leaps and bounds in the postwar period. Contributions have come from neurosurgeons, psychologists, mathematicians, engineers, physiologists, and pharmacologists. Numerous symposia have been held to discuss the operation of the central nervous system, or the effects of drugs, etc., on that system. One hardly knows where to begin, so vast has the literature become, and the listing given here includes only the most useful of the not-too-technical works.

E. D. Adrian's *The Physical Background of Perception* (Oxford University Press, 1947) is excellent. W. Ross Ashby's *Design for a Brain: The Origins of Adaptive Behavior* (John Wiley, 1960) is also extremely good, based on a cybernetic conception of the nervous system. Alan D. Bass's *Evolution of Nervous Control from Primitive Organisms to Man* (American Association for the Advancement of Science, Publication No. 52, 1959) is suggestive. Julian Blackburn's *Psychology and the Social Pattern* (Kegan Paul, Trench, and Tubner, 1945) is useful, but less interesting than his *Framework of Human Behavior* (Kegan Paul, Trench, and Tubner, 1947). E. D. Adrian's *Mechanisms of Nervous Action* (University of Pennsylvania Press, 1959) is difficult but excellent. W. R. Ashby's *Introduction to Cybernetics* (John Wiley, 1956) provides a useful supplement to his *Design for a Brain.* Russell Brain's *Some Reflections on Genius* (Pitman Medical Publications, 1960) is good. Two symposia edited by

Seymour M. Farber and Roger H. L. Wilson are superb; *Man and Civilization: Control of the Mind* (McGraw–Hill, 1961) and *Man and Civilization: Conflict and Creativity,* (McGraw–Hill, 1963). Mary A. B. Brazier's *The Electrical Activity of the Nervous System* (Josiah Macy Jr. Foundation and National Science Foundation, 1959) is good but technical. William Feindel's (ed.) *Memory, Learning, and Language: The Physical Basis of Mind* (University of Toronto Press, 1959) contains some very good things. Ragnar Granit's *Receptors and Sensory Perception* (Yale University Press, 1955) is really excellent though difficult. Ward C. Halstead's *Brain and Intelligence: A Quantitative Study of the Frontal Lobes* (University of Chicago Press, 1947) is a fine summary of a life's work on a very difficult area of the cortex. Lloyd A. Jeffress's (ed.) *Cerebral Mechanism in Behavior* (John Wiley, 1951) is one of the best general works available. Warren S. McCulloch, who seems almost a modern Renaissance man, is always worth reading though his writings are scattered. See "Information in the Head," in *Current Trends in Information Theory* (University of Pittsburgh Press, 1953) as well as his contribution to the symposium edited by Jeffress for typical examples. John von Neumann's *The Computer and the Brain* (Yale University Press, 1958) is a noteworthy book by one of the world's foremost mathematicians. Wilder Penfield and Lamar Roberts' *Speech and Brain Mechanisms* (Princeton University Press, 1959) is a classic by one of the great neurosurgeons of our time. F. N. L. Poynter's *The Brain and Its Functions* (Oxford University Press, 1958) and *History and Philosophy of Knowledge of the Brain and Its Functions* (Oxford University Press, 1959) are both good. W. Ritchie Russell's *Brain, Memory, Learning: A Neurologist's View* (Oxford University Press, 1959) is excellent. Ronald Fletcher's *Instinct in Man* (International University Press, 1957) is extremely suggestive about the role of instincts in modern behavior theory. Daniel E. Sheer's (ed.) *Electrical Stimulation of the Brain* (University of Texas Press, 1961) contains several good things, particularly chap. xxxix by Karl H. Pribram, and a magnificent bibliography. Sir Charles Sherrington's classic works on the brain deserve reading still, especially *Man on His Nature* (Doubleday, 1955). Robert Thompson's little book, *The Psychology of Thinking* (Penguin, 1959) is a good antidote to an overdose of formalism. Philip E. Vernon's *The Structure of Human Abilities* (Methuen, 1961) is excellent. W. Gray Walter's *The Living Brain* (W. W. Norton, 1953) is dated somewhat but very readable. Dean E. Woolridge's *The Machinery of the Brain* (McGraw–Hill, 1963) is perhaps the finest general, nontechnical survey available. J. Z. Young's *Doubt and Certainty in Science: A Biologist's Reflections on the Brain* (Oxford University Press, 1960) is also very stimulating.

CHAPTER FOUR

EXPLANATION I: TYPES

THE ultimate goal of inquiry is explanation. It follows that the manner in which explanation is defined, the concept of an adequate explanation that is aimed at, will have a considerable bearing on the manner in which inquiry is conducted and the kinds of results that will be produced. The kinds of explanations that are considered desirable, or possible, in a discipline will help determine the approach to the subject matter, the phenomena selected for investigation, the information sought, the manner in which data are treated, and the verification procedures employed in the inquiry. It is assumed without argument that the logic of explanation is independent of the subject matter, hence there need be no distinctions made between explanation in science and in political science, though the nature of the subject matter will influence the kinds of explanations that are possible in political science and their relative strength or power. One of the most damaging criticisms that can be made of political science as a discipline is that it shows little concern for the logic of explanation and has, for the most part, failed to train its students to an adequate level of formal competence. In fact, this accounts for much of the uninformed criticism that has been directed against "behavioral" political science, and against attempts to construct political or social theory. And much of the speculation that passes for theory in political science ignores the logic of explanation completely.

Informally, to explain means to answer questions, chiefly those which begin "how" or "why." The questions will always refer to some phenomenon, presumably some empirical phenomenon if empirical is broadly defined. It is most important to realize that all explanations begin with a phenomenon, with something that requires explanation; until the phenomenon is defined, explanation cannot even begin. When we ask "Why does a stick appear to bend if one end is placed in water?" or "Why do political parties appear in all democratic societies?" we are asking for an explanation in this sense of the term. We try to answer such questions —to explain—by showing that if what is already known is taken into consideration, the event could not be other than it appears to be; or we can try to show that if certain conditions are satisfied, given the present state of our knowledge, then the event is to be expected.

The bent stick in the water, a favorite of philosophers of science, is explained by referring to our knowledge of optics; political parties are explained, if indeed explanation is possible at the present time, by reference to what is known about political associations. This informal conception of explanation has the disadvantage of making it appear that explanation amounts to no more than the reduction of the unfamiliar to the familiar, and that is decidedly not the case.

On occasion, explanation may amount to this, but in many important cases it does not, and that construction of explanation would in any case be useless until we could decide the question "familiar to whom?"

For this reason, it is best to begin with an analysis of the formal properties of explanation and proceed from there to discuss its meaning in informal terms with reference to particular subject matter and that is the procedure we will follow here.

In a preliminary and tentative way, let us define explana-

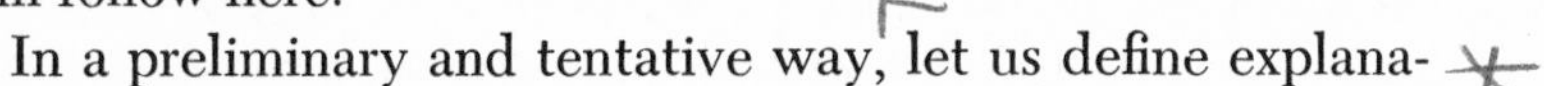

tion as a process by which singular events (explicanda) are related to other events through the use of appropriate general statements. Singular events and isolated phenomena have no meaning; they are only facts. Without explanations facts have no significance, no usefulness. Indeed, we can hardly speak of having knowledge until facts have been related in an explanation structure of some kind. It is the function of inquiry to provide such explanations, or, as R. B. Braithwaite has made the point in relation to science:

> The function of science . . . is to establish general laws covering the behavior of empirical events or objects with which the science in question is concerned, and thereby to enable us to connect together our knowledge of the separately known events, and to make reliable predictions of events as yet unknown. . . . If the science is in a highly developed state, as in physics, the laws which have been established will form a hierarchy in which many special laws appear as logical consequences of a small number of highly general laws expressed in a very sophisticated manner; if the science is in an early stage of development . . . the laws may be merely the generalizations involved in classifying things into various classes.[1]

The formal properties of scientific explanations have been investigated quite rigorously in contemporary philosophy, and this offers a good point of departure for the study of explanations in political science. However, it must be emphasized that not all of the problems related to the explanation of political, or scientific, phenomena have been settled. Further, the logic of explanation is not a panacea, and it is not a guaranteed means of achieving quality results. It is only a guide to investigation and validation, a means of assessing claims to knowledge, or perhaps a form of systematic self-consciousness. Like any other tool, the logic of explanation must be wisely used if it is to produce valid and useful results.

[1] Richard B. Braithwaite, *Scientific Explanation* (New York: Harper & Bros., 1960), p. 1. This seminal work was first published in 1953.

GENERALIZATIONS

The key to the explanatory process is the general statement or generalization. Such statements attribute particular properties to some or all of the members of a well-defined, nonvacuous class and thus provide a link among the members of that class, or they may state relationships among events or classes of events. The extent to which a discipline can generalize its data will in large measure determine its ability to produce satisfactory and useful explanations. In fact, as Braithwaite has pointed out, a generalization is the simplest form of explanation. Clearly, the ability to generalize is in some degree contingent on the nature of the subject matter; some objects are more easily drawn into general statements than others. It follows that a profound knowledge of the subject matter is a prime factor in the capacity to generalize. Though knowledge of the facts is not alone sufficient to ensure that generalizations will be produced, without a knowledge of the subject matter, generalizations are patently impossible. But without some knowledge of the logic of explanation, it would be extremely difficult, and perhaps impossible to validate the generalization, or an explanatory structure that made use of the generalization. The logical and the empirical are inextricably bound in all forms of inquiry, implicitly if not explicitly.

Generalizations may appear in a variety of linguistic forms but we will make use of three comparatively simple and classic formulations, for example, "All *A* is *B*," "*n* percent of *A* is *B*," and "Some *A* is *B*." All general propositions can be reduced to these three forms without difficulty: "If *A* then *B*" is logically equivalent to "All *A* is *B*," or "*A* tends to *B*" is equivalent to "Some *A* is *B*." The first form of the generalization, "All *A* is *B*," is referred to variously as a universal generalization, a nomic generalization, or in some cases, a law. The term "law" is never applied to any generalization that is not universal in form but is not applied to

all universal generalizations; its use is apparently a matter of historic accident rather than any particular set of criteria logically applied. The second form of generalization we shall refer to as "probabilistic," and limit the term strictly to general statements in which a numerical class ratio is stated as part of the generalization, either as a fraction or a percentage. The third form of the generalization, "Some *A* is *B*," or "*A* tends to *B*," we shall call a tendency statement, following the usage in Quentin Gibson's *Logic of Social Enquiry*. Actually, both the second and third forms of generalization are "probabilistic" in that it is only probable that the properties stated in the generalization apply to a particular member of the class to which the generalization applies; but it is useful to make a distinction between statements which contain a definite numerical class ratio and those that merely state a tendency, particularly for political scientists, since the latter type of generalization makes up the bulk of the general statements available in the field.

Generalizations differ widely in scope, precision, and usefulness. Some are quite limited, and perhaps do no more than relate a few simple facts; others are very broad and link whole classes of divergent phenomena. They also differ in their reliability and force. Some, like the "Laws of Nature," are almost absolute and can be assumed to hold in all cases; others are tentative and uncertain, or weak, and must be used with caution. The quality of the generalizations available in a field will influence directly the strength of the explanations that field can offer for the phenomena it is concerned with. Some writers rank scientific generalizations according to their relative strength, for example, into laws, hypotheses, etc., but usage differs widely, and there are no agreed criteria for the classification; therefore, we shall simply use the term "generalization" in all cases except those where the formal requirements of explanation enforce the use of the term "law."

A generalization is a simple form of explanation, and a

simple classification is a good example of both. Statements like "All butterflies have wings" are in a sense part of a real definition of butterflies, the basis on which living organisms are classified as butterflies. On the other hand, they are an adequate response to the question "Why does *that* butterfly have wings?" though they cannot answer the question "Why do butterflies have wings?" For the latter question we need to refer to a higher level of generalization, actually to some kind of developmental theory in genetics and biology. Classification depends upon uniformities and similarities; at the lowest level of generality, things with the same structural or behavior properties, perhaps grossly defined, are grouped together. As the classification system increases in sophistication, the properties are defined with increasing precision. It is not accidental that well-developed sciences like physics and chemistry have classification systems that are very complex and detailed, usually defined by precise measurements, while underdeveloped disciplines are still involved in classification problems. Political science has yet to produce more than the rudiments of a classification system.

Generalizations in political science

It is worth asking whether the relative success of some disciplines is entirely a matter of the skill of their practitioners, or whether there is something more involved. It is, of course, possible that political scientists, despite the long history of the discipline, have simply failed to uncover or produce an adequate classification system for lack of skill and talent, but a more reasonable explanation, for a political scientist at least, is that the peculiarities of the subject matter make it exceptionally difficult to classify. One can imagine the physicist's position if his atoms and molecules could adapt to their environment and change behavior patterns accordingly; every classification system based on behavior would have to be abandoned for the tacit assumption

behind every scientific classification scheme is that identical behavior implies identical event. If the same material exhibited one set of atomic weights on one occasion and another set at a different time, the classification would be quite worthless. To argue that since no classification system for political phenomena has yet been discovered and that it is unlikely that any classification system is possible is to commit a simple logical fallacy, and there are no theoretical grounds on which the possibility of classification can be rejected out of hand. But the absence of an adequate classification scheme does provide some evidence for the difficulty of the task, and the source of that difficulty almost certainly lies in the recalcitrance of the subject matter rather than the capacity of the investigators.

This raises a rather interesting question of strategy of inquiry for political science. The physical scientist has traditionally sought regularities and uniformities in the behavior of his phenomena; political scientists, like historians, have most often been concerned with the uniqueness of each social phenomenon they investigate. Is this an error in strategy on the part of political scientists, or an illustration of a fundamental distinction between the two kinds of inquiry? Generalizations depend primarily on regularities in behavior, to be sure, and no one disputes the existence of regularities in human behavior as well. But is it the regularities and uniformities, or the unique properties of a political phenomenon that best explain the phenomenon? Can an adequate explanation of human behavior be grounded in observed regularities, or must it take into account the unique properties of each action? Is the eating more important than the food being eaten? Is a particular marriage best explained by citing the unique events leading to its consummation? By reference to the function of marriage in society? By citing statistics about the number of marriages that occur in a given year in a given society?

The answer, of course, is that the "best" explanation is

defined by the point of view of the person seeking an explanation. The sociologist may be more concerned with the cultural aspects of the marriage, described in general terms; the bridegroom, seeking desperately to be happy though married, doubtless is better satisfied by an explanation that refers to the unique properties of his entry into the married state. Explanation is not some simple absolute operation that can only be handled in one way; there are many explanations for some events, and perhaps for most events, and we must decide which explanation best suits our purposes. For example, if every human being on earth was observed to engage in behavior ϕ under conditions we may call A, and if no men had ever been observed to do anything but ϕ when conditions were A, the generalization "All men do ϕ under condition A" would be extremely powerful—a lawlike or universal statement applicable without exception when the conditions were satisfied. Yet it is doubtful that reference to this generalization would, in all cases and for all persons, satisfy the demand for explanation. We then ask, *should* this explanation satisfy everyone at all times? I believe the answer is no, at least in reference to human behavior. For one thing, very few cases of human behavior can be shown to be absolutely necessary, so that men "Do ϕ" because they must. This opens the door for further explanation of some sort. And even if the behavior can be shown to be necessary, as in the generalization "All men die," that would not be taken as an adequate explanation of the phenomenon "Jones died today." In human behavior, more commonly, it is almost always possible that under the conditions specified, ϕ will not occur. Of course, physical scientists also accept this same theoretical possibility; for example, there is an infinitesimally small probability that the sun will not rise tomorrow morning, or the sun will cease throwing off energy, or the earth will stop turning on its axis. But few scientists really believe that when organization and structure remain the same, and external conditions do not vary,

that behavior pattern may still change. It is inconsistent with their naturalism, and with the logical structure they have erected. Furthermore, it does not happen in practice. The Law of Gravity does not fail; in fact the number of laws in science is mute testimony to the strength of the argument. Social behavior, on the other hand, does change despite what seem to be identical or very similar circumstances, and such changes are not confined to the behavior of wives. Perhaps this is an illusion, brought about by our limited capacity to specify precise conditions and behavior patterns. The practical force of the argument, however, seems to me overwhelming.

The point is that explanations have formal and psychological consequences and it has yet to be demonstrated that once the formal requirements of explanation have been satisfied the explanation is necessarily adequate for the political scientist. In many cases, the formal requirements of explanation cannot be stated, as we shall see in the following chapter when we consider the grounds on which we agree to accept and use theories.

At the very least, we are entitled to consider explanations of human behavior incomplete if they are not psychologically satisfying to those who are competent in the subject matter. The justification of that position can be obtained from the subject matter itself. When an individual human action can be brought under the terms of a generalization based strictly on empirical observations, we all realize that intentions, purposes, etc., have been ignored in the generalization, and we are aware of the possibility that these subjective factors may be important in the phenomena in question. A slight feeling of unease in these circumstances seems honestly come by. If the physicist knew that his atoms and molecules were capable of acting out of antipathy or liking for other atoms and molecules, he too might feel just a little less certain about the adequacy of generalizations based on strict empirical evidence. Granted that the question "Why" is sometimes asked under circumstances in which the asker is completely in the dark about the kind of explanation he would be prepared to accept, it is also the case that explanations of human behavior are examined not only in terms of the canons of logic but in terms of personal, subjective knowledge about the internal states of human beings. It is always possible that further advances in psychology will produce theories and generalizations that will link observed behavior with internal states with some degree of accuracy, thus reducing the scope of the problem, but until that stage of development is reached, there is some element of "every man his own psychologist" in any evaluation of explanation in political science. The question deserves careful consideration. What has been said here is speculative, but the importance of the general problem raised will be evident as we probe more deeply into the nature of explanation.

TYPES OF EXPLANATIONS

Logically, the classification of explanations is based upon the kinds of generalizations that the explanation employs. There are two parent types: first, *deductive* (sometimes called deductive-nomological) explanations which make use of generalizations that are universal in form (All *X* is *Y*); second, *probabilistic* explanations which make use of generalizations that express an arithmetical class ratio between two events, or generalizations that express tendencies. In a deductive explanation, a particular event is explained by showing that it can be deduced from an established universal generalization, as when we explain the fall of a particular apple to earth by showing that this can be deduced from the Law of Gravity. In a probabilistic explanation, the relationship between the event to be explained and the generalization is not deductive (except in a special case to be explained later), but the event is explained by bringing it within the framework of a probabilistic generalization or a tendency statement. That is, the generalization *provides evidence for* the event; the event cannot be deduced from the generalization.

There are four special cases of explanation which will be treated separately (because of their importance in political science), though logically they can be shown to be examples of either deductive or probabilistic explanation. First, a *causal* explanation relates the explicandum to a set of antecedent conditions that are necessary and/or sufficient to generate the explicandum. Second, a *functional* explanation relates the explicandum to a larger context by showing the function it performs, as when we explain the liver by showing the function it performs in maintaining the body. Third, a *teleological* explanation relates the explicandum to some goal or purpose on the part of the actor or system, as when animal behavior is explained as a search for food or human behavior as an attempt to achieve a particular goal or purpose. There is a fourth type of explanation, called *genetic* or historical explanation, which consists of tracing the antecedents of a particular event and showing how it evolved.

Each kind of explanation has its own merits, its own uses, its own limitations. In general, deductive explanations are more powerful than probabilistic explanations, and they are considered by some to be the ideal explanatory form. This is not necessarily the case, however, particularly in political science, as we shall see in due course. Biologists make frequent use of functional and teleological explanations, as do anthropologists; physicists tend to eschew both if possible. Causal explanations, according to Braithwaite, usually appear in the early stages of a discipline's development and they are later replaced by deductive systems. The validation of generalizations and theories is another difficult problem, particularly for probabilistic explanations, for, unlike deductive explanation, it cannot be discredited by particular empirical evidence. Our problem is to determine as accurately as we can the formal requirements, uses, and applications of each type of explanation and evaluate them in terms of the subject matter of political science. In this chapter, we confine ourselves to simple generalizations and simpler forms of explanations. In the chapter that follows we deal with complex explanations and the role played by theories and models in such explanations.

DEDUCTIVE EXPLANATIONS

A deductive explanation requires the following basic elements: *(a)* a general empirical law or universal generalization; *(b)* a statement of the conditions under which the generalization holds true; *(c)* an event to be explained (explicandum); and *(d)* the rules of logic. The explicandum is "explained" by showing that it is a logical consequence of the generalization under the conditions specified. Formally, the premises in a deductive explanation must include at least one generalization that is lawlike in form (All *X* is *Y*) and enough singular statements to establish precisely the conditions under which the generalization holds true. Deductive explanations can be applied to either singular facts or to universals. If the explicandum is singular, a deductive structure can be used to specify the cause of the event, for example, to state the conditions which are necessary and sufficient to produce it under the conditions specified. The cause of universals cannot be specified. Since a deductive explanation makes use of universal generalizations, validation is a comparatively simple matter, for a single empirical instance to the contrary is sufficient to invalidate the structure. Thus the general statement "All swans are white" (another philosopher's favorite) is a sufficient answer to the question "Why is that swan white?" or in the universal form, "Why are swans white?" But if a single swan of another color is found (black swans are found in Australia), the generalization ceases to be universal and the deductive explanation must be abandoned. A probabilistic generalization, weaker but still useful, could be salvaged, or, if the scope of the generalization was reduced, the universal form could be retained, for example, by asserting "All European swans are white" (which is true), a deductive explanation of the whiteness of a European swan would still be possible. The scope of the class is reduced, but the universality of the generalization with reference to the class can be retained.

Without universal generalizations, deductive explanations are impossible, a matter of some importance for political scientists. In those disciplines where deductive explanations are common, we often find a regular hierarchy of generalizations, each level being deducible from the level immediately above it in the hierarchy. If the hierarchy is sufficiently extended, it becomes an axiomatic structure, resembling geometry in form. That is, there will be a few fundamental generalizations called axioms at the top of the pyramid, and each of the generalizations in the succeeding levels of the hierarchy can be deduced from these few axioms. The status of axioms is uncertain, for what is today the top level of a deductive hierarchy may tomorrow be subsumed within a theory of even greater power and generality, and in theory science could never know with certainty that it had reached an ultimate stage of explanation and could go no further. When a deductive explanation reaches the axioms of the system, it simply stops and it is pointless to demand an explanation of the axioms themselves.

To follow a typical deductive explanation from the bare physical phenomenon let us begin with a stone thrown into the air and ask a physicist for an explanation of its return to earth. His explanation will ignore the wishes or desires of the person who threw the stone and concentrate solely on the physical characteristics of the phenomenon. At the first stage of explanation, he would simply cite the Law of

Gravity and point out that if all objects exercise a mutual attraction on one another the stone could be expected to behave in the same way with reference to the earth. He might even demonstrate that by using the Law of Gravity and certain other statements fixing the conditions under which it holds true, he could actually predict the flight of the stone very accurately. This would constitute a single-stage explanation of the phenomenon, employing a universal generalization. If the listener then demanded to know why the Law of Gravity ought to be accepted, the physicist could argue in two ways: first, he could assert that no single empirical instance to the contrary had even been recorded; second, if that did not provide satisfaction, he would have recourse to a generalization, or set of generalizations, of greater generality than the Law of Gravity, to explain the law. He would point out that according to Einstein's Theory of Relativity, the Law of Gravity is a special consequence of the relationship between space and time that obtains in the kind of universe that Einstein postulated. If then asked why Relativity Theory should be accepted, he could once again point out that certain kinds of observations support the theory, though there are some remaining problems; hence, that it is the most acceptable theory available to physics at this time. If asked whether the theory is true or false, the physicist could only reply that there is no way for science to assert the truth or falsity of theories. If the questioner continued to demand an explanation of Relativity Theory, the physicist could only stop the discussion and point out that science has no theory capable of explaining Relativity Theory; hence, the person asking for an explanation could have no possible answer in mind. Much simplified, this is the essence of a deductive hierarchy.

It is sometimes said that deductive explanations are no more than a summation or description of observed facts,  and that this "descriptive" quality lessens their value as explanation, particularly in the social sciences. However, this is a misconception rather than a criticism. If a deductive explanation did no more than refer to the facts from which it was derived, then it would in fact be circular. But the essential feature of a generalization is that it purports to encompass all cases that fall within the class to which it applies: present, past, or future, observed, or unobserved. A universal generalization is a kind of open prediction about a particular class of events where not all of the members of the class have been observed. Each new observation provides a means of verifying, or disverifying, the generalization; hence, validating or invalidating the explanations in which it is employed. This, incidentally, is one of the principal reasons for asserting the assumption in science of some principle of uniformity of nature, for if nature were not uniform it is hard to see how the generalization could be extended to unobserved phenomena; and if the extension were not made, then the generalization would be circular and descriptive.

Although scientific laws are universal in form, they do not make absolute assertions about the universe, or about man's perceptions of the universe. For one thing, every  generalization is conditional and the conditions under which it applies must be specified. More important, science has no means of proving, in the positive sense, any generalization; it can only disprove it. Any particular bit of empirical evidence can destroy a universal general statement, but it cannot prove it beyond doubt. Each new bit of data provides another test of the generalization, and failure to survive the test invalidates the generalization but passing the test only opens the way for yet more testing. If the universe  were "really" orderly and uniform, then scientific generalizations might actually be proved, and if it appears, on the basis of past behavior, that this is really the case, and even if it seems that experimental scientists make this assumption for their work, the assumption is not, strictly speaking, either necessary or justified. Science discussed human perceptions, not absolute properties of the universe.[2]

A second quality of universal generalizations, particularly those referred to as natural laws, is their imprecision. The relation between an empirical law and the data it explains is always experimentally imperfect. The laws are, in effect, idealizations of empirical data and not exact reproductions of observed results. A theory or law will usually approximate its data but not fit them perfectly.

The importance of testability in any explanatory system is obvious; Popper, for one, claims that it is the most important part of the scientific process. Two points need to be made about testing or validation: first, it may at times be very difficult to decide whether a given test does or does not substantiate a theory; second, there is a great deal of difference between a test and an illustration. The significance of a particular test will depend on the nature and usefulness of the theory, and on its precision. Theories may sometimes be retained even if it is known that they are faulty. And it is not always a simple problem to decide whether the evidence supports or confutes a theory. The distinction between testing and illustrating is particularly important for political science, where data are very commonly used for the latter purpose. A genuine test involves the whole range of pertinent data. The generalization must be formulated in terms that are open to testing, and the test must be precise enough to allow valid inference from the results. Popper's strictures on psychiatric and social theory are particularly apt here, and his assertion that both Marx and Freud have been so interpreted that they explain everything, and are not open to testing, is well grounded. One brief example may illustrate the point. If

[2] There is an excellent discussion of the "Principle of Uniformity of Nature" in chap. v of Stephen Toulmin's *Philosophy of Science: An Introduction* (Hutchinson University Library, 1953).

the Oedipus complex is taken as a theory, the fact that a particular male child is attached to its female parent may be said to be evidence for the theory, and the fact that another male child disliked its female parent intensely would constitute evidence to the contrary. When the orthodox Freudian asserts that in the second case the child has "sublimated" or "displaced" its Oedipus complex, he removes the theory from all possibility of testing, for the theory now explains everything and cannot be refuted by any kind of evidence.[3]

The discipline that can produce deductive explanations is extremely fortunate, for they are more useful than explanations in any other form. They permit accurate prediction, since it is relatively easy to deduce particular events from universal generalizations and such deduced particulars are in effect predictions. They are easily verified, for deduced particulars can be compared with empirical evidence and the standard of disverification is easy to apply; for example, a single contrary instance is sufficient to invalidate the generalization. They are more readily treated mathematically and logically, for strict deductive relations can be handled much more accurately and easily than statistical or probabilistic relations. The physical sciences prefer deductive explanations to all others, and they are a prominent part of the explanatory apparatus of well-developed fields like physics or chemistry. Unfortunately for the political scientist, deductive explanations require universal generalizations, and the latter are not made by the investigator at his discretion; they must be based upon regularities in the behavior of the subject matter. If empirical laws cannot be produced by a discipline, the deductive form of explanation simply cannot be used. This, regretfully, seems to be the case at the present time in political science.

[3] Karl Popper, *Conjectures and Refutations* (Routledge and Kegan Paul, 1963), chap. 1.

DEDUCTIVE EXPLANATIONS IN POLITICAL SCIENCE

Are there, or can there be, universal generalizations in political science? Do we have, or can we produce, "Laws of Politics"? The answer seems to be that at present there are no empirical laws in the discipline, or at best only a very few, and that the outlook for the future is dubious. F. Kaufmann asserts flatly that there are no laws in social science and that none can be produced. Ernest Nagel, after examining the objections raised against the possibility that empirical laws may be discovered in the future, concludes that laws are in principle possible but agrees that there are formidable practical difficulties to be overcome. Quentin Gibson accepts the possibility that empirical laws may be discovered, and cites the "Iron Law of Oligarchy" as an example, but concludes that it is so unlikely that they will ever be numerous that deductive explanation is unlikely to play any major role in the explanation of social phenomena. There seems to be no logical reason why political scientists cannot produce empirical laws; let us therefore grant the possibility in principle and examine the practical reasons why they are unlikely to become available in any substantial numbers.

Complexity

The complexity of the subject matter is usually offered as a practical argument against the discovery of empirical laws governing human behavior. That is, individual and group behavior occurs in a social–physical context that involves so many possible influences on any given action that a full specification of these influences and their relative influence in given situations is out of the question. Clearly, this point is not tenable in principle, for the same argument could be leveled against some branches of science—yet empirical laws have been discovered there. In practical terms, however, the order of complexity that mitigates against a

precise classification system also inhibits the discovery of empirical laws. An empirical law designates the behavior of a specified class of events in specified circumstances, and political science is simply unable to specify accurately at this stage in its development. This is not to say that if a classification could be discovered based solely on observation of human behavior, ignoring subjective influences, the law would not be valid. It would. But the point is that we have not yet been able to produce such laws, and the reason that suggests itself is that until nonobservable influences are included in the classification, the categories are not sufficiently stable to allow universalization of behavior patterns.

Experimentation

The inability of political scientists to experiment widely and under controlled conditions with their subject matter is offered as a second reason why empirical laws of behavior are not forthcoming. Even if the term "experiment" is defined broadly enough to include controlled field research, and granting that some experimental evidence is now being produced, it remains true that experimentation is limited fundamentally by the relation between the investigator and the subject matter. In practice, it is very difficult if not impossible to establish lawlike generalizations without experimental evidence; the experiment permits the investigator to vary his conditions so as to winnow out possible interfering factors in a way that cannot be achieved through uncontrolled observation, however systematic. We should not overstate the case on behalf of the physical scientists, of course, for in practice their ability to control perfectly all of the variables in a given situation is never complete. But in comparison with the materials of politics, the subject matter of physical science is much more amenable to laboratory test and this is doubtless an important reason why the scientist has managed to produce a wider range of experimental laws than the political scientist has available.

Learning

The human capacity to learn and alter behavior through experience seems also to limit the possibility of discovering empirical laws in political science simply because this quality will actually reduce the possibility that such laws exist or can be discovered. In one sense, an empirical law asserts that under particular circumstances a given event *must* occur; if it does not, the law is not a law. In principle, it would seem that the learning capacity of man reduces the number of cases in which it can be said that men *must* act in a particular manner. Of course, every scientific generalization, lawlike or not, is liable to change, but in practice science would soon founder if its laws proved unreliable. In politics, it seems that men in fact do not always behave in the same way under the same circumstances (if they did, we would have more empirical laws), and man's ability to learn and alter his behavior probably accounts in part for this behavioral instability.

Cultural relativity

An additional barrier to the development of universal generalizations in political science is the fact of cultural relativity. There is not just one social context in which political theorists can work but many such contexts; hence, actions with a given meaning and significance in one culture may have quite a different meaning in another environment, just as words are notoriously misleading when we move from one culture to another. Universal generalizations ought to be transcultural and, in practical terms, the fact of cultural relativity makes the task more difficult, though it does not affect the principle. In contemporary political theory, for example, it often appears that the generalizations available are very much culture-conditioned; hence, limited in application. Can we apply a conception of the role of violence in politics arrived at by a study of Western political development to the political conditions that obtain in the underdeveloped nations, particularly those recently freed from colonial rule? To what extent could a theory of political parties based on American experience be transferred even to Western Europe without major changes in structure? One of the most hopeful trends in recent political science, from the theorist's standpoint, is the growth of a genuine attempt at comparative study of politics, for the availability of detailed comparisons of the political process in different cultural and institutional surroundings will certainly help to winnow out the universal from the culturally determined and thus start the discipline on the road toward firmly grounded empirical theory.

Values

A corollary to cultural relativism, as an influence on the capacity of the discipline to produce lawlike generalizations, is the influence of values and preferences on the social investigator and on his conception of the subject matter. This is not the same as the question whether the social inquirer can maintain his objectivity under conditions that are certainly more trying for the political scientist than for the physicist. The physicist, through the use of special terminology and symbols, seeks to minimize the influence of values and culture on his work and his subject matter seems amenable to this kind of treatment. But in political science, both language and learning conspire to influence professional work. There is no special vocabulary of politics, despite Professor Weldon's pioneer attempt to deal with the problem. Further, the problems of politics are so closely intermingled with our educational system and the mass media that it is almost impossible to avoid some measure of preconditioning that will influence the outcome of inquiry. More important for our problem, however, is the fact that political science deals with phenomena that are so heavily impregnated with values that the separation of fact from value may be a formidable or even an impossible task. Indirectly, this can influence the production of generalizations, for the extent to which the data of politics are impregnated with inseparate value connotations they decline qualitatively, using empirical standards, and it is harder to produce laws with poorly defined or faulty data than with data that are crisply defined and unambiguous.

In sum, political scientists are unlikely to make use of deductive explanation in the immediate future for lack of an adequate supply of empirical laws. Even the "Iron Law of Oligarchy," to which there seems no empirical exception, may, in fact, be a definition rather than a generalization, as many of the "laws" of economics are logical derivatives of the axioms of economic theory and not generalizations from observed data. We shall have occasion to return to this question in our discussion of theories and models.

PROBABILISTIC EXPLANATIONS

For the immediate future, explanations of political phenomena can be expected to assume the probabilistic rather than the deductive form. That is, political events will be explained by reference to one or more generalizations that are probabilistic and not universal in form; for example, they assert that "Some part of *X* (less than 100 percent) is *Y*." Two different cases are possible: first, the generalization can specify with a fraction or percentage exactly what part of *X* is *Y;* second, the generalization can include some relative term like "some," "most," or "tends to," without specifying how much or what part. The first case we will refer to as a probabilistic generalization; the second, following Quentin Gibson, will be called a tendency statement. A probabilistic generalization asserts that an event will occur with a given probability, meaning roughly that it will appear with a certain relative frequency in a long sequence of events or within a large population. The index of probability is stated as an arithmetical ratio. A tendency statement asserts that "All *X* is *Y* *except* for interfering conditions," and the interfering conditions cannot be specified fully. Indeed, the amount of interference that can be anticipated is also beyond specification, otherwise the tendency statement would become a probability statement. A typical probabilistic generalization might assert that "82 percent of the registered voters participated in the last primary election in West Virginia," or "51 percent of all human births are male children." A typical tendency statement could be, "In a multiparty political system, the government is likely to be controlled by a coalition of parties rather than a single party," or "Voters tend to adopt the political party of the male parent." Tendency statements are less precise than probability statements; hence, they are harder to validate or disprove, but that does not mean that they are necessarily less useful or powerful. A good tendency statement may be far more useful in the explanation of political phenomena than a precise statistical generalization that deals with trivia.

In a probabilistic explanation, the explicandum is related to the generalization, but not deductively, excepting one special case. Hence, we cannot simply substitute probabilistic generalizations for universal generalizations and deduce consequences in particular cases. Logically, no singular event can be deduced from any statistical generalization. The most that can be said is that the generalization provides evidence for the event. The major exception, arising out of the so-called "Law of Large Numbers," produces deductive statements of a peculiar sort. If we know that a certain statistical relationship holds for a particular event, for example, that 51 percent of all infants are males, we can then deduce that *the chances are good* that this relationship will hold in a large population. Similarly, if we know that the probability of tossing a head on any given flip of a coin is 1:2, we can deduce from this that there is a good chance that 50 percent of the tosses in a long series will result in heads. But we must have the original probability on other evidence; we must, in other words, know that in any particular case the odds are 51–49 that a particular embryo will develop into a male infant.

There is, of course, a formal logic for handling probabilistic generalizations, though it is far too complex to be considered here in any detail. The rules differ from normal logical deduction, particularly with relation to singular events. The basic point to remember is that nothing can be deduced about an individual member of a class from the properties of the whole class. If, for example, we know that 80 percent of the members of a religious group voted for the Democratic party in every election for the past forty years, we still cannot assert that the probability that a particular member of the group voted Democratic is 8/10. The reason is that other factors, besides membership in the particular class of which the generalization is true, may influence the behavior under discussion. The particular person may also be a member of a very wealthy family with a long tradition of Republican political leaning and this factor may outweigh the influence of his religious affiliation. Furthermore, a statistical relationship between two classes of events does not and cannot establish a causal relationship between the two classes; causal relationships must be established independently and empirically. A statistical correlation between income and voting behavior does not mean that income level is in some way the "cause" of voting behavior. Statistical correlations may be considered evidence for the existence of a causal relationship but they cannot demonstrate that the causal relationship exists. And if a one-to-one relationship between class membership and a particular behavior pattern could be established, the generalization would then be universal in form and not probabilistic at all, at least with relation to that particular class. The absence of a one-to-one relationship also constitutes evidence for the belief

that multiple influences are at work in a particular case, and in any factor theory of this sort the outcome of particular combinations cannot be predicted unless the direction and strength of each influence can be identified and measured, as in vector analysis.

One device that is used to eliminate some of the problems arising out of the multiplicity of potential causes of human behavior is to increase the complexity of the class definition by including more of the factors involved in the behavior. Thus the voting habits of farmers as a class can be studied with greater precision by redefining the class. Instead of generalizing about farmers, for example, we may generalize about farmers with a particular religious background, a particular income level, a particular geographic location, and so on, through various limiting conditions. However, there are practical limits to the usefulness of the technique. As the classification grows increasingly complex it becomes more accurate, and that is to the good. But, at the same time the number of events that fall into the class is reduced, the generalizations based on the class become less useful. Reducing the size of the class in order to obtain more precision is ultimately self-defeating for as the class is reduced in size, the generality of its properties decreases in direct ratio. Moreover, as the number of factors used to define the class increases, the complexity of the calculations needed to manipulate the data increases very rapidly and it soon becomes impracticable. We arrive at a position very much like that asserted in the Heisenberg "Uncertainty Principle"; we increase precision in one area only at a cost to be paid in another. We cannot have both.

Probabilistic explanations are substantially weaker than deductive explanations. The former do not, for example, have very much predictive capacity, since it is not possible to deduce singular statements from general statements that are probabilistic in form. Furthermore, probabilistic explanations are sometimes difficult to verify or substantiate. If the general statement includes an arithmetical coefficient of probability, it can usually be verified by adequate sampling. But at what point can we say that the statement "Some X is Y" has been disproved? Finally, as we shall see in the following chapter, it is easier to construct theories with universal generalizations than with probabilistic generalizations. In the former case, the general statements in a theory will be related logically, and its implications can be explored fully by the various tools available to the logician and mathematician. When theories are constructed from probabilistic statements, the general statements are not related logically and the implications of the theory are much less clearly defined. For the political scientist, this is a serious handicap, and we cannot hope to achieve the level of precision, or generality, that physical science has already attained. There are various "cross-referencing" techniques that can be employed when probabilistic statements are used in explanation which will do much to tighten the chain of reasoning in an explanation, and the drawbacks to probabilistic explanation are probably less serious in practice than they appear in formal analysis. But it is reasonably clear that political scientists will be called upon to exercise informal judgment more often, and in more significant cases, than is the case in physical science. The discipline will remain less formal, more uncertain, more personal, perhaps, than physical science. This may be obvious, but it is still worthwhile to pinpoint the reasons why such conditions are likely to continue.

PROBABILISTIC EXPLANATIONS AND POLITICS

Probabilistic explanations may make use of statistical generalizations which include a coefficient of probability or tendency statements which are less precise. It is unlikely that probability statements which include a numerical class-ratio will be anything like so numerous as tendency state-

ments, chiefly because the former require a more stringent set of conditions before they can be asserted. Probability can only be stated in numerical terms when the phenomena to which it relates can be measured additively. In political science, that class of measurable phenomena is quite limited and it is obvious that many significant events cannot be so measured, though they are worth explaining. We can produce precise statements about voting behavior, or population movements, or various phases of economic activity, but the range of phenomena is narrow and the boundaries of the phenomena are not easily defined. Voting statistics, for example, refer only to the physical action that we designate to be "casting a vote," and in strict terms there is no way of inferring from such data to any subjective conditions that may precede or accompany the act. Before that is possible, we need an established theory that will provide some reliable link between observable data and subjective motivation or intention, and that is not available. This does not mean that voting statistics are worthless. In the absence of other information, they may be the best data we can obtain in quantified form. But it does mean that political scientists must be extremely careful about the inferences they draw from the statistical generalizations, and about the use that is made of such generalizations in explanation.

Although statistics are widely used in social science, their use in explanation is not always satisfactory. For one thing, there is always the psychological dissatisfaction that comes from the realization that statistical data based on empirical observation omit influences or relationships that we believe, on subjective grounds, to be important. A formal problem in the use of such generalizations is more serious. Statistical generalizations are explained by reference to further generalizations or combinations of generalizations (theories), one of which must contain a statistical term, yet be of greater generality than the general statement to be explained. Alternatively, statistical generalizations are explained by reference to strict empirical laws. Since these latter generalizations are not available in political science, we will have to depend upon second-order statistical generalizations, and they are not easily obtained. That is, a general statement about voting behavior phrased in statistical terms would have to be explained by further generalizations about political phenomena, also statistical, of even greater generality. These we do not at present have.

Finally, political science often requires an explanation of individual behavior, and it is not really possible to explain individual actions by statistical generalizations. They can only refer to the descriptive aspects of the action and, as H. L. A. Hart has pointed out, it is an error to suppose that actions can be described adequately in terms that are purely descriptive. The concept of an action is a social concept, and its meaning depends upon accepted rules of conduct.

> It is fundamentally not descriptive but ascriptive in character; and it is a defeasible concept to be defined through exceptions and not by a set of necessary and sufficient conditions, whether physical or psychological.[4]

If Hart is correct, no set of empirical general statements referring solely to the observable elements of human behavior would suffice to define human actions adequately. An explanation of the action would probably include some general statements of this type, but it would also have to include generalizations about nondescriptive aspects of the behavior. An explanation comprised wholly of statistical generalizations could not satisfy this requirement.

This suggests that the bulk of the task of political explanation will have to be handled through the use of tendency statements. Again, tendency statements, like probabilistic statements, are of limited use in the explanation of individual behavior; they provide evidence, not deductive

[4] H. L. A. Hart, "The Ascription of Responsibility and Rights," in A. G. N. Flew (ed.), *Logic and Language*, First Series (Basil Blackwell, 1960), pp. 161–62.

proof, for a particular proposition. A more serious shortcoming of tendency statements, however, is that they impose no predetermined limit on the evidence; they are exceptionally difficult to verify, for verification is an act of judgment—not the application of a criterion. Taken alone, a single tendency statement is almost useless; it must be bound with other statements into a coherent theory before it acquires significant explanatory power. This is a problem that we will take up in detail in the next chapter.

OTHER FORMS OF EXPLANATION

Bearing in mind the general properties of the two fundamental modes of explanation, we can now examine four more specific kinds of explanations that are widely used in political science and the other social sciences. Logically, all four can be reduced to one of the two fundamental forms, but they are sufficiently distinct to be worth separate consideration. (1) A *causal* explanation, which is used to explain singular events, does so by specifying the antecedent conditions that are necessary and/or sufficient to generate the event. The phenomenon is explained by showing how it is caused. (2) A *functional* explanation makes use of expressions that relate a particular phenomenon to the system in which it occurs—it shows the function that the explicandum performs in the system. (3) A *teleological* explanation identifies the goal or purpose that particular events fulfill. It is very close to a functional explanation in form but will be kept separate here. (4) *Genetic* explanations trace the past history of a particular event, presumably to a point where the inquirer understands how the event came to occur. Each of these explanatory structures has a wide range of uses in political science.

Causal explanations

Causal explanations, as R. B. Braithwaite has noted, have

proved unusually fruitful and satisfying in the sciences; when events can be fitted into a causal chain the result is particularly satisfying psychologically and, if the chain is deductive, the exploration of its implications can be unusually fruitful. However, not all causal explanations are of equal quality, and a distinction has to be drawn between a causal explanation that includes the sufficient conditions for an event and one that includes only the necessary conditions. When causal explanations occur in physical science, they are usually part of a deductive system, and the relationship between events is Humean, implying no more than a constant conjunction of properties or an invariable sequential relationship between successive events. If one billiard ball strikes another, the second ball will move, and everyday usage asserts that the first ball caused the second to move. Hume destroyed causality as an observed relationship, but the essence of the interaction implied can be retained without the term "cause" if we consider events as invariably related in nonreversible order. When the sufficient conditions for an event can be specified, the logical form (simplified) is then "If *A* then *B*" which is equivalent to "All *A* is *B*." The statement is, therefore, universal and unrestricted and it can be related deductively to other phenomena; it becomes a "causal law." If, however, only the necessary conditions for an event are known, the general statement is probabilistic and it cannot be related deductively to particular events. Both forms of causal explanation occur in science, though the former is preferred for obvious reasons.

Political scientists, like physical scientists, have long sought the "cause of things," but we must note that if they are able to assert both the necessary and the sufficient cause of a given political phenomenon, they are, in fact, in possession of a very powerful kind of universal generalization. This, as we have already noted, is very unlikely because of the peculiar properties of political phenomena. In fact we find that if it is often possible to state the conditions necessary to a particular event, it is extremely difficult to state the conditions that are sufficient to generate the event. Causal explanations of war, divorce, social disintegration, or particular policies are common, but only rarely can the investigator state more than the necessary conditions for these events. Usually, other variables of unknown content and power must be assumed to influence the system. The predictive power of such explanations is obviously very limited since prediction requires a knowledge of sufficient conditions; with the necessary conditions we are in a position only to make tendency statements. Causal explanations that depend on tendency statements are considerably less powerful and fruitful than causal explanations that include the sufficient conditions for an event.

Nationalism, for example, is certainly a factor in producing war; so are armaments, family jealousies, pride, greed, and ambition in particular individuals. But no single-factor theory will be adequate to account for all wars, and until all of the factors necessary to produce war can be specified, the causal explanation is incomplete and useless for prediction. Further, a multifactor theory of war would have to be able to weigh each of the factors and produce a criterion for war in which each would have a place. Further, the inability of political scientists to conduct the kind of controlled experiments that would be needed to provide the evidence on which a multifactor theory could be based makes it very difficult to establish a causal explanation that is wholly unambiguous. When behavioral regularities do appear, and statistical treatment can narrow the range of potential causes to some extent, quite adequate statements of the conditions necessary for a particular political phenomenon to occur are quite possible. But they will only rarely attain the power and precision of a truly deductive causal explanation in which the relationships are treated deductively. Most of the attempts at causal explanations in political science, in relation to war, for example, are more an exercise in ingenuity than attempts at formal explanation.

Functional explanations

Functional explanations, though widely used in biology, are not very common in the physical sciences. A functional explanation requires a conception of a dynamic system in which each part has a function in maintaining the dynamic of the whole. C. G. Hempel argues that functional explanations do not satisfy the logical requirements of explanation because of an unwarranted inference, made in the following manner:[5]

(1) A system (S) functions adequately in a specified setting at a specified time and is then characterized by particular conditions and properties.
(2) The system functions adequately in a given setting only if a certain necessary condition is present.
(3) If a particular trait is present, the conditions necessary for maintaining the system are satisfied, as an effect of that trait.
(4) Therefore, the trait is present at that time.

As Hempel notes, (4) would follow *only* if the particular trait being explained was the only means of satisfying the necessary conditions for the event. This, he claims, is questionable on empirical grounds, for there are few phenomena for which no equivalent can be found, and some functionalists like Robert K. Merton insist that functional equivalents must be accepted as a possibility in principle.

Hempel's analysis is very rigorous, and it may be that we cannot hope to find any explanation of social phenomena that will meet this kind of standard at this time. Certainly, there has been an enormous upsurge of interest in functional explanation in sociology and the other social sciences in recent years, and many sociologists and political scientists

[5] C. G. Hempel, "The Logic of Functional Analysis," in L. Gross (ed.), *Symposium on Sociological Theory* (New York: Harper and Row, 1959), p. 284 f.

believe it offers the best route to the development of an adequate social theory.[6] Some of the practical problems facing the functionalist searching for social theory should be noted. First, the boundaries of the system may be very difficult to draw; for example, the statement of the factors included in the system and influencing its operation may be incomplete, not because the investigator has committed a logical error but simply because our knowledge of the operation of the system is not complete. As an example, let us assume the present world of national states as a system, though in fact it would be peculiarly difficult to define the properties of that system very accurately. Each national state would then become a subsystem within the international system and the function of the former in maintaining the latter would be the basis for explanation. But each state is also a collection of subsystems, some if not all of which have influence on the way in which the state functions as an international entity; and the subsystems in turn are open to the same kind of analysis. At what point in the analysis of the total system is the proliferation of subsystems to stop? Presumably at a level where the interaction of subsystems is adequate to explain the functioning of the larger system. And there seems no way of evading the full specification of the system in which explanation is framed, for even if the goal is the explanation of a particular action by a particular nation, the whole structure must be called in to supply the conditions which the particular phenomenon acts to maintain.

There are other dangers involved in the concept of system and function, too. For one thing, the inquirer may assume

[6] Typical "functionalist" approaches to explanation and theory can be found in A. R. Radcliffe-Brown, *A Natural Science of Society* (Glencoe, Ill.: The Free Press, 1957); David Easton, *The Political System* (New York: Alfred Knopf, 1953); Eugene Burdick and A. Brodbeck, *American Voting Behavior* (The Free Press, 1959); Robert K. Merton, *Social Theory and Social Structure* (rev. ed.; The Free Press, 1957); Talcott Parsons, *The Social System* (The Free Press, 1951).

without warrant that everything either has a function or can be explained in terms of function, and this is not always the case. That is, the problem of relevance must be solved and that depends upon the adequacy of the analysis of the system. More important, there is always the danger of attributing a necessary quality to what is, in fact, accidental. Functionalist explanations of phenomena like foreign relations, for example, sometimes appear to take for granted that a particular set of goals formulated for a system at a given point of time are, in fact, *the* goals of the system in a Platonic sense. Finally, it is very easy to slip from statements of function to statements of purpose, particularly in the treatment of social institutions; for example, to a "personification" of phenomena that is not warranted.

When this much has been said, however, it remains true that functionalism offers a means of explaining a great deal of human behavior, and indeed the behavior of any living organism. While the view that only functional explanations are acceptable in behavioral science is nonsense, the use of functional explanation is quite acceptable and valid. If generalizations can be established relating to function, they can be used in either deductive or probabilistic explanation just as easily as generalizations about any other aspect of human society. The predictive capacity of functional explanations is limited, for they depend upon the demonstration of necessary and sufficient properties of the system and this is rarely achieved.

Teleological explanations

The difference between functional explanation and teleological explanation is very slight, logically, but nonetheless quite important for political science. In a functional explanation, there are goals or ends involved, but they are not necessarily foreseen by the actors involved. In a teleological explanation, as the term is used here, the goals *are*

foreseen and the action is explained as a purposeful move-

ment in the direction of predetermined ends. Any explanation of human behavior that involved reference to the motivation of the actor, for example, would qualify as a teleological explanation, and the distinction between functional and motivational or purposive explanations seems to me worth preserving. Again, there is a danger of assuming that every social phenomena can be explained in motivational terms, producing what Kaplan has called a "conspiratorial theory" of society. However, any form of explanation can be overextended, and it is no argument against the validity of teleological explanation or function explanation to show that they can be misused. Nor does the fact that physical scientists avoid them mean that they are unacceptable. As Braithwaite states the case:

> . . . in general irreducible teleological explanations are no less worthy of credence than ordinary causal explanations. A teleological explanation of a particular event is intellectually valuable if it cannot be deduced from known causal laws; other things being equal, it is more valuable the wider the variancy of the conditions and hence the greater the plasticity of the behavior concerned. It is because we are acquainted with systems—organisms and parts of organisms—which exhibit greater plasticity that we make use of teleological explanations.[7]

Considering the lack of causal laws in political science, teleological explanations and functional explanations can fill a serious gap in our explanatory structure, adding another dimension to the pattern of explanation available to the discipline.

Teleological explanations seem peculiarly well suited to the explanation of human behavior, for they allow the expression of unique sets of conditions leading to particular actions by individual persons. Assertions about human intentions are subjectively desirable and accord with common-

[7] R. B. Braithwaite, *op. cit.*, p. 334. The discussion of this form of explanation on pages 328–41 is excellent. He does not make the distinction between functional and teleological explanation that is used here but the logic of explanation applies equally in both cases.

sense observations about the foundations of our own behavior. Further, they allow us to take into account the characteristic human quality of persistence in the direction of goals in the face of obstacles. As Braithwaite has noted, such explanations are particularly valuable when our knowledge of the relevant factors in a given act of behavior has been obtained independently of the causal laws which account for goal-directed behavior, for this is precisely the situation in which teleological explanation is most frequently undertaken. For when no causal relations can be established, future behavior is most easily inferred by making use of some external factor—like goals or purposes—to account for the direction in which behavior tends.

Genetic explanations

Genetic or historical explanations are subject to some dispute among logicians, and they have been denied status as explanations by Brodbeck and others on the ground that a mere statement of an historical sequence is not explanation. This can be granted without impugning them completely, for if an historical explanation describes and accounts for the evolution of a particular event it is very closely related to a causal explanation, though it is weaker since the premises do not suffice to establish the event deductively. The point is that any historical or genetic explanation requires the observer to select certain sequences rather than others, and in order to do this some assumptions must be made about causal significance. Nagel asserts that historians are forced to rely upon "guesses" when they choose one pattern of genetic explanation rather than another, and his argument is impressive.[8] Nevertheless, genetic explanations may be very satisfying psychologically, and if it is difficult to establish criteria of relevance for given historical chains, it is not impossible if we do not seek to

[8] E. Nagel, *op. cit.*, chap. xv, esp. pp. 583–88.

force all explanation into a rigorous deductive framework. Some histories are doubtless little more than chronicles and that is not explanation. But history well done, which seeks to weigh and evaluate influences, can be extremely useful and illuminating. A classic case is Max Weber's study of the "Protestant ethic," which is open to formal criticism and to historical criticism but remains, nonetheless, a very significant and stimulating historical study. Of course, the problems that arise when we seek to formalize the results of such studies are formidable, but neither political scientists nor historians can, at this stage of their development, afford to discard whatever lies beyond formal specification as worthless. The problem seems rather to find means of sifting what is valuable from what is not.

Thus far, we have been dealing with the bare fundamentals of explanation, conceived at the lowest level. It remains now to consider more generalized explanatory structures—theories and models and their uses and limits. Already, however, it is possible to trace certain distinctions between explanation in physical science and explanation in political science that are of some significance. The deductive pattern of explanation that science prefers (but does not always achieve by any means) is presently well beyond our reach; most political explanations will be probabilistic in form, hence subject to the limitations that this form of explanation enforces. Further, it is unlikely that political scientists will be able to rely heavily upon probabilistic explanations that incorporate arithmetical coefficients of probability but will employ tendency statements in most of their explanatory structures. Limited causal explanations, rather than deductive structures, are likely to be the rule in politics. And the special forms of explanation that physical science tends to eschew, functional and teleological explanations, seem peculiarly well suited to the explanation of political phenomena and their use is fully justified by subjective understanding of the importance of motivations and purposes in human behavior.

What seems implied for political scientists is that formal criteria cannot be established arbitrarily and enforced rigorously or the discipline may suffer. What is needed is criteria of adequacy of explanation that are suited particularly to the subject matter and needs of political scientists. For certain purposes, statistical generalizations may be quite adequate; for other purposes they may need to be supplemented by other types of generalizations. In all cases, we must work with the tools that are available, realizing that the results will often be faulty, for tentative explanations that are subject to correction are surely better than no explanation at all. As we shall see in the following chapter, political explanations are weaker, more partial, less able to predict accurately, and perhaps are less comprehensive, than scientific explanations. We can suggest certain steps that may be taken to raise the general standard of explanation in the discipline, particularly growing self-consciousness about the methodological principles employed in political inquiry, but there is no magic key that will open the door to rigorous explanation and axiomatization.

BIBLIOGRAPHICAL NOTE

For explanation in social science, Ernest Nagel's *Structure of Science* is still the best general introduction available though it should be read with Abraham Kaplan's *Conduct of Inquiry* and R. B. Braithwaite's *Scientific Explanation.* Israel Scheffler's *The Anatomy of Inquiry* (Knopf, 1963) is difficult but Part I, which deals with explanation, repays careful study. F. Kaufmann's *Methodology of the Social Sciences* (Oxford University Press, 1944) is still worth reading, but F. S. C. Northrup's *Logic of the Sciences and the Humanities* is not. Karl Popper's works are essential, including the *Logic of Scientific Discovery, The Poverty of Historicism,* and the *Open Society and Its Enemies.* Robert Brown's *Explanation in Social Science* (Aldine Publishing Co., 1963) is good, and Max Weber's methodological writings should be included, though not uncritically. Don Martindale's *The Nature and Types of Sociological Theory* (Houghton Mifflin, 1960) is lucid and informative. L. Gross's (ed.) *Sympo-*

sium on Sociological Theory (Harper and Row, 1959) contains some very fine articles, as does Maurice Natanson's (ed.) *Philosophy of the Social Sciences: A Reader* (Random House, 1963), especially those by Nagel and Hempel.

Some of the fundamental articles and shorter papers on the subject of explanation are: C. G. Hempel's "Explanation in Science and in History," in Robert G. Colodny's (ed.) *Frontiers of Science and Philosophy* (University of Pittsburgh Press, 1962); A. M. MacIver's "Historical Explanation," in A. G. N. Flew's (ed.) *Logic and Language* (Second Series) (Philosophical Library, 1953); John Hosper's "What Is Explanation?" in A. G. N. Flew's (ed.) *Essays in Conceptual Analysis* (Macmillan, 1960); C. G. Hempel and P. Oppenheim's "The Logic of Explanation" in *Philosophy of Science*, 15 (1948), pp. 135–75; E. Nagel and C. G. Hempel's "Concepts and Theory in the Social Sciences" in *Language, Science, and Human Rights* (American Philosophical Association, 1952).

CHAPTER FIVE

EXPLANATION II: THEORY

IN the conduct of inquiry, no other form of activity can match the importance of theorizing, and no accomplishment can surpass its satisfactions. A theory is an act of creation and a work of art. Good theories are things of beauty and esthetic worth: fertile, suggestive, simple, productive, and satisfying. To grasp a new and important theory, to see its implications fully and clearly, is one of the great joys of study; to discern the extraordinary in the commonplace, the unsuspected connection, is a delightful surprise. It need hardly be said that the process by which theories are formed cannot be taught for it is not known. We can, however, learn to appreciate and understand the role that theory plays in explanation, and from *post hoc* examination of established theories come to know something of their internal structure. The logical aspects of theory relate to explanation as harmony, counterpoint, and orchestration relate to great music. Knowledge of these matters will not necessarily generate great accomplishments, though it may increase our appreciation of what has been done by others; without some knowledge of the underlying structure of theory, however, creativeness must move blindly and inefficiently, and perhaps without effect.

In political science, as in most other social sciences, terms like "theory" and "model" have been badly served. Usage is so confusing that it is not uncommon to find the same construction variously identified as theory, model, neither theory nor model, and both theory and model; a construction praised by one group is denounced by another, often on grounds that seem quite irrelevant. Finally, the use of highly ambiguous terms like "heuristic device" to praise or justify a particular intellectual construction only adds to the confusion. The resulting muddle has some very unfortunate consequences for the standards of explanation employed in the discipline and the kind of training imparted to its students. For the question what is or is not a theory cannot be answered arbitrarily; theories have a definite function to perform in explanation, and that function can be stated fairly precisely. It is pointless, if not definitely harmful, to give the name "theory" to a construction that cannot perform these functions.

THEORY

Theories are explanatory devices, and something more. In an explanation, isolated observable phenomena, loosely defined, are brought together and related systematically. As a first step, general statements of various sorts classify observables according to their properties, and a classification system is the simplest form of single-step explanation. Particular events are explained by "bringing them under" the general statements in the classification system, deductively or in some other way. The explanatory hierarchy is always open at the top, for it is always reasonable to demand an explanation of the general statements used in explanation, and then to demand a further explanation of the structure used to explain the generalizations. At any given time, some level of explanation exhausts our knowledge, it lies beyond further explanation, but only in practice and never in principle.

A theory is a generalization, or set of generalizations, that explains general statements, or explains other theories. Common usage, even in philosophy of science, is not exactly clear about the distinction, largely because certain applications of terminology were historically determined, but the general principle is safe. The answer to a request for an explanation of a general statement or law is always a theory. The relation between theory and observables is always indirect; generalizations mediate between theory and direct evidence. Theories explain general statements by relating them to one another, much as general statements relate individual phenomena, deductively or in some other way. A theory supplies the larger conceptual scheme in which generalizations find a place and thereby are explained. And like a good generalization, a strong theory does more than simply relate what has already been observed. It "spills over" into areas as yet unexplored, suggesting relationships not yet observed and generalizations not yet asserted. A theory is more than a means of explaining; it is also a guide to research, a means of substantiating other theories, an aid to discovery.

On this view, a theory is simply an instrument for ordering and arranging general statements that man creates for his own purposes and not, in some way, a map or picture of "reality." This is the "instrumentalist" conception of theory, and though it is sometimes disputed by philosophers of the "realist" school, the dispute is best left to philosophy of science. The significant point for the political scientist is that there are no good grounds for asserting that one type of theory is "more scientific" than another if theories are instruments. Man may use any and all theories that explain and, hopefully, assist him to discover new knowledge and integrate what is already known. Nor is a construction to be despised because it performs only some, not all, of the functions of theory. A theory may explain but not predict, for example, and if that is a weakness, it is not a reason for discarding the theory. All that can ever be decided is whether or not a given theory is useful in a particular inquiry, and here the subject-matter specialist is king. If the theory explains, if it suggests new relationships and generalizations, if it opens new lines of inquiry, or if it "satisfies" the person familiar with the data—if it does one or more of these things—then it is a "good" theory and worth using. The grounds on which theories are evaluated are somewhat vague. When a theory relates generalizations deductively, validation is relatively simple, but not entirely cut and dried; when theories are partial and weak, as is likely to be the case in political science on most occasions, evaluation is an act of judgment, not the application of formal rules of validation. In all cases, the value of a theory will depend upon its "usefulness" to the inquiry in which it is employed.

Theories and generalizations

Theories explain or relate generalizations. This is a useful minimal criterion for a theory. In practice, however, some general statements, like the "Laws of Nature," are so broad and powerful that they actually explain other generalizations, though they are commonly referred to as "laws." There is no conflict in principle here; terminology, particularly when it originates in the distant past, is not standardized. Furthermore, a theory may contain only one general statement, though more often it contains several. So long as the structure is able to explain generalizations, we will consider it to be a theory, disregarding current usage. The distinction between law and theory is not quite so clear as we might wish, even in physical science, but a brief comparison of the two types of constructions will help define the properties of each and thus set them apart reasonably well.

General statements are related to observables directly and immediately; theories relate to observables only indirectly—through general statements. This is a useful means of separating the two types of constructs. A generalization classifies observable phenomena (loosely defined to avoid confusion with scientific constructions like atoms or genes which are not, strictly speaking, observables) according to their properties. Each general statement is an independent proposition, established by its own body of evidence; it can be considered an inductive generalization from a body of observed data. The meaning of a generalization is independent of any theory in which it may appear and its validity depends primarily upon its relationship to singular facts. This is not the case with a theory.

Theories are abstract and symbolic constructions, and not descriptions of data or inductive generalizations from observations. Theories relate general statements by appealing to underlying similarities, not to observable properties. Theories supply a wider framework in which generalizations appear as special cases of broader principles. The link between theory and generalization is conceptual and not empirical. Some of the nonlogical terms in a theory will refer to observables, but others will refer to nothing that is directly observable. These "theoretical terms" are extremely important, for they give a theory its generalizing power and provide the linkage between theory and generalizations. "Gravity," for example, is a theoretical term, as are terms like "instinct," or "motive," used to explain human behavior.

The relationship between theoretical concepts and observables is always a little vague. Of course, some inferential relationship must exist, for theories are meant to explain observed phenomena—they are not merely logical constructions. But the exact meaning of theoretical terms is defined implicitly by the terms of the theory, and not explicitly and precisely in terms of observables. A theory must include some statements that relate theoretical terms to observable data, but not all of the theoretical terms are so related, and even when the relationship is specified, it is often loose and imprecise.

The loose fit between theoretical terms and observable

data is worth a great deal of emphasis. Theories often employ terms that are idealizations of observed phenomena (frictionless motion or absolute zero, for example); no physicist really expects his experimental data to fit theories employing such terms precisely. But even in those cases where the terms are not idealizations, the results of observation will not fit exactly. For that reason, theories cannot be proved or disproved in absolute terms. There is always some element of judgment involved in the evaluation of a theory, in the decision to accept or reject it. A theory is not simply an attempt to generalize or describe the real world in terms of observables. It is a conceptual structure —using abstract, symbolic terms—in which empirical generalizations find a place through their relationship to these symbols. The observable referrents of the symbols are imprecise. The symbol is "more general" than the observables it implies in a theory. This is the reason why theories are powerful explanatory tools. The looseness of fit, in other words, is an asset, not a liability.

The structure of theories

An empirical generalization is always a single statement. A theory *may* be a single statement but more often it comprises a number of general statements linked together in various complex ways. In the first case, the theory *is* the general statement; in the second, the theory is the sum of the general statements and the set of relationships that bind them. Often, the set of relations really define a theory; for example, in factor theories, where none of the generalizations employed are sufficiently broad to include other generalizations, the theory consists of the *selection* of general statements and the rules of interaction governing their application.

We will classify theories into two broad types, depending upon the kind of relationship that obtains between the various elements of the structure. If the relationship is

deductive, the theory forms a hierarchical construction and the general statements in the theory (theorems) are logical derivatives of a few basic axioms or postulates. We will refer to theories of this type as hierarchical or *deductive* theories. If the general statements in the theory are not related deductively but held together by some other factor  like relevance to a common class of phenomena, we will refer to them as *concatenated* theories, following Abraham Kaplan. Kaplan's terminology is preferred to Quentin Gibson's use of "factor" theories because it is broader and therefore more useful in political science. Social theories are at  present all of the concatenated type, and even the limited form of factor theory that Gibson favors is often more than political science can produce. In philosophy of science, a common definition of a theory is "a deductively related group of general statements," and discussions of theory center around this conception. But that is far too strict for political science, for it requires the use of universal general statements and they are not found in abundance in politics. There seems no good reason why concatenated theories  cannot perform various useful and legitimate functions in the study of politics, and if the restricted form of deductive theory is easier to use, and more powerful, that is not a good reason for eliminating concatenated theories from consideration. Indeed, I shall suggest, in another part of the chapter, the use of concatenated theories or "quasi-theories" so loose and weak that they can hardly be called "theories" at all, though they seem likely to prove useful in the discipline.[1]

The division of theories into deductive and concatenated types underlines the importance of the kinds of general

[1] The discussion of theory in Quentin Gibson, *The Logic of Social Enquiry* (Routledge and Kegan Paul, 1960), chap. xiii, and Abraham Kaplan, *The Conduct of Inquiry: Methodology for Behavioral Science* (Chandler Publishing Co., 1964), chap. viii is excellent. It is interesting to note that neither R. B. Braithwaite nor Ernest Nagel deal with nondeductive theories in their respective works on scientific explanation.

statements that are available in a discipline. Without empirical laws, or universal general statements, deductive theories are impossible. If political science were limited to deductive theory there could be no political theory, for most of the general statements that political science disposes are tendency statements and they cannot be combined deductively. Political theories, if we are to have them, must be connected nondeductively—an awkward statement implying only that the relationships among the general statements in a theory are not formal or logical. Concatenated theories will not be able to perform all of the functions that deductive theories perform, but that need not impugn their status for not everything in man's universe is logical. The weakness of political theory is not fatal; it only makes discovery a more difficult task, and it opens up a wider area for individual judgment and disagreement. But so long as political scientists are aware of the nature and source of the weakness and evaluate their work accordingly, this can do no harm. The chief danger in the use of weak theories arises out of a failure to appreciate their weakness, to demand too much of them.

Unfortunately, philosophers and methodologists have paid very little attention to nondeductive theories, and the social scientists themselves have not exploited them systematically. What follows is, therefore, somewhat speculative and incomplete. Nevertheless, a beginning must be made, and exposure to criticism seems the best way to increase the quality of the formulation. And, in any case, the best strategy open to political science is clearly to exploit the possibilities of such theories as we are able to produce at the present time, continuing the search for a deductive base that can augment the weaker forms now in use.

DEDUCTIVE THEORIES

The axioms in a deductive system may be universal general statements or they may include some probabilistic generalizations of a particular type. The type of generalization admissible to the theory is contingent on its amenability to deductive treatment. When all of the general statements are universals, or empirical laws, the theory is extremely powerful and closely knit. When probabilistic generalizations are included, the theory is weaker and more complex. We will deal here with these two basic subclasses of deductive theories. There are, of course, many other ways in which deductive theories can be classified; for example, as causal theories, functional theories, high-level or low-level theories, and so on, depending on their use, range of applicability, number of deductive levels and other properties. These aspects of theory may be important, but the classification standards are always somewhat ambiguous. It is impossible to say, for example, what is meant by terms like "middle-range theories," or even "empirical theories," for all theories relate ultimately to empirical data and the "range" of a theory cannot be known with certainty. In any event, these considerations do not affect the logic of theory, and causal theories, etc., can always be classified according to their logical form. The classification of theories as deductive and nondeductive underlines a fundamental logical distinction; classification by "level" or "range" does not.

A deductive theory begins with one or more axioms or postulates, universal in form, and not deducible from any other statements in the theory. We will illustrate the form of the theory using a structure with but a single axiom; but in larger and more complex structures, the same principles apply to the internal relationships of the theory. The axioms mark the stopping point in any deductive explanation that makes use of the theory; they are taken as given. The usefulness of the axioms depends on the kinds of propositions that can be deduced from them and the relationship between these deduced propositions and observable data. Of course, it is always possible that a new theory will be put

forward in which the axioms of the older theory appear as deductions from the new set of axioms, but that is only an indication of the incompleteness of human knowledge.

Since the axioms in a deductive theory are universal in form (All *A* is *B*), any general statement that is also universal in form which can link either *A* or *B* to another set of properties can be included in the hierarchy and explained by the theory. For example, if an axiom of the deductive theory asserts an invariable relationship between religious affiliation and voting preference, then any other general statement that relates either religious affiliation or voting preference to any other factor whatsoever can be linked with every other part of the hierarchy. And these further relationships are again potential sources of even wider links among different kinds of knowledge. The problem, for political science, is that each generalization must be universal, otherwise the relationships cannot be deductive. When these conditions are satisfied, the result is an extraordinarily powerful tool for inquiry.

All deductive theories have the same fundamental structure or hierarchical arrangement:

(1) $A \rightarrow B$
(2) $X \rightarrow A;\ Y \rightarrow A;\ Z \rightarrow A$
(3) $X \rightarrow Y;\ X \rightarrow Z;\ Y \rightarrow Z;\ X \rightarrow B;\ Y \rightarrow B;$ etc.

The initial axiom of the theory (1) is a universal generalization in the form "All *A* is *B*." It will contain at least one theoretical term not defined precisely in observable terms. It provides a link among the three empirical laws at the second level (2) leading to the set of deductive relationships at (3). Each of the general statements must be deducible from the axioms. In addition, each must have its own independent existence as a generalization that relates empirical data. Every statement in the structure is related logically to every other statement. The number of statements that appear in even a simple structure is indicative of the fruitfulness of the method of development; a small handful of broad axioms can link an enormous substructure of less general statements. That is the principal reason why deductive theory is a powerful tool for exploration, since the relationships will hold so long as the general statements are universally valid and the axioms hold good. It is possible to infer easily from what is known to what has not yet been explored. The theory links what is known and what may be known in time, the former providing evidence for the theory and the theory suggesting sources of further evidence. Although we tend to think of empirical generalizations as preceding theory, theories also suggest new generalizations. Obviously, any further general statement that can link other observables to any part of the hierarchical structure expands the usefulness of the theory. The addition of new axioms has the same effect. Deductive theories grow by accretion as well as the exploration of their internal logic. They become, in a peculiar sense, self-fulfilling ordinances.

This may seem a large claim for so simple a structure, but the simplicity of the symbolism employed is misleading. The axioms are usually very complex propositions. For example, "All *A* is *B*" may mean "every physical object in the universe attracts every other physical object in the universe," or "every human being is driven by a primitive urge that is instinctual and inherited that aims at the domination of others." So long as the axioms state an invariant relationship between fully defined classes, the complexity of the class definition is limited only by the fertility of human imagination.

The use of symbols is characteristic of formal, deductive theories. The descriptive and theoretical terms in the theory are replaced by abstract symbols, or, to put the point another way, the theory is transformed into an abstract calculus. It follows that the empirical meaning of the theory cannot be determined until rules are provided that link the abstract symbols in the calculus to observable data. Although this has the disadvantage of loosening the relation between theory and data, it is nevertheless very advantageous in the long run. The deductive operations are more easily and accurately performed in the abstract calculus than in more complex observable terms, and this facilitates a full exploration of the theory. A good example of the function of formal calculi can be found in R. B. Braithwaite's *Scientific Explanation,* and it deserves careful study.[2]

A formalized deductive theory, then, consists of a formal calculus and a set of rules of correspondence that link the terms of the calculus to observable data. In addition, the theory may be accompanied by a model or isomorph. The meaning of "model" is very severe in this context; it is a representation of the calculus of the theory. Different kinds of models can be produced (models *of* theories, and models *for* theories, for example) but such epistemic distinctions need not concern us here. What matters is that a model is a simple way of picturing the structure of a theory. Some scientists seem to feel that a theory is not really understandable until a good model has been produced, but a model actually has no explanatory usefulness, and there is no causal relationship between model and theory. Models are simply analogs or isomorphs, constructed of words (semantic models) or of physical parts. They facilitate understanding of theory, and are much easier to discuss or explain than the formal calculus of theories; hence, they are widely used in teaching.

The simple, single-axiom theory we have been considering can be elaborated almost endlessly by adding new axioms or discovering new generalizations that provide a link to wider ranges of observations. Whole deductive systems can be linked by showing that they share axioms or that the axioms of one can be derived from the axioms of the other. What is called "unification" or "reduction" of theories con-

[2] R. B. Braithwaite, *Scientific Explanation* (New York: Harper & Bros., 1960), chaps. ii and iii.

sists of demonstrating that they can be derived from a common set of axioms, and science is often successful in the attempt to do this. Complex theoretical structures may have a number of layers of deductions between the axioms at the top of the hierarchy and the singular statements that relate to particular observables at the bottom. So long as the generalizations are universal, and the relationship remains deductive, the status of any proposition in the system can be established. When more than one axiom is employed, the theoretical difficulties increase. For one thing, the theorist must be careful not to include axioms that are not needed in the theory. Otherwise, it would be a simple matter to append dubious postulates to an established theory in which they have no function and assume that the validity of the theory extends to the postulates. Validation of multi-axiom theories is also more difficult, for a failure of the theory to accord with observable data merely indicates that one of the axioms is false, but does not indicate which axiom should be altered. Locating the fault may be a very complex task.

There are no deductive theories in political science, nor are any to be found in sociology. Economics, more than any other social science, makes use of deductive theory and formal models, but they tend to be technical and complex and not too useful as illustrations.[3] The reader interested in examples of deductive theories can make use of any standard text in philosophy of science. We will confine our illustrations to nondeductive theories, which are more relevant to the present state of political science.

Advantages of deductive theory

Deductive theory is usually considered the "ideal" form,

[3] A very good, nontechnical discussion of John M. Keynes' *General Theory of Employment, Interest, and Money* can be found in Lawrence R. Klein's *The Keynesian Revolution* (New York: Macmillan, 1954). Chapters i–iii show very clearly the nature of the theory, and the model used to explain it.

and for obvious reasons; it is powerful, reliable, easily assessed, and fertile or fruitful. Because each general statement is a universal, and all relationships are deductive, powerful mathematical techniques can be employed and the deductive consequences of a given set of axioms and theorems (general statements deduced from axioms) can be explored fully and accurately, however large the system may be. In large complex structures, where it is almost impossible to work by visual inspection of the theory, this is an enormous advantage, facilitating the discovery of lacuna, and promoting exploration of new fields. A formal mathematical treatment of a theory will examine the full range of inference, suggest relationships that need further exploration, and indicate areas in which new generalizations may appear. Nor do the advantages of deductive theory end here. Formal deductive relations are usually more easily grasped than irregular relationships that depend upon a profound knowledge of the subject matter. Formal structures are more easily converted into useful models than nonformal systems, and the models themselves can be made more accurate. Complex structures of thought are handled more easily and freely when the machinery of inference is well established and comparatively easy to use. Finally, the validation of formal theory is a much simpler task than the validation of concatenated theory. In absolute terms, no theory can be proved or disproved, but the assessment of theory is much simplified when fixed relations between theory and data must hold.

The four basic means for testing theories suggested by Karl Popper, for example, are all more easily applied to deductive systems than to concatenated theories, if indeed they can be applied to the latter. (1) The conceptions employed in a theory are examined for internal consistency. (2) The logical form of the theory is examined to determine whether its propositions are empirical or tautological; for example, whether they are true by definition or open to empirical test. (3) Theories are compared to other theories to determine logical compatibility. And (4), conclusions deduced from theory are compared with empirical data as a final test (for Popper) of validity.[4] Each of these tests is clearly intended for application to deductive theory; in some cases, they could not be applied to nondeductive theory at all.

A word of warning is in order here about the significance of validation in relation to theory, even when the theory is deductive. The fit between theory and data is never perfect, and validation is not simply a matter of confronting theory with evidence. The range of the data explained by the theory, and its heterogeneity, must be assessed, along with other factors to be explored more fully later in the chapter. A theory must fit its own facts, of course, but that is only part of the story. Even in physical science, as Philip Frank has pointed out, "agreement with observations," and "simplicity," must be compromised in some degree when validations are carried out.[5] What is very easy to forget is that the practical applications of a theory, so highly regarded in naïve conceptions of science and its methods, are neither necessary nor sufficient to establish the logical validity of a theory. Any given application of a theory may either fail or succeed for reasons that have nothing to do with the theory. We shall return to the point in our discussion of the validation of nondeductive theories.

Probabilistic–deductive theories

When a probabilistic generalization is introduced into a deductive theory, or when we seek a theory to explain probabilistic generalizations, certain consequences follow

[4] Karl Popper, *The Logic of Scientific Discovery* (Science Editions, 1961), p. 34.

[5] Philip Frank, "The Variety of Reasons for Acceptance of Scientific Theories," in Philip Frank (ed.), *The Validation of Scientific Theories* (Collier Books, 1961). Other essays in this volume offer suggestive insights into the standards actually employed in physical and social science.

for the logic of the theory. As we might expect, the ensuing structure is more complex and cumbersome and much less powerful and useful than a deductive theory employing universal generalizations. Because probabilistic generalizations do appear in political science, however, it is worth noting in some detail the extent to which they can be incorporated in deductive structures.

The precise meaning of "probability" we shall leave to philosophers of science and mathematicians. In general, the kind of probability statement that can be used in a deductive theory will give a precise numerical value for the relationship between two classes of events, and it will refer, roughly, to the relative frequency with which events occur or to the probability of a given outcome in a given case, as when a coin is flipped. When probable is used as a synonym for likely or reasonable, without a numerical coefficient of "likelihood," it may be very useful, but as Braithwaite notes, ". . . it is by no means certain that probability as the reasonableness of a hypothesis has characteristics which permit a number to be attached to it."[6]

Even in those cases where probability statements do include a numerical coefficient, we cannot simply substitute them for universal statements and continue deduction. The calculus of probability severely restricts deductive inferences. The most common form of deduction relies upon the so-called Law of Large Numbers, and this requires a very special set of conditions for application. When we can state the probability of a particular outcome in a given case, for example, that the probability of tossing a head is 1:2 for any given toss, then the law permits a deductive inference from that statement to the *probability that* one half of a long sequence of tosses will be heads. Statements of this kind are used in physical science, as in the theory of gases, but they are rare in political science because we can

[6] Braithwaite, *op. cit.*, p. 120.

seldom state the probability of a particular outcome in a given case. That is, the Law of Large Numbers depends upon the ability of the investigator to attach a particular probability figure to a given outcome in a stipulated instance.

Even if deductive theories can make use of probabilistic generalizations, they remain beyond the political scientist's reach for the moment. And their usefulness is limited. No probabilistic statement can explain a singular event, and no single event can be deduced from a probabilistic generalization. This limits the predictive value of theories that include them, and their usefulness in discovery. Further, since no particular observation suffices to invalidate a theory using probabilistic generalizations, it is more difficult to validate these theories than theories using universal statements. As Braithwaite has shown, a theory that has been rejected on the basis of available evidence may later be reinstated when new evidence is available.

Furthermore, the logical structure of a deductive system that includes probabilistic statements is far more complex than the structure needed to link universal statements. The logic of probability is more limited and more complex than formal deductive logic. This sets practical limits on the number of statements that can be handled with available techniques, and on the usefulness of the results that are obtained. The rules of combination do not follow ordinary deductive patterns, often with quite peculiar results. For example, when two probabilistic statements are combined, the probability of their combination is equal to the product of their individual probabilities (conjunction theorem) and since probabilities are always stated in fractions, the product will always be much less than the two original probabilities.

Finally, and perhaps most important for political scientists, the psychological satisfaction obtained from the use of a straight deductive theory is missing when probabilistic generalizations are included in the theory. We usually expect independent evidence for statistical explanations, not references to yet another statistical generalization. That is, if an explanation of a probabilistic statement does not include some reference to causes, purposes, intentions, past history, etc., it is likely to be considered unsatisfactory. For example, if *n* percent of all American farmers voted for the Republican candidate in all presidential elections between 1920 and 1960, the explanation of this generalization is likely to be complex. The Law of Large Numbers cannot apply, for there is no way of saying that farmers as a class are likely to vote Republican or Democratic with a given probability. And in any case, an adequate explanation of the generalization would require some reference to matters like party platforms, legislative programs, past tradition, farm problems, farm organizations, and so on. The fact is that we know far too much about farmers and voting to accept a statistical generalization as an adequate explanation of the phenomenon. Statistical generalizations may help explain certain phenomena, but in many, and perhaps all, cases those familiar with politics would expect to see references to the relevant factors as well.

This rather brief summary of the nature and function of deductive theories indicates something of their value and desirability. Regretfully, it is unlikely that political science will produce many deductive explanations in the near future for the empirical laws needed for deductive explanation cannot be obtained. The great deductive systems of physics or chemistry are hopelessly beyond reach, and if it is some consolation to know that other physical scientists must also regard the physicist with envy, that does not help the political theorist very much.

CONCATENATED THEORIES

So far as philosophy of science is concerned, we have said all there is to say about theory. Theory means deductive theory, and nothing more, to that discipline. Yet there are significant political generalizations that cannot be related deductively, and it is unlikely that they will ultimately appear in a form that permits deductive inferences, whether from theory to generalization or from generalization to empirical data. These general statements are worth explaining, and if they are to be explained, a theory is needed. The problem, then, is to find theories that will relate general statements in some meaningful and useful pattern without recourse to strict logical inference. More specifically, political scientists have produced a wide range of generalizations of the statistical sort, plus a great many useful tendency statements. Since statistical statements can be reduced to tendency statements, the discussion can be confined to the latter, for the logic of explanation is not altered by the addition of a percentage to the proposition. What is needed is a theoretical structure that will link tendency statements; since the tendency statements are not universal in form, the linkage cannot be deductive. Of course, that does not open the door to all sorts of illogical or absurd proposals, for nonlogical and illogical are two quite different things, and if the former is permissible, the latter is not. Failing this, political science must simply resign itself to doing without theories until it can establish universal general statements.

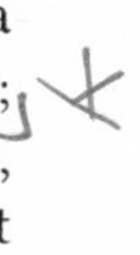

WHAT THEORY IS NOT

It will help to begin by eliminating from consideration certain kinds of intellectual constructions which, if they are often mistaken for theories, in fact perform no explanatory functions. It would be a hopeless task to seek a complete enumeration of such structures, but the major sources of confusion are fairly readily identified. In fact, they often include the term "theory" in their nomenclature, as is the case with "field theory" and "power theory."

Series of definitions

No series of nominal definitions is a theory.[7] Although some of the nonlogical terms in a theory may be nominally defined, some at least must be tied to observables if the theory is to explain. A logical structure, or a sequence of vaguely related definitions that has no connection to observable evidence, cannot explain anything; the whole of pure mathematics falls into this category. "Game theory," for example, is a well-developed mathematical structure but it is in no sense a social theory or a scientific theory; it is only a formal logical system. Of course, formal structures can be transformed into theories, they can be applied to observable data, if, and only if, the axioms of the system can be linked to observable data through a set of rules of correspondence. Plane geometry, for example, is a formal structure, but it can be applied by surveyors, on the earth's surface at least, because conditions on earth fit the axioms of the system. Similarly, if a social situation can be found in which the axioms of the mathematical theory of games are fulfilled, then the implications of that situation can be explored through the use of the mathematical structure. In political science, this has thus far proved almost impossible. In any event, when formal theories are applied, they cease to be nominally defined and are linked directly to observable data.

List of factors

A theory is not simply a list of factors that may influence a given phenomenon, no matter how complete and exhaustive the list may be. That would be roughly equivalent to telling an author that everything he might conceivably have to say could be found in one book—a dictionary. Now factor theories do, as we shall see, involve the enumeration of factors involved in a particular phenomenon, but the list is always selective; no factor can be included in the

[7] See Robert Bierstedt, "Real and Nominal Definitions," in L. Gross (ed.), *Symposium on Sociological Theory* (Harper and Row, 1959).

theory unless it is relevant and operative, and no factor should be omitted when it is influential. A mere list of potential factors explains nothing. Indeed, a list that is purportedly exhaustive may well retard theoretical development by prejudging the issue. In any case, there can be no grounds for making this assertion. If a list of factors is derived by logical inference from nominal definitions, the result is a formal system of the type discussed above in (1) and subject to the same limits. If the list has been adduced from empirical observation there can be no grounds for asserting that it is exhaustive. In no case should a list of factors be given status that might inhibit the search for new points of view.

Approaches

A theory is not merely an "approach" to a discipline or topic—a suggested framework for investigation. What is sometimes called "power theory," for example, is no more than a statement that, in principle, generalizations about political behavior ought to be stated in terms of the power-seeking propensities of individuals. "Systems theory," similarly, implies no more than the view that society is best investigated within a framework provided by a "system," nominally defined. Neither of these conceptions is a theory, and it is puzzling to try and think out the reasons why men would be willing to argue in favor of the primacy of one or another of these approaches. A theory could, certainly, be constructed within this framework; theories can function with any kind of generalization, whatever the terms they employ. But theories are definite and particular; they are attempts to explain real phenomena. Power theories and systems theories are research strategies, or statements about the content that political generalizations ought to include. The assertion that they are the best possible research strategies is logically and practically dubious. Systems theory, to take one example, is open to very serious methodological criticism.[8] The concept of a "system" is highly ambiguous, as is the concept of function which is needed to clarify the operation of the system. It is very easy to confuse "system" with "association'" or to take one as model for the other. The precise boundaries of any system are empirically difficult to define. And a meaningful system, like a human society, is so fearfully complex that the task of describing its "state," a necessary feature of systems analysis, seems unlikely to be fulfilled. When we add the problem of showing how a given phenomena contributes to the maintenance of the system, which is the basic strategy of explanation employed in systems theory, there seem to be formidable limits and restrictions on the use of the approach.

"Field theory" offers another illustration of the use of the term "theory" to identify what is essentially only a method —a strategy for analyzing social relations. Kurt Lewin, one of the leading proponents of field theory, defined the status of the structure very accurately:

> If one proceeds in physics from a special law of theory . . . to more general theories . . . one does *not* finally come to field theory. . . . In other words, field theory can hardly be called a theory in the usual sense. Field theory is probably best characterized as a method: namely, a method of analyzing causal relations and building scientific constructs.[9]

Again, a theory can certainly be constructed that will explain general statements phrased in "field" terms, and such theories are quite popular in physical science. But the generic conception of field theory has no explanatory value whatever.

[8] See particularly, C. G. Hempel, "The Logic of Functional Analysis," in L. Gross (ed.), *Symposium on Sociological Theory* (New York: Harper and Row, 1959), and Ernest Nagel, *Structure of Science,* pp. 520–35. The criticisms in both works seem to me to be devastating and unanswerable.

[9] Kurt Lewin, *Field Theory in Social Science* (Harper, 1951), p. 45. Italics in the original.

Models

Finally, a theory should be differentiated clearly from a model. A model is not an explanatory instrument, in the sense that theory explains generalizations. Models are an aid to understanding, and they may contribute indirectly to explanation, but they do not have a part in the process. A model, very generally, is an analogy, an isomorphic construction that is similar in some, but not all, respects to the theory or phenomenon for which it is a model. To use a model is to use an analogy, and it is subject to all of the limits imposed on analogous reasoning. In no case is the model causally related to the theory or object, and in all cases the model is a simplification, a partial isomorph.[10]

Models are very useful tools, of course, and a model of a complex theory or phenomenon can facilitate comprehension and discussion enormously. What are called "postulational" models, formal structures in which the postulates are "educated guesses," can aid the exploration of observable phenomena and relationships. Max Weber's "Ideal types," which are essentially models and not theories, do this very well, as do many of the models used in economics. Such "quasi-theories" have an important role to play in political science, as I hope to show presently, but they are not properly entitled to be called theories.

The uses of models in engineering, medicine, biology, science, and elsewhere are so obvious and manifold that they hardly need further elaboration here. But the results obtained from the study of models are not knowledge, and strictly speaking a model is not an explanatory tool. Models can perform some of the functions of theories, properly employed. But the very properties that make models useful also make their use dangerous. It is very easy to confuse

[10] Abraham Kaplan, *op. cit.*, chap. vii, contains an excellent discussion of the role of models and their limitations.

model and theory, to assume that a property of a model is a property of a theory or object. It is also easy to forget that models are always partial and incomplete, that some variables have been eliminated, that some relationships have been dropped, that structure has been simplified. No amount of study of formal models can produce knowledge unless the axioms of the model are linked to observables by rules; in that case, the model becomes a theory. Finally, as Kaplan rightly points out, extensive reliance upon models can lead to overemphasis on rigor and precision, hence to unrealistic and unattainable criteria of inquiry. In the world of observable facts, rigor must always be sacrificed to human capacity and precision is limited by the tools of inquiry. Rigor may be bread and butter to the logician but it can be an extremely expensive luxury for the field worker in social science.

FACTOR THEORIES

A theory, according to our minimal definition of the term, is an intellectual construction that relates general statements and thus explains them. The relationship may be logical, or it may be based on other considerations; our concern here is with this latter group of nonlogical theories. Ideally, any theory will do more than explain a given body of data; it will facilitate discovery, help direct research, suggest new areas of inquiry, and so on. Deductive theories perform well in all these respects. Nondeductive theories, as we might expect, do not. They are less powerful and flexible. One structure may explain well but fail to predict; another will prove a useful guide to research but a weak explanatory system. Most nondeductive theories are harder to evaluate than deductive theories, so much so that we shall have to give special consideration to the problems of evaluation when nondeductive relationships are employed in theory. The point, surely, is that any theoretical structure which can perform some useful service for the discipline ought to be used. All we can reasonably require is that the investigator make use of his tools with a clear understanding of their strengths and weaknesses.

Factor theories, which seem likely to play a major role in political theory in the near future, explain general statements by relating them to a particular phenomenon or class of events. The use of factor theories is already widespread in political science, though they are more often implicit and not explicitly stated. Whenever a political scientist enumerates the factors leading to a particular development or the motives involved in a particular behavior pattern, he is stating a weak factor theory. In fact, almost every effort at causal explanation involves the use of a factor theory.

The general statements in a factor theory may be empirical laws, statistical generalizations, or tendency statements. When empirical laws are available, a very powerful deductive theory can be produced, but since political science lacks universal statements, the discussion will center on factor theories that explain tendency statements. Each tendency statement is logically independent of the others, and rests on its own evidence. The general form of the structure of a factor theory is quite simple, though it complicates rapidly as the number of factors increases:

(1) *A* tends to *X* (or 40 percent of *A* is *X*)
(2) *B* tends to *X*
(3) *C* tends to *X*
(4) *A, B, C,* tend to *X*

The theory states that when *A, B,* and *C* are present, *X* is to be expected; in some cases, a probability coefficient can be established for the complete theory; for example, when *A, B, C,* then *X* in 70 percent of all cases. The coefficient must also be established independently, for even if *A, B,* and *C* all favor *X*, it does not follow logically that the combination is also favorable to *X*. Nonlogically, it may seem reasonable that an outcome is more likely when three favorable factors are present than when only one is present, but an extensive assumption is needed to establish "reasonability."

The two essentials of any factor theory are: (1) the selection of factors to be included and excluded; and (2) the stipulation of the rules by which the factors combine. Except in very simple cases, a large number of possible factors have to be considered by the theorist, some favoring a given outcome and others tending in quite different directions. Factor theory seeks a selection of significant factors that will include everything important, both positive and negative, and exclude all factors that have no influence. Ideally, each factor should be measurable, in terms of both direction and strength, so that the interaction of factors can be handled mathematically, as is done by the parallelogram rule in classical dynamics. In practice, political scientists will do well to stipulate the necessary factors in a theory and indicate relative strength and relative direction of influence in rough terms.

A distinction ought to be drawn here between a factor theory and the "systems" approach to political science. A factor theory can, certainly, be produced within the framework that systems theory supplies, but the specification of a system is not the same as the formulation of a factor theory. In general, proponents of the use of systems theory like Talcott Parsons, David Easton, or Gabriel Almond use the concept of "system" as a basis for comparing data, much as Max Weber used his "Ideal Type" for comparing historical data.[11] Almond's comparative system, for example, argues that general statements about politics ought to include certain kinds of information, systematized in terms of

[11] See David Easton, *The Political System* (Alfred Knopf, 1953); Talcott Parsons and Edward Shils, *Toward a General Theory of Action* (Harvard University Press, 1962); or Gabriel Almond, "Introduction: A Functional Approach to Comparative Politics," in Gabriel A. Almond and James S. Coleman (eds.), *The Politics of Developing Areas* (Princeton University Press, 1960).

stipulated "inputs" and "outputs." To the extent that the defined categories can be taken as necessary conditions for the operation of particular political structures, a weak form of theory may be produced, but the system definitely is not a factor theory. Rather, it is a schematic structure that can be used to classify data from various sources. A theory is a device for relating general statements about empirical data and not a program of study or a framework for making comparisons. The concept of "system" can be very useful in political science, particularly as a guide to research and classification, but it is not, strictly speaking, a theory.

Factor theories will usually deal with the causes of common phenomena or with their genesis, explaining them by reference to the various factors associated with their occurrence. Obviously, a factor theory that can stipulate both the necessary and the sufficient conditions for an event is an extremely powerful and effective instrument—deductive in form. Failing this level of precision, factor theories vary in strength depending upon the precision with which the factors are stipulated and the accuracy of the rules governing their interaction. If all of the factors included in the theory are necessary to the phenomenon, a good theory may be produced. If the factors can be measured, well and good, but if not the theory is still useful if it can indicate strength and direction of influence in comparative rather than absolute terms. Thus a factor theory explaining two-party systems would presumably include tendency statements dealing with factors like tradition, type of constituency, social homogeneity, election laws, ideological commitments, and so on. Other statements in the theory would assert the relationships expected to hold among these factors and assess their relative strength and influence. The result, though weak, would still be useful.

An illustration

A typical example of the use of factor theories in political science can be found in the various studies of voting behavior. The factors that influence significantly the amount of activity and interest on the part of the voter, for example, are well known. Lipset, for example, has correlated income level, education, occupational group, race, sex, age, length of residence in the community, nationality, marital status, relevance of government policies, access to information, group pressures, and cross pressures, to voting turnout.[12] Each of these factors can be expressed as a tendency statement, and perhaps as a statistical generalization. Together, they form a weak theory of political activism. As Lipset himself points out, the various factors are almost impossible to isolate; hence, it has not yet proved possible to make general statements about the interrelationships of the factors, or their relative strength. But the theory provides a very useful summation of what is known about political participation, facilitating teaching and the transfer of information. Moreover, a factor theory of this sort readily suggests areas in which further information is needed. Until the influence of each factor has been analyzed more accurately, the theory is a very weak predictor, obviously, but as the necessary factors in the theory are identified, and their interaction and relative influence are assessed, the theory gains strength and usefulness. A wide range of similar theories, of varying strength and applicability, is already available in political science.

Notice particularly that Lipset's generalizations are empirically based, they are not merely categories about which more information is needed. This quality sets a factor theory apart from a "systems theory." The latter contains proposed categories, not actual general statements based on empirical evidence. This assumes a close working relationship between theory and research, particularly in the poorly developed disciplines. Factor theories must begin with the general statements that have been established empirically, and the

[12] Seymour Martin Lipset, *Political Man: The Social Bases of Politics* (Doubleday, 1960), adapted from pp. 188–91.

development of a factor theory will stimulate further research. The theorist, for example, will want to know whether income is more important than education as a determinant of political activity, and, ideally, how much more important in relative or absolute terms. He will want an evaluation of the relative importance of different kinds of group affiliations so that this information too can be included in the theory. All such questions must be answered empirically. Factor theories are peculiarly useful in this respect, for they allow the cumulative development of theory over time. The work of many different persons can be combined quite readily in factor theories, for they absorb new information readily. The goal is always a necessary and sufficient explanation of the phenomenon under investigation and any information which contributes to that end is acceptable and useful.

Uses of factor theories

For the moment, factor theories in political science are likely to remain partial and incomplete. Only rarely, if at all, can a necessary and sufficient explanation of a given phenomenon be offered. But even in a very weak form, when the theory can do little more than assert some of the conditions necessary to a phenomenon, the theory is worth having. For one thing, all theories reduce what is known in a given area to manageable proportions. By organizing the available data, they eliminate the need to rehash the same material over and over again. Theories, even when they are partial, facilitate the transfer of information from one generation to the next by providing a framework in which particular information can be understood and stored. Finally, since each factor theory is in effect a "cluster" of general statements, the multiplication of available theories should facilitate the task of generating more comprehensive theories dealing with the properties of clusters and not with individual general statements.

The chief disadvantage of factor theories is that they lack predictive capacity; hence, they are not very useful in discovery and exploration. We may explain the appearance of a two-party system by using a factor theory but we are not likely to be able to predict the appearance of a two-party system using the same theory. There are simply too many factors, and their interrelationships become too complex for accurate calculation. Partial factor theories reveal little of the future, and we can expect serious discrepancies between theory and data when they are applied. From the standpoint of pure theory, this is not a serious matter; the theory is simply corrected for the new circumstances. But pure theory is not always easily separated from the decision-making process, and when theories are employed in everyday politics, the lack of predictive power can be a serious shortcoming. A further problem is, of course, the extent to which factor theories become unmanageable as the number of factors involved in the theory increases. Interrelationships increase exponentially as new factors are added, and there are limits to the size of the apparatus that we can manipulate freely and accurately. Finally, political scientists will find it very difficult, if not impossible, to achieve the kind of precision and accuracy in measuring the strength and direction of the influence of individual factors that would enable them to calculate the interaction of factors accurately. A factor theory in politics will not reach the level of usefulness of factor theories in dynamics, for example, until measurement is brought to a level of precision far beyond what is presently possible. Factor theory is not, in short, a panacea for the ills of political theory. It offers a useful approach to theory, and it can be developed systematically in many areas of political inquiry, but there will still remain serious theoretical problems in the discipline that factor theories cannot solve. Other theoretical structures will have to be produced before political science can be considered to be firmly grounded.

EVALUATING THEORIES

Of the three major forms of theory (deductive-nomological, deductive-probabilistic, and factor theory), only factor theories are likely to be produced by political scientists in the near future, and they cannot provide a really adequate theoretical base for the discipline. The extent of the inadequacy is readily apparent when we consider the things that we would like to have theory do for the discipline, the standards by which theories are evaluated. Three are particularly important: (1) the explanatory power of available theories; (2) the usefulness of theories to the discipline; and (3) the esthetic and psychological satisfaction that theories afford.

Explanatory power

The explanatory power of a theory depends upon its range, the heterogeneity of the data it explains, and the importance of that data. It also depends upon the kind of relationship that it provides between generalizations—for example, deductive or nondeductive—and upon its verifiability. These properties are in some degree interdependent, yet it is desirable to try to separate them when theories are being evaluated. Generally, a theory that deals with a wide range of data is more desirable than a theory that deals with one narrow class of phenomena, and a deductively-related theory is preferable to a nondeductive theory. A theory that can be disverified is more acceptable than one that cannot be disproved easily. The difficulty lies with the *ceteris paribus*, for other things are not always, or even usually, equal. It is better to have a theory that deals with significant data nondeductively than a theory that handles trivia by strict deductive inference. It is better, usually, to have a theory that relates weakly to a wide range of significant data, even though it cannot be disverified easily, than a deductive theory dealing with a narrow range of data.

It is too easy to concentrate on logical properties and ignore the empirical significance of theories.

Furthermore, the relation between theory, explanation, and prediction is not so sharply defined as we might think. Even in the physical sciences, it is possible to explain without being able to predict, or predict without being able to explain. Evolutionary theory, for example, offers a perfectly adequate explanation of existing species of plants and animals without providing a means for predicting the species that will appear in the future. Conversely, the statistician can predict quite accurately the number of deaths that will occur in a given year among the members of a specified population without being able to explain the phenomena he predicts. The explanatory power of a theory does not, in other words, depend on predictive capacity alone, although some philosophers of science insist that prediction is the real hallmark of a theory. The criterion is too severe, even for physical science, and if it were adopted in political science it would literally put an end to theorizing. Prediction is certainly a desirable quality of theories but it is not essential.

Usefulness

The usefulness of a theory is related to, but separate from, explanatory power. It refers to the assistance that a theory can provide in the discovery and exploration of new fields, new generalizations, new theories, and new points of view. A theory that is weak as an explanation may still prove very useful in this sense. It may suggest research projects that are likely to prove fruitful, or new modes of classification that will throw new light on old phenomena or illuminate corners of the field hitherto left untouched. The process is rather vague, and it is not really possible to formulate rules for evaluating the fruitfulness of theories, yet this "suggestive" element in theories is extremely important, and a discipline can well afford to make use of useful and fruitful theories even though they may be difficult to verify and only loosely related to data.

A theory may be "useful" in another sense when it is employed by those responsible for policy making in the decision-making process. Here, the criterion that is likely to weigh most heavily is predictability. The policy maker is concerned with the consequences of varying alternative solutions to given problems, and a theory is useful to him to the degree that it can predict accurately. This use of theories is academically irrelevant, so far as the theorist is concerned, and it suggests a criterion for evaluating theories that is, in fact, unrelated to their explanatory power or logical validity except indirectly. Predictability depends on the logical properties of the theory, and they are evaluated differently by practicing politician and academic inquirer.

Satisfaction

Finally, theories may be evaluated according to the psychological and esthetic satisfaction that they provide for the informed student in the field. This may seem a rather flimsy criterion to include in a discussion of the formal properties of theory, but it ought not to be ignored completely. A theory that is "satisfying" to an informed observer, even though he is unable to specify what it is about the theory that "satisfies" him, is to be preferred to a theory that is displeasing or irritating, other things being equal. We do not yet know enough about human thinking to be able to say with any confidence that we have exhausted our critical faculty when we have stipulated every reaction to a given theory that can be put into words. I do not mean that there is some "higher" faculty that some men possess and others do not. But those with great familiarity with a subject matter may respond to theories out of experience which they are unable to stipulate precisely, and such responses can be valuable. Evaluations of this sort need to be used with caution, certainly, but they do add another dimension to our appreciation or evaluation of theory that ought not to be overlooked.

If we examine political theories in these terms, particularly the factor theories that political science may be able to produce, it is clear that they leave much to be desired. The weakness of the relation between theory and data, the absence of logical connection, complicates the task of evaluation. The practical limits on the number of factors that can be handled within the framework of a given theory limits the range of data that can be included, and the predictive power of the structure is limited. Worst of all, however, factor theories are not very useful in discovery. A factor theory is usually concerned with a single phenomenon, and each factor theory tends to be independent of others. It does not readily suggest other generalizations because a factor theory is not itself a generalization but a selection and arrangement of general statements focused on a definite phenomenon. In broad terms, factor theories tend to atomize inquiry; they focus narrowly and not broadly.

Deductive theories, which perform well in all respects, offer a means of avoiding these limitations, but that alternative seems presently to be closed to political science. Other means must be found to augment factor theories and further political inquiry. To that end I would like to suggest, very tentatively and under suitable safeguards, the use of certain constructions that are not theories, strictly speaking, but that can perform some of the functions of theories. We will call them "quasi-theories." So long as their limits are understood and respected, quasi-theories can contribute substantially to the development of political theories and to the extension of political inquiry. They are not, of course, substitutes for deductive theories, or even for factor theories.

QUASI-THEORIES

A quasi-theory, as the term is used here, refers to any intellectual construction that is a useful tool for the political theorist, though it cannot meet the standards employed in deductive or factor theories. In particular, quasi-theories serve as aids to classification, exploration, and discovery—three areas that are peculiarly difficult for factor theories. Actually, constructions of this sort are widely used in political science, though more often than not they are simply referred to as "theories." Max Weber's "Ideal Types," the postulational structures suggested by Talcott Parsons, the mathematical theory of games, cybernetics, communications theory, "functional" theory, and so on all fall into this category. The structures range from a fairly simple classification system to complex mathematical networks; they may be hierarchical, or concatenated in form. They do not "explain," in the strict sense of the term, but they can be very useful indeed in theory.[13]

Approaches

The simplest of the quasi-theories is the "approach" that has been systematized to produce a classification system for data. Almond's "systems theory" approach to comparative politics is a good example of this type of structure. What Almond suggests is a comparative examination of political systems employing four "inputs" (political socialization and recruitment, interest articulation, interest aggregation, and political communication) and three "outputs" (actually legislation, execution, and adjudication). This is a

[13] See Max Weber, *The Theory of Social and Economic Organization*, Talcott Parsons (ed.), (Free Press of Glencoe, 1964); Anthony Downs, *An Economic Theory of Democracy* (Harper, 1957); Robert Presthus, *The Organizational Society* (Alfred Knopf, 1962); Robert A. Dahl and Charles E. Lindblohm, *Politics, Economics, and Welfare* (Harper, 1953); Gabriel A. Almond and James S. Coleman (eds.), *The Politics of the Developing Areas* (Princeton University Press, 1960) for typical examples.

gross oversimplification of the program of action that Almond favors but it indicates in broad outline the nature of the structure he proposes.[14]

Almond's "system" does not consist of a set of logically related nominal definitions; no connection between "inputs" and "outputs" is stipulated. Literally, it suggests only that the accumulation of information about these particular features of political associations would be useful. Its usefulness is, therefore, strictly limited. It can provide a basis for making comparisons between two or more independent systems, and it can lead to a standardization of political data. In a weak sense of the term, it can also provide some guidance for research and exploration. Obviously, it can explain nothing, though an explanation could be formulated in these terms. The principal drawback to Almond's schema is that the stipulated classifications may be too broad to be useful, yet in fact omit significant information. To be told that we ought to compare the legislative, executive, and judicial functions when we are undertaking a comparative study of politics is not particularly useful. At best, then, "systems theories" can be expected to produce reasonably well-organized information of a comparative sort, and perhaps to suggest areas in which further research is needed. They are far too weak to be considered theories, and they perform none of the essential functions of theory.

Models

A much more significant form of quasi-theory is the model, for it can perform many of the functions of theory, properly employed. In a model, the initial postulates are related deductively, hence the model is more than a program for classifying empirical data. Given the initial postulates of a model, certain consequences will follow, and the exploration of these consequences can be very "productive," theoretical-

[14] Gabriel A. Almond and James Coleman, *op cit.*, chap. i.

ly. Models can suggest new areas for exploration, or even derived postulates that can be investigated empirically.

A good example of this kind of quasi-theory is Anthony Downs' *An Economic Theory of Democracy.* Downs builds a model of the democratic state, using three postulates borrowed from economic theory: (1) each voter seeks to maximize his personal utilities when he goes to the polls; (2) each political party seeks to gain and keep office; (3) both parties and voters act rationally in the pursuit of these goals. By adding uncertainty to the model (imperfect information), Downs produces a very interesting, if limited, analog for the political process in a democratic society and suggests some extremely interesting relationships between political and economic behavior. A substantial body of testable propositions can be derived from close analysis of the properties of the model. So long as we realize that the model is not an explanation, that it proves nothing whatever about empirical relations, it can be a fruitful source of research suggestions and possible relationships. Models may be constructed from any set of axioms, and whole systems can be borrowed directly from pure mathematics and studied for their relevance to and significance for political theory.

Speculations

A third form of quasi-theory, similar in some respects to formal models, is a postulational system in which the initial axioms or postulates are frankly speculative though they are, of course, related to some body of data. One of the best examples of this kind of speculative structure is Freudian psychology. Despite its obvious weaknesses, and even if it should prove totally worthless in the long run, the fruitfulness of the theory is beyond question. The impact on psychology of the various Freudian theories has been immense and it is unthinkable that the same amount and kind of influence could have followed from a more formal and logical theory confined within stricter limits. There is a need for balance, for a respect for facts that keeps the theorist from returning to the web-spinning universalism of the great system builders of the nineteenth century. But there is also room for boldness and daring, which readily find an outlet in speculation. They keep a discipline from debilitating into Neo–Scholasticism and parochialism. Freedom to speculate opens the door to abuse but freedom implies responsibility, in academic life as in politics, and it would be a mistake to inhibit speculation merely because it may be abused. The final form of Freud's instinct theory, for example, employing the tripartite division into Ego, Super-Ego, and Id, was abused by many of Freud's followers, and perhaps by Freud himself, for the theory was indefeasible as interpreted, each digression from theory being treated as a consequence of factors external to the theory. This led Karl Popper to denounce the theory in *The Poverty of Historicism* because it could not be tested. Popper is correct, formally; hence, the designation "quasi-theory." But Popper is criticizing the explanatory power of the theory, and not its usefulness.

Obviously, some criteria, however weak, are needed to inhibit absurd and useless speculative rambling from political theory, and a few minimal standards can be supplied. For one thing, no theory that is patently absurd, that contradicts accepted scientific principles, is acceptable. Quasi-theories that depend on assumptions about vital forces, or Lamarckian genetics, for example, can be ruled out immediately. Logical examination can also eliminate certain theoretical structures, for any theory that explains everything, that is tautologous or circular, is worthless. Finally, speculative theories must be credible, acceptable on the basis of what is known. These are very weak criteria indeed. If, in addition, we concentrate on the usefulness of speculative theories rather than their explanatory power, evaluating them according to their use in research, exploration, and discovery, it should be possible to keep speculation within reasonable bounds. The "correctness" of a theory is, in any case, less important than its usefulness, and much can be learned from mistakes—given time and an open mind. A theory that deals with significant phenomena is to some degree a self-correcting device, and given time it should either prove its worth or reveal its shortcomings. Even if the theory should prove to be hopelessly wrong, it may provide a route to another more viable structure. Of course, it would be much simpler and easier to begin with valid theories and develop them but a discipline that lacks theories has little choice in the matter. As a basic strategy for developing theory, speculation has merit. Used cautiously, it can be a source of sound theoretical conceptions and useful guides to discovery and exploration.

An illustration

A hypothetical example of a speculative theory or quasi-theory may illustrate some of their uses and properties. Consider the following postulates, comprised in the "Ant-Hill Theory of Politics":

1) In any two political systems, differences in procedures, institutions, and values will vanish in the long run.
2) The rate at which differentials between political systems vanish is directly proportional to their physical proximity, the size of their respective resource bases, and the amount of communication and interaction between them.
3) Procedures, institutions, and values in the two systems will stabilize at a point that reflects the needs of the largest and wealthiest urban population included in the two areas.

The theory is not, of course, intended seriously as here stated, but I have tried to formulate the postulates in a way that would illustrate the desirable properties of a speculative theory.

Although the theory is very general, and a number of concepts employed in the postulates would have to be linked to empirical data by a set of transformation rules, it is not circular. The propositions are significant, they do not state absurdities, and the complete structure is open to empirical verification. The range of the theory is substantial and the data it relates are variegated and heterogeneous. Once established, the theory would have considerable explanatory power and perhaps some measure of predictive power as well. It would serve as a useful guide to research, though it is not a "system" or suggested framework for collecting information; the theory makes statements about real political phenomena and the process of "filling in" the data would produce a verification of the theory and not a classification. Since the theory is significant, its negation would also be significant, and a demonstration of the falsity of the theory, or of the conditions under which the theory does not hold, would be worthwhile. Because the postulates in the theory are universal in form, its implications can be explored by strict, formal logic, and a model of the theory could be constructed quite easily, though it would doubtless require additional postulates. In short, a speculative theory of this sort could perform many if not all of the functions of regular theory. Given a still more speculative system, employing more theoretical terms and more vaguely related to empirical data, this would be less true but the ensuing structure could still prove useful and fruitful.

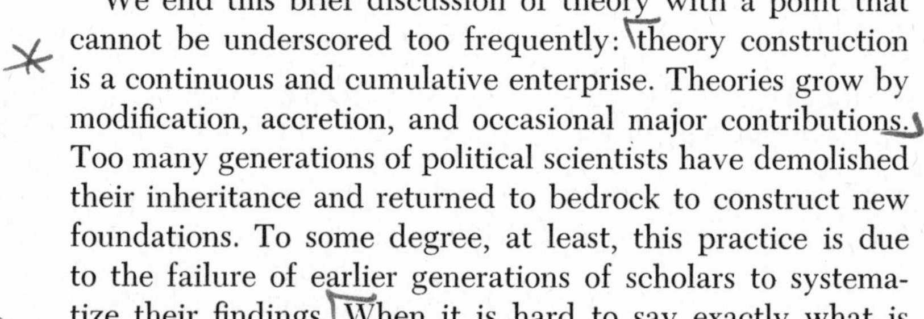

We end this brief discussion of theory with a point that cannot be underscored too frequently: theory construction is a continuous and cumulative enterprise. Theories grow by modification, accretion, and occasional major contributions. Too many generations of political scientists have demolished their inheritance and returned to bedrock to construct new foundations. To some degree, at least, this practice is due to the failure of earlier generations of scholars to systematize their findings. When it is hard to say exactly what is known about a given subject, it is often easier to assume that nothing is known and start anew. Well-established

theories can do much to prevent wasteful reiteration in research. Inquiry, after all, seeks to generate knowledge; theory is knowledge consolidated into a form that is more readily comprehended and transmitted than any other. Possession of facts is not knowledge; facts must be related. Political science has at its disposal a great many well-established generalizations, but they are widely dispersed and not readily accessible. This is the greatest handicap to the development of theory faced by the discipline, for theory must begin with what is known and seek to relate facts and general statements. Disperse knowledge and the theorist is helpless. Systematize what is known, make it widely available, and theory can begin to play its rightful part in the process of inquiry and analysis.

BIBLIOGRAPHICAL NOTE

The paucity of material on theory in political science is astonishing; virtually everything available on the subject comes from philosophy of science or sociology. I have found most useful the following: R. B. Braithwaite, *Scientific Explanation,* particularly for formal, deductive theory, and the explanation of probabilistic generalizations; Ernest Nagel, *The Structure of Science,* again chiefly for deductive theory and functional explanation; Abraham Kaplan, *The Conduct of Inquiry,* for both theory and models, though he does not discuss the properties of theories in detail; the essays by Hempel and Oppenheim, Ernest Nagel, and J. W. N. Watkins in Herbert Feigl and May Brodbeck (eds.), *Readings in the Philosophy of Science* (Appleton-Century-Crofts, 1953); essays by Bierstedt, Edel, C. G. Hempel, F. H. George, May Brodbeck, L. Gross, and Anatol Rapoport in L. Gross (ed.), *Symposium on Sociological Theory,* dealing with both theory and models; Henry E. Kyburg, Jr. and Ernest Nagel (eds.), *Induction: Some Current Issues* (Wesleyan Press, 1963), especially the Introduction by Ernest Nagel; Ernest Nagel, Patrick Suppes and Alfred Tarski (eds.), *Logic, Methodology, and Philosophy of Science;* Proceedings of the 1960 International Congress (Stanford University Press, 1962), especially Parts IV, VIII, and X; Philip G. Frank (ed.), *The Validation of Scientific*

Theories (Collier Books, 1961); J. H. Woodger, *The Technique of Theory Construction,* IEUS, Vol. II, No. 5 (University of Chicago Press, 1939) to be read in conjunction with J. J. C. Smart, "Theory Construction," in A. G. N. Flew (ed.), *Logic and Language* (Second Series) (Basil Blackwell, 1959); Karl Popper, *The Logic of Scientific Discovery,* Science Editions (1961), especially chaps. i, iii, iv, articles by Ernest Nagel, Hans Jonas, Alfred Schutz, and Maurice Natanson in Maurice Natanson (ed.), *Philosophy of the Social Sciences: A Reader* (Random House, 1963); Hans L. Zetterberg, *On Theory and Verification in Sociology* (rev. ed.; Bedminster Press, 1963); Nicholas S. Timasheff, *Sociological Theory: Its Nature and Growth* (Doubleday and Co., 1955), chap. i is a good illustration of the nebulous conception of theory taught in standard texts; Max Weber, *The Theory of Social and Economic Organization,* trans. by A. M. Henderson and Talcott Parsons (Free Press of Glencoe, 1964), especially Parsons' introduction and chap. i; Robert K. Merton, *Social Theory and Social Structure* (rev. ed.; The Free Press, 1957); Earl W. Count and Gordon T. Bowles, *Fact and Theory in Social Science* (Syracuse University Press, 1964) includes a useful article by Talcott Parsons in chap. ix, pp. 140–58; more of Parsons' views on theory can be found in *Essays in Sociological Theory* (rev. ed.; The Free Press of Glencoe, 1954), especially Nos. XI (1945), XVII (1950); John Rex, *Key Problems of Sociological Theory* (Routledge and Kegan Paul, 1961); Robert Brown, *Explanation in Social Science* (Aldine Publishing Co., 1963).

The best work available, in my judgment, is Quentin Gibson's *The Logic of Social Enquiry* (Routledge and Kegan Paul, 1960) and I have relied heavily upon his construction of factor theories. Unfortunately, Gibson does not go into the structure of non-deductive theories nearly as deeply as one would wish.

Anyone interested in the results of analyzing theory in formal terms should look at David Rapoport's *The Structure of Psychoanalytic Theory* (International Universities Press, 1960). It is beautifully done.

CHAPTER SIX

EPISTEMOLOGY

THE need for a clear and unambiguous definition of knowledge, for a set of criteria that can be used to determine the status of propositions, is classic. Reasoned argument or explanation is not possible until the standards of evidence have been defined and agreed. A good part of the polemic over methodology in political science can be traced to fundamental disagreement about epistemological requirements, and many of the distinctions that can be drawn between political science and physical science may be attributed in large measure to epistemic differences. If the political scientist could simply adopt the epistemological standards of the physicist for his own, a great many troublesome problems of technique, method, and research strategy would disappear, and it has sometimes been suggested that this be done. Unfortunately, or perhaps fortunately, this solution to our problems will not do; a political scientist restricted by the strict epistemological standards of the physicist could not perform the tasks of his own discipline. Why this is so, and what its implications may be for political science, I hope to demonstrate in this chapter and in those that follow. The point may be formal, but its significance for the discipline can hardly be overestimated.

EMPIRICISM

That political science should define its standards of evidence in empirical terms seems beyond argument. Empiricism has its faults, and is not always easy to apply, but in general it accords so well with what is known about the human mental apparatus and its operation that the accumulation of evidence to demonstrate the force of the argument would only be tedious. That human thought, human action, and human experience are necessarily related to the operation of the central nervous system seems established beyond doubt. However, it is not enough to agree that empirical evidence alone ought to be allowed in argument; the term itself is not concise and wholly unambiguous. Although empiricism can be distinguished from other epistemologies easily enough, a whole range of possible standards can be defined within this very broad framework. In practice it is usually more difficult to decide which of the many possible standards of empirical evidence ought to be used than to agree on the need to be empirical in the broad sense of the term. In the last analysis, we select our epistemic standards pragmatically, or more accurately, according to the instrumentalist's point of view. Before a claim to knowledge can be evaluated, an epistemic standard is needed, but if that standard is so rigid that no claim to knowledge can be advanced in the discipline, then it is not very useful and should not be accepted. This may sound contradictory, but in fact no inquiry begins in a vacuum and it would not be possible, even if it were desirable, to reason ourselves back to the Cartesian void and begin anew. The selection of an epistemology is a change in course made after a voyage has begun and not a program of action that must be outlined before the ship leaves harbor. What is already known, however imperfectly, conditions our beliefs about knowing, and standards of evidence must in some way accord with accumulated experience and established procedures of inquiry.

Definition

Broadly construed, empiricism is the doctrine that man can have no knowledge of the universe that is not a consequence of perception and experience. The philosophical problems that arise out of the relationship between direct perception and conceptualization can be left to philosophy and psychology; our concern here is with some of the practical consequences of epistemology for the conduct of inquiry.[1] This minimal definition of empiricism implies, at the very least, that claims to know based upon a mystique —extrasensory perception, divine revelation, or inexplicable insights—cannot be accepted. Such "knowledge" may, of course, be valid; the empiricist must be agnostic and not atheist with regard to these claims. Nor does the empiricist deny the possibility of useful "intuitions," though he uses the term merely to designate an intellectual construction arrived at by a train of thought that is beyond precise specification, as when the mathematician reaches a solution to a problem without being able to say precisely how he did so. Of course, if a person wholly unfamiliar with mathematics suddenly produced a solution to a major problem in the field, which seems not to have occurred outside the writings of Plato, that position would have to be reexamined with some care.

If knowledge is acquired solely through the use of the perceptive apparatus, suitably augmented by various instruments, and the manipulation of these primitive inputs in 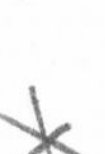 the central nervous system, we have a basis for making some discriminations, but the definition remains weak. The manipulations that occur in the central nervous system are influenced by the accumulated experience of the individual, and that is a very complex structure. If a proposition begins with concepts whose meaning is agreed, logic can serve as an instrument for differentiating the valid from the unac-

[1] A good, brief statement of some of these problems can be found in chap. ii of Abraham Kaplan's *The Conduct of Inquiry* (Chandler, 1964).

ceptable. Our problem comes one step before. There is, in other words, a difference between asserting on logical grounds that a proposition is untenable because the inferences it makes are illegitimate and asserting that a proposition is inadmissible because it errs perceptively. What is needed, briefly, is a standard that will differentiate claims that are based on perception, but involve different conceptions of the meaning of perception. In particular, the status of "subjective" as against "objective" perceptions must be agreed.

Formally, empiricism is the doctrine that all synthetic propositions must be verified by observation before they can be accepted as evidence. That is, any proposition that claims to add to the sum of human knowledge, and not to be a logical derivative of what is already known, must be verified by observation, a term yet to be defined. This draws the classic distinction between empirical propositions and logical propositions; the latter follow necessarily from a given set of premises, while the former do not have their predicates contained within their subjects. A logical proposition is true if it can be demonstrated that the proposition follows according to the canons of logic from the premises assumed; an empirical proposition is true only if it accords with human experience, or with observation. There is no implication here that empirical truth in some way corresponds with or represents the "real" world; the standard is human perception of the external universe and not the properties of that universe, defined in nonhuman terms. Further, the term "truth" does not have quite the same meaning in reference to logical and empirical propositions, respectively. Logical truth is absolute in a peculiar sense, for it is impossible to accept the premises and refuse the conclusions of a logical argument without self-contradiction, though that might not deter an obstinate woman. Empirical truth can, however, be disputed without self-contradiction simply by questioning the standards used to define the truth of the proposition. An interesting question about the relationship between logical and empirical truth in some of the exact sciences, like physics, has been raised but remains unsettled, for example, whether it is possible that in a fully deductive scientific structure the distinction disappears.

Complications

Empiricism, as it has been defined thus far, sounds sensible and innocuous—a generalization of man's common-sense beliefs about the world in which he lives. Indeed, everyday behavior is so firmly interwoven with sensory perceptions, and men are so thoroughly accustomed to rely upon them, that few pause to examine the relationship systematically and fewer still take the necessary time to seek a precise definition of the relationship between perception and knowledge. The kind of naïve realism that common sense tends to favor is only tenable so long as it is coupled with an awareness of the limits of human perception and of the practical difficulties involved in the refinement of observational standards and the elimination of vagueness and ambiguity from the results. Common sense is, in fact, remarkably metaphysical, all too often in precisely those situations in which metaphysics and empiricism clash most violently. Empiricism depends upon sophisticated criticism of the relation between perception, knowledge, and thought. It is only a relative standard and not an absolute; there is an irreducible element of subjective judgment that can be minimized but not eliminated. Empiricism defines truth in much the same way that the statute law defines justice, by asserting rules that men have created for their own purposes and not by reference to natural absolutes that are discovered and not created. The statute law does not guarantee that justice will be done, if by "justice" we mean some absolute standard; it states what will be done in particular cases, and if someone chooses to argue that what is done is unjust, there can be no reply beyond asking the

critic to state precisely his meaning of "justice" and his source of the definition. Empirical truth may also be inferior to some other "higher truth," and it most certainly is not an absolute statement about reality. What empiricism can do, however, is produce a human standard of truth that will guarantee the quality of the evidence that is accepted in argument in a given inquiry. No single definition of empiricism is the "correct" definition; there are many empiricisms, each giving a different standard of evidence. And we may choose the one that best suits our purposes, so long as we stipulate our choice and do not seek to use evidence obtained from one standard as an argument against propositions based on another.

If empirical facts are taken to include everything that men observe and experience, which is a tenable form of empiricism, the level of precision is so low that the results are not very useful. Observation and experience are extremely broad terms, and what can be experienced or observed, in some senses of these terms, may be considered inadmissible. We can, for example, accept every human experience that relates to the sensory apparatus as equal; that would include all perceptions of the external world plus all perceptions of internal states—all subjective experience. The result would be a mass of undifferentiated information of varied quality. Some standard is needed that will separate propositions arising from this broad range of observations according to their quality. The simplest solution to the problem is to classify observations according to the number of observers; for example, to separate observations open to only one observer from those that are open to plural observation. This is the classic distinction between subjective and objective data, and it is very useful. When the data used in inquiry are limited to observations of "public" phenomena, to perceptions of phenomena located outside the observer, every observation is open to verification by another suitably located and trained observer. If, however, a lower standard is used, subjective evidence relating to emotional responses and other psychic states can be used as evidence. Verification, of course, is no longer possible.

The basic choice lies between a definition of empirical fact that produces precise, verifiable data relating to a restricted range of phenomena and a definition of empiricism that widens the range of phenomena but lowers the quality of the evidence. The choice depends on the nature of the subject matter and the needs of the discipline. Political scientists, for example, need to ask themselves whether they can accomplish their task of explaining political phenomena if they rely on the first of these standards (public phenomena only), or whether it is necessary to use evidence that is subjective, and not open to verification.

Scientific empiricism

The physical scientist employs a very rigid and narrow form of empiricism. At a minimum, the scientist makes use only of observations that are public, that can be shared by two or more competent observers; subjective evidence, in the sense that it refers to an individual's perceptions of his own internal states, is eliminated completely. This is perhaps misleading if taken too literally. The biologist or neurologist, for example, may very well be influenced or aided by information that is subjective and not verifiable, but he does not employ such evidence in his scientific arguments. Similarly, there is an epistemic sense in which the subjective or psychic factor is involved in *every* observation and cannot be eliminated. In any event, the physical scientist commonly insists upon plural observers as a minimum requirement for adequate evidence. Moreover, he adds, wherever he can, the further requirement that observations be measured or quantified. "Nothing is known until it has been measured," is an extreme but not entirely unfair statement of the scientific ideal—an ideal achieved far more often than not in science. Quantification obviously limits still further the classes of events that can be observed and the kinds of propositions that can be made about them, but it pays handsome dividends in the form of accuracy of data and the elimination of uncontrolled subjective interpretation of observations. Two scientists may agree that the object before them is "large" but propositions that use relative terms of this sort are comparatively weak; when the assertion is made that a particular object is 38.653567 millimeters in diameter, on the other hand, the comparative term is eliminated and with it the evaluation. All that can then be questioned is the accuracy of the measurement, a matter that is open to statistical treatment when a number of measurements have been made. As the use of scientific instruments has spread, scientific observations have tended more and more to become what Percy Bridgman has called "pointer readings." For a scientific instrument is, in most cases, a device for making accurate measurements of a specified class of events; the information obtained through the use of instruments is already quantified. This has proved a very successful strategy, needless to say, and science has not been handicapped in the least by the need to adhere to rigid empirical standards. More important, perhaps, there is no reason why the scientific community should seek other standards. Nothing that has been learned about the behavior of inanimate objects, or even the lower life forms, leads to the conclusion that important aspects of these objects and their behavior are omitted because of strict empiricism. The social scientist, obviously, faces quite a different situation.

One further point needs to be made relating to the scientific definition of empirical fact. Science does not depend upon brute observation alone for its specification of facts, and scientific observations are not accepted simply because they have been observed. The "meaning" of observations must first be clarified, and the observations themselves must be related to the existing body of scientific information. The difficulty lies not with the precision of observations or perceptions but with their meaning. Once we move beyond a very simple conception of observed fact, the exact nature of what has been observed is not easily specified. Measurements are always "interpreted" in some measure, or converted into conceptions employed in the sciences. An "atom" or "particle" is not identical with the perceptions from which it is derived, and there is always room for error between perception and conceptualization. By bringing in the facts and theories already established in the sciences, new data offer a means of verifying established theories, and the theories offer a way of verifying the results of observation. The procedure is corrective, keeping the body of scientific information up to date, and maintaining the standards of evidence at a high level. Errors appear as discrepancies between theory and observation, or even between fact and observation; serious discrepancies will lead to a revision of theory, a reinterpretation of perceptions, or perhaps a reinvestigation of the phenomenon in question.

EMPIRICISM AND POLITICAL SCIENCE

Few persons would argue that political science ought not to be, or need not be, empirical. And virtually everyone would agree that we ought to employ the most stringent construction of empiricism compatible with the conduct of inquiry into political science. But it is clear that the rigid form of empiricism that physics employs would emasculate political science and, in any case, the fact that physics has been enormously successful while remaining within specified limits is not prima-facie evidence in favor of the belief that political science could do the same. Assuming that political science is a legitimate intellectual enterprise, with its own phenomena to explain as best it can, nothing would be gained by limiting evidence to events that would satisfy a rigorous definition of evidence but eliminate significant data from consideration. The best strategy for political science, surely, is to try as hard as possible to be strictly empirical, but to realize that the goal cannot be achieved. So long as the variations in quality of evidence are known, no harm can come from their use. The possibility of error in the interpretative transfer of data into concepts, of course, increases sharply as the rigor of empirical standards is relaxed, and this point needs to be scrutinized very closely in any empirical study.

Scientific empiricism and political science

The principal reason why political science cannot maintain the standards of empiricism that physics requires is fairly obvious; it would exclude from consideration any event whose full significance could not be conveyed by an accurate description of its public properties in quantified form. The objects of science are defined as the sum of their observed properties and their logical relationships. An atom of oxygen, for example, is a construction whose meaning is defined by the properties by which the scientist asserts its presence. Science has no reason to believe that any further qualities influence its behavior in a way that can be known to man. If, on the other hand, an atom of oxygen refused to combine with an atom of hydrogen, science would be in a dilemma. Ordinarily, an atom that would not combine with hydrogen could not be an oxygen atom. If, however, it could be established that it was in fact an oxygen atom (only possible, if in all other respects the atom in question behaves as oxygen atoms behave), science would have to postulate the existence of a subclass of oxygen atoms with this peculiar behavioral property. But if some scientist could somehow isolate oxygen atoms for a period of time and then he found that they had changed some of their behavioral properties, science would really be in a pickle. Presumably, a few isolated cases could be handled by assigning statistical probabilities to such changes in behavior based on experimental evidence, but if the phenomenon were common science could no longer proceed on its present course. Actually, of course, this seems never to happen and for practical purposes the scientist can assume that it does not happen. Event X is presumed when a, b, c, and d are present; behavioral variants are handled by introducing subclassifications of X. Given this procedure, science would have no way of knowing that the kind of change postulated above really did occur in any case.

The political scientist, unlike his colleagues in physics, *knows*, on the basis of subjective empirical evidence, that there are factors influencing the behavior of human beings that are beyond direct observation and measurement. Men act because of certain motives, they pursue identified goals, and their behavior reflects, partially at least, a wide range of psychic states. Communication among men, however imperfect it may be, seems adequate to establish these properties as true of all men. Men cannot make this assertion about any other part of the natural universe, though we sometimes project such human qualities to the lower orders of living things, as when we assert that the family pet "wants his dinner" when he behaves in a particular way. Given this unique property of human beings, political science must choose between a limited number of alternative strategies. The significance of subjective or psychic factors in human behavior may be denied, though that position hardly seems tenable at the present time. Alternatively, it may be asserted that psychic states can be inferred from the study of the observable behavior of the organism. However, that would require a linking theory, a means of connecting observable data to subjective state, and psychology cannot presently provide that connecting link. Finally, we can seek to investigate the psychic element in human behavior with those means at our disposal. Necessarily, this requires a weakening of the standards of empirical evidence imposed on the inquiry.

There is a great deal of difference between denying the importance of the subjective aspects of human behavior and asserting that the study of man can proceed through the observation of public data, ignoring or omitting subjective data. It must be admitted at once that certain kinds of political phenomena can be explained by theories and generalizations that rest entirely upon observed data. But that does not imply that the whole of politics can be explained without reference to psychological states, and on balance it seems rather more likely that psychological explanations will prove superior to purely empirical generalizations as explanations of political phenomena. Theories that refer to motivation, purposes, or goals cannot be replaced completely by theories that refer to observable behavior patterns. It follows that the study of political phenomena cannot be limited to observables in the strict sense of the term, even if the requirement of measurability is dropped. Whatever the better short-range strategy may be, in the

long run political science will have to come to terms with the psychic element in behavior.

Once the exploration of the psyche is undertaken, standards of evidence will drop. Inferences from public data to private conscious states necessarily involve the application of theory and the interpretation of perceptions and this softens the rigor of the total inquiry. That cannot be helped,

and it is always possible that psychology and other related disciplines will in time produce a stronger apparatus for conducting such investigations. The point is that political scientists do not face a choice between strict empiricism and metaphysics, as some of the earlier logical positivists seemed to think. The standard of evidence used in any

particular inquiry will depend upon the nature of the inquiry. Studies of public opinion will employ evidence obtained by a variety of techniques (questionnaires, interviews, analysis of publications, and so on) and though the value of the findings will depend upon an evaluation of the

standards employed to gather evidence, there are no grounds for asserting that such studies are worthless. When the results obtained from the application of two standards of evidence come into conflict, it may be difficult to find grounds for accepting one rather than the other, and the quality of the data will certainly count heavily. But the value of evidence obtained from, say, a major political figure through an interview may be much greater than the value of strict empirical evidence obtained by a precise study of observables. Precision at the expense of quality of content would be an expensive luxury, and to reduce politics to the study of trivia in the name of "being scientific"—to take the extreme case—would seem a regression to medieval scholasticism and not a step toward a stronger discipline. Fortunately, few persons advocate anything quite so drastic as this, though it is implied in proposals for research and study rather too often for comfort. In broad areas of human behavior, the facts are very dim indeed; yet the task of clarifying the facts, and linking them together into some sort of structure that can provide a foothold for another step forward, is a most worthy enterprise. It would be tragic if political scientists refused to inquire in any areas except those where the facts could be determined clearly and precisely.

Politics involves the behavior of man—individually and socially—and if the richness and diversity of human behavior is the despair of the system builder and if the factors of subjective motivation and value preference are the monkey wrench in the systematic theorist's gear box, these are not sufficient reasons for either denying the existence of the problem or oversimplifying it grossly. However imperfectly, we can study the goals men seek, the justifications they employ, the motivations that drive them, the social machinery they construct for these purposes, and the effect of that machinery, and of each other, on the behavior of individuals and groups. The results obtained from such study will be less precise than a chemical experiment; they need not be less useful or significant.

The physical scientist is a fortunate fellow. He does not have to deal with a living creature whose intentions are known only to himself—with a creature having the capacity to alter external behavior according to internal desires and aims. The scientist's objects are without guile or wit or intelligence; they learn nothing and they cannot dissimulate. There is an attractive simplicity to a subject matter so amenable to strict logical reasoning. Yet there is no reason here for consuming envy unless we adopt the scientist's standards of accomplishment—and every reason why this should not be done. Men are capable of stable and orderly performance, and it is possible, and even likely, that the vast majority of human actions fall into categories that can be defined and related with reasonable precision. Hopefully, there will remain an element of caprice, unpredictability, and perhaps sheer cussedness to disturb the symmetry of behavior. The influence of the expansion of knowledge is never wholly predictable. By comparison, atoms and molecules, or even ants and apes, seem dull and simplistic affairs.

Neither the "subjectivist" nor the "objectivist" argument is tenable in its extreme form. The denial of strict empiricism does not mean that all kinds of evidence must be allowed into the study of politics on equal footing; the denial of subjectivity can hardly imply a denial of the subjective element in human behavior. Broad ranges of human behavior are open to public observation and even to quantification, and the empirical evidence that can be obtained in this way can provide the discipline with a stable foundation. The body of empirical evidence available to political science can be maximized by careful research design, by the use of new experimental techniques, and by careful borrowing from allied disciplines like psychology, sociology, and even some of the physical sciences. Already, a great deal has been done under the influence of the "behavioral" movement. So long as scientific empiricism is conceived as an ideal rather than a limit, nothing but good can flow from the attempt to achieve it.

The limits of empiricism in political science

There is another side to the empiricist coin that is too easily overlooked. We have used empiricism as a guide to the evaluation of evidence and no more. Carried to extremes, it can become an unwarranted burden on the discipline. As Robert Bierstedt has pointed out, there is no philosophical justification for relying exclusively on empirical data in social science, and its ultimate logical consequences are either "Berkeleian idealism or solipsism." And on purely logical grounds, observation and experiment are never sufficient for generalization unless the universe of data is so limited that complete enumeration is possible. Further, excessive emphasis on empiricism can lead to highly undesirable consequences, enumerated by Bierstedt for the benefit of sociologists, but no less applicable to political science. First, it can lead to the aimless collection of facts "for facts' sake." Second, it can force research into certain channels not always of practical importance to the discipline. Third, it acts to reverse the role of theory and research; for example, to make theory a subordinate of research work; whereas, as we have already seen, theory has a prime explanatory function as well as an obligation to aid research. Fourth, it tends to place the burden of constructing systematic theory on the textbook writers (an assertion about sociology that has some parallel in political science). Fifth, it makes it very difficult to distinguish principles, generalizations, and laws against a discordant welter of unrelated facts. Additionally, it tends to give statistical data a privileged position in the discipline, not warranted by their explanatory significance in many cases, urges a search for accurate description as against an inquiry into causal relations, and leads to the neglect of historical material. Like

Bierstedt, I would not choose to opt for rationalism as a substitute for empiricism, but an appreciation of the shortcomings of empiricism is a necessary corollary to its intelligent use.[2]

When everything that can be done has been done, political science will still be a long way indeed from an empirical discipline in the sense that physics or chemistry is an empirical discipline. The amount of quantified direct evidence available will be only a small portion of the relevant data available for any particular inquiry. This need not prescribe a fatalistic or indifferent attitude toward matters of epistemology, nor is it sufficient warrant for impugning the accomplishment of present or preceding generations of scholars in the field to note that their data cannot meet scientific standards. That would be a slander the facts do not justify. A great many competent men and women have pursued knowledge of politics to the best of their abilities and with all of the means available to them.

The lack of empirical data in the strict sense does not mean that the field is in a state of utter anarchy and chaos, nor that political scientists are peculiarly insensitive to questions of quality. To the contrary, the standards of evidence have improved steadily in this century.

What is sometimes overlooked, I believe, is that the problems involved in the study of political phenomena have been evident for a very long time and a significant part of the training that any student receives in his special field in politics is, in fact, intended to teach him how to use the

available resources critically and intelligently. The standards that are taught are not always framed in self-conscious methodological terms, and they are certainly less clear and formal than the standards used in science, but they are

[2] I know of no better introduction to these shortcomings and their significance for the study of human society than the article from which this paragraph was taken, "A Critique of Empiricism in Sociology," *American Sociological Review*, Vol. XIV, No. 5 (October, 1949). I can only hope I have done justice to his argument in this brief synopsis.

not meaningless. Informal standards of this type are more difficult to learn, doubtless, than formal procedures, and they call for the exercise of more judgment than the student fully equipped with formal procedures needs, but that cannot be helped. To insist arbitrarily, as sometimes occurs, that political science must meet criteria of a given type or abandon its right to be taken seriously is mere childishness. To concentrate on methodological questions to the exclusion of matters of substance is a very serious error. It is heartening to see more time devoted to the discussion of methodology in politics, and it can be assumed that the discussion will prove fruitful in the years ahead. But those whose prime concern is methodology must realize that the discussion of procedural matters ought not to be prolonged unduly, and that we cannot stop working and await the methodological millenium. Any attempt to tailor a discipline to the Procrustean bed of a particular epistemic requirement may prove fatal to the patient.

What is probably more important in our context is that even if it can be agreed that social inquiry must deal with psychic states and that evidence for these states and their behavioral consequences is more difficult to obtain than evidence for public aspects of behavior, that does not mean that the logical canons used to evaluate the evidence or explain the phenomena in question are any different in one case than in another. The belief that the student of politics, because he is a human being, has some peculiar insight into human behavior that transcends the limits of formal inquiry cannot be accepted. It is true that the experienced political scientist may have "insights" into political phenomena that are difficult to formalize. He may also claim to have "sensations" of various sorts about his subject matter, but they can have no academic significance until the sensations are reproduced as symbolic representations that are open to verification by some criteria of evidence. The kind of data that political science can produce will influence the manner in which political phenomena are explained, and the need to take into consideration the psychic states of individual actors in a social situation makes it likely that causal, functional, and teleological explanations will play a much greater part in political science than in physical science. But the rules of criticism—and explanation—remain the same.

CHAPTER SEVEN

METHOD AND TECHNIQUE

IN a society where science and technology and "getting things done" are valued highly, we can expect to find a considerable amount of emphasis placed on method and technique—in schools, in industry, in government, or in academic life. The phenomenon is a prime illustration of that "rationalization" of domination that Max Weber postulated as a corollary to the development of large-scale industrial and urban societies. Unfortunately it is dangerously easy to slide from an appreciation of the importance of method and technique to an overstatement of their significance in inquiry. Even the academic community has not been immune to the influence of methodological "fads" and to the overvaluation of techniques. In many cases the error has arisen out of a mistaken assumption about the role played by particular methods and techniques in physical science, or out of a failure to appreciate the importance of the subject matter in any assessment of the usefulness of technique or method. In this chapter we examine some of the fundamental techniques and methods employed in political science, suitably generalized for maximum usefulness. The aim is a clear statement of their uses and limits, and particularly of the conditions that must be satisfied before the results obtained through their application to the subject matter of politics can be used.

PRELIMINARY OBSERVATIONS

The extent to which method and technique are dependent upon other aspects of inquiry is worth further emphasis, even at a risk of exaggerating the obvious. The physical scientist employs techniques that are not merely compatible with his epistemology; they are enforced by it. Epistemic assumptions, principles of verification, patterns of explanation, methods of approaching the subject matter, and techniques for acquiring data are all of one piece. The physical sciences, for example, have combined strict empiricism, quantification, analytic methods, precise instrumentation, and highly developed experimental techniques into a tool of great power and flexibility for the investigation of natural phenomena. The validity, and value, of any particular element in the structure is contingent upon the whole. There is nothing intrinsically valuable about quantification or the analytic method, so far as the scientist is concerned; they are valuable in the framework supplied by the other qualities of scientific inquiry. And in all cases the total structure is meaningful only because it is applicable to the phenomena with which inquiry is concerned.

This is easily demonstrated. Given the strict empiricism that science accepts (because it has proved compatible with its data), inquiry proceeds from the observation of public phenomena; the quality of observation is highest when the objects observed can be classified fully and unambiguously and specified accurately, hence, the emphasis that science places on quantification. This, in turn, facilitates the use of logical and mathematical techniques. Scientific instruments, which are essentially precise measuring devices, broaden the range of observations that scientists can make and, at the same time, increase the precision of the observations by quantifying the results. Experimentation, which implies the capacity to control the environment with some measure of precision, aids in carrying out these procedures and upholds the analytic method of approaching the phenomena. Logical tools, similarly, further rigorous analysis of the inferences that can be drawn from the findings, facilitating the production of the generalizations on which scientific explanation depends. One aspect of scientific inquiry tends to facilitate or generate the others, and the conjunction of elements is not accidental. Because the parts of the system of inquiry are easily discerned, the unity of the total structure is perhaps too easily overlooked. And those seeking to borrow from the sciences sometimes fail to realize that the worth of a particular tool in the scientific context may be quite different from its value in another form of enterprise. Intrinsically, the tool has no value whatever.

No technique and no method can be assumed to be useful in discipline A simply because it has proved useful in discipline B, particularly when the two disciplines differ widely in the stage of their development and investigate phenomena that are practically or logically distinct or incompatible. In every case, the validity of a method or technique depends upon the nature of the phenomena under investigation, the kind of information that is desired, and the purpose for which the information will be used. It is futile to seek information with a technique that will not produce it, to apply a technique to a phenomenon to which it is not suited, or to use an instrument that depends upon conditions that are not satisfied in the inquiry. The physician, to take a trivial example, may apply a stethoscope to the chest wall as a matter of routine, but it is assumed that his actions are meaningful, and with good grounds. He seeks information about the heart, presumably, or the lungs, and the information conveyed by the instrument must be in some manner related to the state of the organ whose condition he is investigating. There must, in other words,

be some theoretical or empirical relationship between the perceptions obtained through the use of technique and the phenomenon that the inquiry is concerned with. We must be able to connect, on the basis of past experience and accumulated knowledge, the rate of action, regularity, and "sound" of the heartbeat as they appear in the stethoscope to the actual operation of the heart. In this case, the assumptions are so well grounded that they are seldom spelled out explicitly; the physician learns them as a part of his normal training in medicine. He also learns, presumably, the justification for using the instrument, the conditions under which its use is valid, and the circumstances in which it is not sufficiently reliable—when to rely on the stethoscope and when to call for an electrocardiogram, for example. Learning *how* to use a technique is never enough. We must also learn when to use it, and when *not* to use it.

Every method and technique needs to be examined in these terms, not, of course, by every person on every occasion that it is employed, for that would effectively enjoin most human activity. But when the basic methodology of the discipline is being examined or the results of an inquiry are being evaluated, they need close examination. To put the matter differently, every application of technique or method that purports to deliver significant information to a discipline, excluding deliberate fraud, rests on the validity of certain assumptions, usually unstated, concerning the relation between technique and object. Implicit in these assumptions are further assumptions about the nature of the phenomena to which the technique can be applied. There are, in other words, warranted uses of technique and method that can be specified in terms of the conditions needed to make them fruitful, and there are uses that are enjoined strictly. The rote application of a technique produces results that are partial and even meaningless, like the perceptions of a child playing with a stethoscope. Of course, method and technique are usually learned along with the subject matter of a discipline, and it is unfair to designate every application of technique that does not specifically estimate the conditions of application as "rote" application. Yet an assessment of the uses made of technique and method, of their applicability to given phenomena, should be part of the training of the student, and it is sometimes omitted. And when new techniques and methods are introduced into a field of study, particularly where they are borrowed from another field, they need careful evaluation. When a given technique has been employed in a field for some time, it is perhaps possible to rely upon tradition; but when techniques are borrowed there is no tradition to depend upon and the questions raised here need to be answered carefully and rigorously before the data produced by their application is accepted and used.

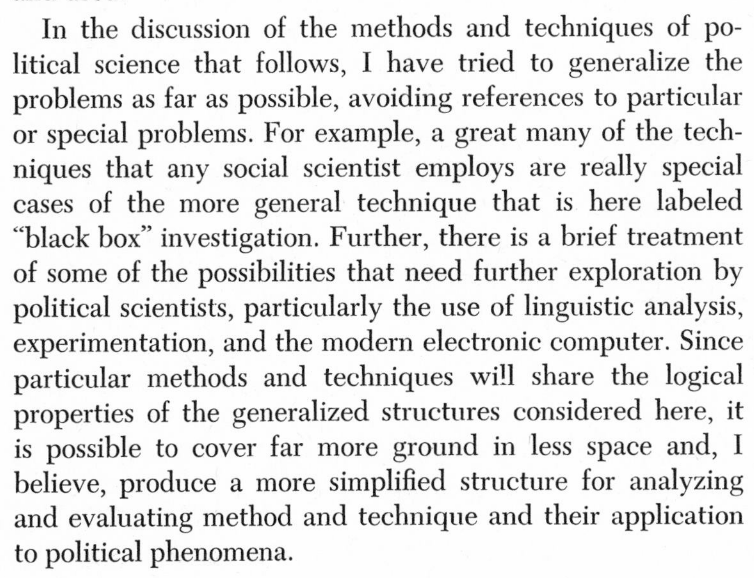

In the discussion of the methods and techniques of political science that follows, I have tried to generalize the problems as far as possible, avoiding references to particular or special problems. For example, a great many of the techniques that any social scientist employs are really special cases of the more general technique that is here labeled "black box" investigation. Further, there is a brief treatment of some of the possibilities that need further exploration by political scientists, particularly the use of linguistic analysis, experimentation, and the modern electronic computer. Since particular methods and techniques will share the logical properties of the generalized structures considered here, it is possible to cover far more ground in less space and, I believe, produce a more simplified structure for analyzing and evaluating method and technique and their application to political phenomena.

MEASUREMENT

The term "measurement" is used in a variety of different ways, some broad and some quite narrow. Basically, a meas-

urement is a procedure for assigning a number to classes of data or members of some class of data according to a definite rule. This is very broad, and it is possible to differentiate the various kinds of measurement that are possible within this framework according to the kinds of rules, or the *scales*, that are employed. The prime distinction lies between what is called *additive* measurement, which permits the use of arithmetical techniques like adding, multiplication, and division with the numbers assigned, and forms of measurement that do not allow this kind of manipulation. Actually, the extent to which it is possible to employ mathematics with the results of measurement depends on both the rule of measurement that is used and the state of development of mathematics. When a measurement is additive, very powerful mathematical methods can be employed to treat the results; when it is not, the problem is, at least for the time being, more complex and less can be done with the findings. As a consequence, some writers do not like to refer to nonadditive measurements as "measurements," reserving that term for strictly additive measurements. There is no harm in this, so long as it is realized that it is chiefly a matter of convenience and that further development in mathematics may alter our standards of desirability.

Direct additive measurement

Additive measurements may be either direct or inferential, though all measurements of this type depend ultimately upon some form of direct measurement. It is very important

to bear in mind that the mathematical treatment of assigned numbers that is made possible by additive measurement is not a property of the numbers assigned to the class of events measured, but depends upon the actual properties of the class of events. When we add two lengths to obtain a cumulative length, we have actually added the *lengths*, and not just the numbers assigned to each length. The reason why we cannot add length and time does not lie in some difference in the quality of the numbers assigned to these properties of objects but in the differences in actual properties. The properties to be treated arithmetically must really be combinable. Kaplan gives four rules or requirements for combination of this type: (1) the outcome of combining two objects must be the same regardless of the object with which the combination begins; (2) the results must be the same regardless of the manner in which the objects are grouped; (3) "the operation must be incremental with respect to the ordering relation: if two objects are equivalent with respect to that relation, then the combination of either of them with some third object is no longer equivalent to the other one but precedes it in the order established by the relation"; and (4) when equivalents are combined with equivalents, the outcomes must be equivalent.[1]

Direct additive measurement requires the specification of number in terms of standard units of magnitude comprised in a fully and unambiguously defined class of events or, in the case of dynamic systems, standard units of magnitude related directly to standard units of time. The class of events to be measured must be observable, repeatable, stable, and homogeneous; otherwise, the rules of combination cannot be satisfied. Each class of measurements must refer to one and only one class of events. The standard unit of measurement, like the class to be measured, must be defined precisely and unambiguously; in fact, the definition here is arbitrary but must be reasonable given the class of events to be measured. Once the class of events to be measured is fully specified, and the standard unit of measurement selected, all that is needed is to count the number of standard units in the class and assign that number to the class; hence the term "additive measurement." Without doubt, this is the most powerful form of measurement available and the most useful. It permits the application of powerful mathe-

[1] A. Kaplan, *The Conduct of Inquiry* (Chandler, 1964), pp. 184–85.

matical techniques (though it is not the only form of measurement that admits of the use of mathematics), and it serves as a basis for a wide range of inferential measurements.

Inferential measurement

When we seek to measure the circumference of the earth, the rate of movement of distant galaxies, or the viscosity (amount of molecular friction) of different liquids, we cannot simply apply a standard unit of measurement to the structure and count. Such phenomena must be measured indirectly or inferentially, combining a direct measurement with

a theoretical structure that relates the direct measurement to the phenomena to be measured inferentially. The measurement depends absolutely on a linking theory, and obviously it is no better than the quality of that theory. The use of inferential measurement widens immeasurably the range of phenomena for which precise quantitative data can be obtained, and it may even be said that practically

all really significant measurements in science today are inferential and not direct. Thus viscosity is measured by comparing the rate of flow of one liquid through a limited aperture with the rate of flow of some arbitrary standard like water. The linking theory asserts that molecular friction will have a direct influence on the rate of flow of the two liquids. Similarly, the astronomer measures the speed of moving galaxies far out in space by measuring the amount of "red shift" produced in a spectroscope when light from that galaxy is examined. He assumes, for good reasons, that the shift in the spectrum is due to the rate of speed at which the distant galaxy is moving. Finally, the psychologist who measures "intelligence," if indeed he really does produce a measurement, must have a theory that links the data produced by the measurement with the hidden property that he is trying to measure. So long as it is clearly understood that every inferential measurement depends on a linking

theory, they are very useful and perfectly valid forms of additive measurement.

Other measurements

Measurements that are not additive—for example, those that assign numbers to irregular ordinal relations, ratios, or preferences—are not all members of a single category of known quality. The evaluation of each measurement must be made uniquely, and it depends on the kind of scale used to produce the measure. Obviously, the usefulness of the results, the extent to which they can be manipulated mathematically, will depend upon the rules used to assign numbers to properties and the kinds of mathematical systems available. These measurements are not useless, of course; it is often quite valuable to know that one factor

is greater than another, or that a certain order of preferences will hold. But it is obviously much less useful than a measurement that will give an index to the precise degree of difference. It is one thing to say that *A* is greater than *B* and quite another matter to say that *A* is twice *B*. So great is the distinction that it seems not unreasonable to hold that anything less than additive measurement ought really to be designated by some other term, and some writers do take this position.[2] We can leave the question of terminology unsettled so long as we remember that what can be done

with any set of measurements depends on the rules by which numbers are assigned to categories or properties and that all nonadditive measurements must be evaluated uniquely. In what follows, the use of additive measurements in political science is dealt with almost exclusively, for

[2] Compare, for example, S. S. Stephens, who favors a broad conception of quantification with Walter A. Rosenblith, who prefers a restrictive definition, in Daniel Lerner (ed.), *Quantity and Quality* (The Free Press, 1961). Aaron V. Cicourel, *Method and Measurement in Sociology* (Free Press of Glencoe, 1964), chap. i, and A. Kaplan, *op. cit.*, Part IV are also worth reading. Kaplan treats measurement quite thoroughly though he does not seek to evaluate nonadditive measurements.

additive measurements can be evaluated generally, and they suggest many of the questions that must be asked with reference to any attempt to measure social phenomena.

Measurement in political science

The desirability of additive measurements in any discipline is beyond argument; they facilitate mathematical treatment, and organization, of data. Unfortunately, it seems unlikely that political scientists will be able to apply additive measurements to political phenomena on any significant scale in the immediate future. Though a number of very ingenious and useful schemes have been designed for applying numbers to classes of data, closer examination suggests that few of the measurements produced are in fact additive. This underlines the importance of the general principle that the quality of data is not assured simply because the data are stated in numerical terms; a great deal of nonsense can be, and has been, stated numerically. A general examination of the difficulties involved in making additive measurements in political science may suggest some of the criteria by which measurements may be evaluated and some of the major limits on measurement that must be observed.

The conditions that must be met for direct additive quantification or measurement are clear: a precise and unambiguously defined class of events and a standard unit of measurement are basic. If the measurement is inferential or indirect, a theory is needed to relate the unobservable phenomenon and the direct measurement. Only rarely can political scientists satisfy these conditions. Although there are many aspects of individual and social behavior that are open to observation—hence, are in principle open to measurement of the direct sort—it is extremely difficult to produce inferential measurements of social phenomena. At present there simply is not the body of theory needed to connect the direct measurement to the inferential data. The situation in the field of psychological testing is a notorious illustration of the point; it is relatively easy to get quantified information but extremely difficult to define the class of events to which the information pertains. Intelligence tests are a good typical example, for however useful the data may be pragmatically, no one has yet succeeded in identifying the "intelligence" that is purportedly measured by such devices. Any act of behavior can be construed as a combination of observable and unobservable factors (as in theories of motivation or instincts) and at present we are unable to infer with confidence from one to another. The problem is complicated by the fluctuations in the environment, which make it singularly difficult to be certain that the same measurement is being made on two successive occasions. Assuming a particular technique *(T)* applied to a given class of events *(φ)*, and designating the results *(R)*, it is clear that *(R)* will follow only when *(T)* and *(φ)* have been reproduced exactly. But it is always possible, in principle, that *(φ)* has not been reproduced exactly when the private element in the event is taken into consideration.

This kind of problem can be avoided, of course, by limiting measurements strictly to what can be observed directly. Unfortunately, that class of events is very limited in scope. Few political phenomena can be described adequately using observable properties alone; both social and individual factors need to be taken into consideration.[3] Furthermore, it is very easy to forget that an observable class of events cannot be used for inference to unobserved properties of events without an adequate theory. That is, it is very easy to slip from a category based purely on physical description to a category that includes, by implication at least, motivations or intentions or other private elements in behavior. For example, when a ballot is cast in an election, the only

[3] H. L. A. Hart, "The Ascription of Responsibility and Rights," in A. G. N. Flew (ed.), *Logic and Language*, First Series (Basil Blackwell, 1960), pp. 145–66.

assertion that can be made on strictly empirical grounds is that "X placed a ballot marked in the following manner into the ballot box." Did X thereby "vote for" a given candidate? Clearly that depends on the meaning of "vote for" and the theory that links that meaning to the physical action recorded by the observer.

Even if this trap can be avoided, a strictly empirical approach to political explanation is likely to meet with unexpected hazards. As Leontieff has noted, the empiricist works

generally by abstracting from his original data in gradual stages, omitting details, averaging, and aggregating his material. Presumably, this procedure can be expected to lead to generalization about the really significant elements of observed phenomena. But this apparently safe and simple process in fact leads to a genuine dilemma:

> (the) . . . essentially unsolvable problems of so-called index-number theory. He (the investigator) winds up either with a system of quantitatively well-defined relationships between qualitatively ill-defined variables or with a set of qualitatively indeterminate . . . relationships between sharply defined variables.[4]

Even if the raw data of political phenomena can be measured very accurately, it might prove a poor strategy to limit the discipline solely to empirical information. Some means of investigating the private or psychic element in social and political behavior seems essential.

"BLACK BOX" TECHNIQUE

The most common means employed to investigate the psychic properties of man is a variant of the "black box" technique employed in science and engineering. It involves the treatment of a complex structure as a single undefined entity; the behavior of the total system is observed under

[4] Wassily Leontief, "The Problem of Quality and Quantity in Economics," in Daniel Lerner (ed.), *op. cit.*, pp. 127–28.

varying stimuli and the results are recorded and measured. Although it is very easy to criticize particular uses of the technique, especially where quantification of data is claimed, some of the results that have been obtained through its use may prove very helpful to political scientists. We must distinguish, however, between the psychologist's probings into the operation of the neural structure, the physiologist's attempt to specify the rules by which the structure functions, and the psychiatrist's efforts to explore the relationship between the content of the mind and the behavior of the organism with an eye to therapy.

The psychiatrist is interested in those aspects of the human psyche that are most clearly applicable to political phenomena, yet the psychiatrist is less concerned with quantification, or even with a full specification of the factors at work in any particular instance of behavior, than either psychologist or physiologist. Though some psychiatrists have tried to generalize their theories and apply them to other fields—Freud himself not least among them—psychiatrists, in general, are usually criticized sharply by both physiologist and psychologist for lack of rigor. Yet it must be said that psychiatry has been more influential in political writings than either of its companions—witness the work of Lasswell, Fromm, and many others. The point is, however, that psychiatry is essentially the practice of medicine, particularly in the United States, and it deals mainly with psychic disorders and their treatment. The technique is not really aimed at investigation or generalization but at therapy; it is slow, tedious, and often very difficult to evaluate. Psychiatric theories tend to be grandiose where they follow Freud or Jung and pragmatic and medical when a clinical psychiatrist is writing. There is little that psychiatry can offer political science at present that is methodologically satisfactory. Indeed, it is a curious fact that although psychiatric theory has produced no major discovery or advance in nearly three decades, and no significant new theory has appeared in years, and psychologist and physiologist alike have subjected it to deadly criticism, psychiatry continues to flourish.

Our prime source of quantified information about the observable elements in human behavior lies with psychology; indeed, a working knowledge of statistics is today virtually a *sine qua non* for studying the field, so heavily have the psychologists been impregnated with the spirit of measurement. Again, this is more typically American than European. For many years, American psychology, under the influence of rigid behaviorism, ignored the work of ethologists like Tinbergen or Lorenz, despite the suggestive and even amusing inferences that can be made from animal behavior to human behavior. Today, this omission is being remedied very rapidly, and studies of the social life of animals, or the rationale of certain kinds of animal behavior, are progressing apace. They are at least a useful antidote to anthropomorphism, and in many cases suggest avenues that political science might do well to explore.[5]

In some branches of psychology, the techniques approach very closely the mode of analysis employed in physiology. But when the psychologist is concerned with the content of the psyche, rather than the physical operation of the nervous system, his principal instrument has been the "black box" technique. The same technique is employed when questionnaires are circulated for completion, when interviews are carried out systematically, and when experiments are conducted with small groups of various sorts; in all these cases, the "black box" technique is being used. We have here, then, a very useful and highly generalized technique for the investigation of the private element in social phenomena, one

[5] For example, W. C. Allee, *The Social Life of Animals* (Beacon Press, 1960), John T. Bonner, *Cells and Societies* (Princeton University Press, 1955), or the Scientific American's *Twentieth Century Bestiary* (no date). Other studies have been made of bees, monkeys, insects of various sorts. and a variety of fish. They make fascinating reading.

worth considering in some detail. Further, the results obtained by this device are easily quantified. The black box can be used as a measuring instrument; hence, it is very important to be perfectly clear about what it can and cannot measure, and what validity can be attached to measurements obtained in this way.

Procedures

When the elements in a complex structure are ignored, and the structure is treated as a unit, it is possible to consider the response of the unit to variations in its environment (changes in inputs to the unit) without worrying about changes taking place within the unit structure. Known stimuli are introduced into the unit and the response of the whole unit—the output of the total structure—is taken as a basic datum. Engineers commonly handle complex electronic apparatus in this way. Since the results are easily reduced to numerical figures it can be considered a form of measurement, though the precise meaning of the measurements remains to be discussed. For explanatory purposes, we will consider the technique to involve three parts: an *input*, the *black box* (a human being, in our case), and an *output* or behavior. In fact, of course, this schema is too simple for there may be "feedback" relationships between the three elements; for example, part of the output of the box may be fed back into the box as an input, immediately or following a period of delay. We shall, however, ignore this possibility here and concentrate on the relationship between input, black box, and output.

Ideally, we proceed to use the black box by isolating it from all environmental influences and introducing a single, carefully defined input into the structure duly recording the consequences in the output of the box. An engineer may introduce an electric current of known voltage and frequency, for example, and measure the output from the circuit to determine what changes have been effected by the input. The psychologist may administer a test, written or oral, to a human being. Asking any question is, in fact, a use of this device, though we seldom bother to structure our questions very carefully. By careful planning, the input can be designed in a way that will probe the unknown qualities of the black box and even disclose some of its configurations, just as a well-designed test can explore a student's knowledge of a given subject. With human subjects, we can explore knowledge, opinion, character traits or personality traits, and a wide range of other properties.

What can be learned in this way? Directly, the observer can learn what the consequences of a particular input are for the output of a particular black box. That seems not to be very much. But by subjecting a single box to a variety of inputs, much can be learned about that particular box, and by comparing the responses of many similar boxes to identical inputs, further useful information can be gathered. But there are some things that *cannot* be done with the technique. For one thing, when identical inputs result in identical outputs, we cannot infer that the boxes are identical. The measurement is too gross; it cannot discriminate very finely. We realize, for example, that even if two students achieve identical scores on a given test, and even if each answers every question in the same manner as the other (without cheating), that does not mean that the two students are identical. Their identity consists only in their achievement on the test, and the "meaning" of that identity is very hard to specify. Second, we cannot infer from outputs and inputs to the actual internal configuration of the box; the larger the number of experimental inputs, and the more closely their relationships are reasoned, the closer we can approach a stipulation of the contents of the system, but it cannot be specified fully. When the box is a human being, the output may be a consequence of such a wide range of internal sequences and effects that inferences from output to internal structure or content are always very risky.

Uses and limits

Obviously, the technique must be used with care. Since it depends in some degree on verbalization of inputs, the terms used to state the stimuli used with human systems must be formulated as precisely and unambiguously as possible, eliminating potential sources of verbal confusion and differences in word meaning. The use of "forced response" structures can facilitate the exploration of specific aspects of the system by a careful choice of terms. And some gross errors can be eliminated by factor analysis and statistical treatment of results. Yet when all that can be done has been done, the technique remains imperfect and the interpretation of results problematic. An intelligence test, for example, certainly provides a measurement of some property or quality of the human nervous system, but it is impossible to define that property. And it has been suggested that the best definition of "intelligence" may well be "the quality measured by an intelligence test." That is not very helpful.

Are the numerical data obtained through the use of "black box" technique direct additive measurements? Clearly not. At best, the psychologist who administers a particular test to a person, or an interviewer who asks a particular set of questions of an interviewee, then has at his disposal the following information: Under specified conditions, this particular human being has responded to this particular input with a particular set of responses. Such responses cannot be cumulated for we cannot know that they are identical in anything but the purely physical sense; rarely are we interested in such physical properties for their own sake. The purpose of the black box is to obtain information that can be used as a springboard to other information. We want information that will provide clues to human motivations, intentions, or thought processes. We need, therefore, some inferential structure that will relate the raw data provided

by a black box to the property being investigated. We need, in brief, a theory.

More information can be obtained either by multiplying inputs to a single box, or by using the same input with a number of boxes. When a test is administered to one person it is of little use; when the same test is administered to thousands of persons we obtain some extremely useful information. Similarly, the administration of a battery of tests to a single individual allows us to explore various aspects of that person's internal structure, and how they are related. If the composite results of a large number of tests using the same input but different persons are reduced to statistical indices, and questionable items are eliminated from the scores, the results obtained from any given box can be compared with statistical generalizations applicable to the entire population. Although this structure has little explanatory value, it can and does serve as a valuable predictor. For example, if a given test produces certain kinds of results from persons who achieve stipulated results in other kinds of activity (academic work, perhaps), it can then be assumed that a person who scores in a similar manner on the test is likely to succeed in the same kind of activity. That is, if n percent of all persons taking a particular test and scoring above the x level succeed in college, it can be assumed on pragmatic—but not logical—grounds that an individual who scores above the x level is likely to succeed in college. This is not a proper formal inference, of course, for no statistical generalization permits inferences to individual members of the population. But in practice, such assumptions work out reasonably well, which is some evidence in favor of the validity of the procedure; hence, their pragmatic usefulness as predictors. Test results cannot explain why a person who scores well on a given test does well in college; there is no causal relationship involved in the interpretation of the results or their use.

A second possible means of expanding the usefulness of

the "black box" technique is to begin with certain assumptions or postulates about the relationship between input, box, and output; the actual results obtained from the test may then serve as evidence for or against the theory. A questionnaire, for example, will usually begin with certain assumptions about, say, the manner in which particular political beliefs will influence responses to particular questions; without such assumptions, it would be impossible to structure a questionnaire properly. If the assumptions are clearly stated, and the theoretical structure reasonably accurate, the quality of the results will depend on the skill with which the investigator has reasoned out his relationships. Too often, of course, the assumptions are implicit and not explicit, and it is frighteningly easy to assign relationships on an improper basis, but the device is still very useful. The results are not, however, additive measurements.

For those who believe that additive measurements are a necessary prerequisite to a legitimate and worthy study of politics, this will appear as a rather dismal recitation of possibilities and limits. It seems quite clear that political scientists cannot expect to obtain strictly quantified information in any substantial amounts. However, if the looser conception of measurement is adopted, the "black box" technique can prove an extremely useful means of probing the private element in human behavior, supplementing and enriching the information that can be obtained from the study of observables. In any case, it has yet to be demonstrated that political science cannot proceed without additive measurements, or even that additive measurements would solve any of the basic problems of the discipline. In general, quantities appear as suitable replies to questions that demand to know "how much," "how often," "how quickly," or "what part"; quantities are not proper answers to questions that begin "why," or "for what purpose." Yet it is this latter class of questions that commands our attention most often in politics. Except in the rather trivial sense that "how many"

votes determines the action taken by society when its political structure rests on a democratic base, only a limited range of political questions is open to quantitative analysis. When we can quantify, we state the terms of our phenomena more precisely and accurately. But it is more important to be able to say that two events are invariably coupled than to be able to specify the events in numerical terms. The failure to measure may be a handicap; it cannot be construed as a catastrophe.

FORMAL LOGICAL SYSTEMS

The use of formal logical systems in political science—mathematics, statistics, game theory, etc.—raises a second class of general problems that is worth careful consideration. We are not here concerned with the need to make use of logical inference, broadly construed, in the explanation of political phenomena. The formal structures whose functions  and uses we are seeking consist of a set of axioms or postulates that is taken as given, a set of defined terms, and a set of rules for manipulating those terms. A fully developed branch of logic or mathematics contains all of the deductive relationships that can be obtained from a given set of axioms, terms, and rules of manipulation. It resembles a  formal deductive theory, but differs in that there is no necessary relationship between the terms in the logical structure and any empirical phenomena. Euclidian geometry is a typical example of the kind of system we are describing, as is common arithmetic. An infinite number of mathematical structures is possible, for any set of axioms can be used as a starting point and as rules for manipulating the terms in the system. Some logical structures have proved to be very useful, while others have not; from the logician's  point of view, that is irrelevant. From the political scientist's point of view, on the other hand, applicability is the most important criterion to be applied to logical constructs. At the present time, only a few mathematical or logical systems are available for use in political science and most of these find their best applications in economics. An increase in that number would be a definite asset, and that requires an understanding on the part of mathematicians and logicians of the political scientist's needs, and some understanding on the part of political scientists of what the logician or mathematician can do.[6]

Three of the basic properties of formal logical systems will help us to understand their uses and see their limitations in political science. First of all, there is no relationship whatever between the terms of a logical construction and the real or empirical world. They are formal, arbitrary, symbolic constructions, based on nominal definitions. Validation depends solely upon the internal consistency of the system; no logical system can be proved or disproved by reference to any external data. As a logical system, then, it cannot be applied to the empirical world; application requires some addition to the formal system.

A second point, often misunderstood, is that mathematics and logic do not depend absolutely upon quantification and strict measurement. When additive measurements are available, the use of mathematics is simplified, and more powerful structures may be employed. But a wide range of mathematical techniques is now available for dealing with information that has not been quantified. Of course, the data must be ordered in some way, but for all practical purposes formal logic can be adapted to any problem that can be specified clearly in ordinary language. For example, the modern electronic computer is a logical machine, but it

[6] See Anatol Rapaport, "Uses and Limitations of Mathematical Models in Social Science," in L. Gross (ed.), *op. cit.* for an excellent discussion of the problem. Also, John G. Kemeny, "Mathematics Without Numbers," in Daniel Lerner (ed.), *op. cit.*, and John G. Kemeny and J. Laurie Snell, *Mathematical Models in the Social Sciences* (Ginn and Co., 1962). The Kemeny–Snell book gives several instances of applied mathematics, chiefly in economics.

can handle any problem that can be stated in words and solved by the application of specified rules. Mathematical systems may deal with order, magnitude, sequence, relational terms, and many types of scales. It follows that the potential use of mathematics in political science has barely been tapped, perhaps because mathematicians have taken little interest in the subject matter, and few political scientists have become competent mathematicians.

Finally, and it cannot be too strongly emphasized, it follows from the first two qualities of logical systems that they cannot be applied until the terms of the axioms can be fitted to empirical data, or, more precisely, until it can be shown that the empirical conditions fit the axioms of the system. Before we can use arithmetic with empirical data, and arithmetic is the logic of numbers, essentially, the data must be combinable, for example, must satisfy the minimum conditions required by the axioms of arithmetic. The surveyor makes use of Euclidian geometry in his work, yet the surface of the earth is not really flat. For practical purposes, the fit is close enough, though not exact. Over the relatively short distances involved in surveying, the axioms of plane geometry are satisfied. The astronomer, on the other hand, cannot use Euclidian geometry because his data do not satisfy the axioms; instead, he uses another form of geometry whose axioms can be satisfied by the available information. Finally, when the mathematical theory of games is applied to political science or economics, it must be demonstrated that the situation to which it is applied approximates reasonably well the axioms of the theory. So important is this point that the first general rule for criticizing the application of *any* logical or mathematical structure in any discipline is to determine the extent to which the data accord with the axioms of the system being used.

Statistics and probability

Statistics have been used extensively in social science, particularly in economics and psychology; in recent decades, they have come into wide use in political science as well. The use of statistics makes it possible to present large masses of data in compact form, and it provides a means for examining the properties of the relationships that obtain among numbers. In addition, statistical techniques can be used to eliminate errors of various sorts and to deal with problems in which the outcome is uncertain or risky. In all cases, the numbers to which statistics applies are additive measurements; the use of statistics depends on the extent to which the data can be fitted into the axioms of the system. For statistics is a formal device, a logic of numbers, that demonstrates the properties of relationships among numbers and no more. It has no empirical content, no "real meaning." Pure statistics, like any form of pure mathematics, is a formal system. Before it can be applied, its axioms must fit the data.

Statistics depends, ultimately, upon a calculus of probability, a formal structure for manipulating probabilities—a  concept that remains undefined in the calculus except for a set of postulates that depend upon the theory of probability that is being used. That is, the theory of probability defines the axioms that define the meaning of "probability" in the calculus. Our concern here is not, however, with the content of the probability calculus, with the rules of combination and inference that it permits. Instead, we are concerned with the nature of the calculus, and with the conditions that must be satisfied before it can be applied. And what is true of statistics is also true of probability:

> No matter how it is axiomatized, the calculus of probability is, in the first instance, a set of purely arithmetical, hence tautologically or logically true, statements about numbers, in this case certain fractions called "probabilities." In the "frequency theory" formulation of the probability calculus, the probability of an event is arithmetically defined as the limit of the relative frequency of that event in an infinite reference class. Packed into the notion of "reference class" are certain arithmetically defined characteristics . . . Certain other concepts . . . are also arithmetically defined. *Before the probability theory can be applied*

these arithmetical notions must all be made to correspond to descriptive or empirical concepts.[7]

The arithmetical notions in a mathematical theory, in other words, must be correlated with descriptive conceptions. When this has been done, the result is a set of laws governing the referents of these terms. If the laws hold good, then the theorems of the calculus can be used to compute further probabilities.[8]

There is nothing in the training program of mathematicians or statisticians that equips them to translate arithmetical concepts into empirical social phenomena; there is nothing in the training of the political scientist that would alert him to the fact that particular situations do fit a set of arithmetical concepts in the probability calculus. Even

if the political scientist is "trained" in statistics, he is usually taught descriptive procedures, standard techniques for correcting errors and calculating correlations, and other commonly used manipulations. Rarely is he taught the foundations of statistics and probability, or made aware of the definitions of the fundamental concepts employed in the calculus. If a choice must be made, however, it seems far more important that political scientists learn the meaning of the axioms and definitions in the mathematical structure than learn how to carry out their own calculations. Learning *when* to apply statistical techniques, rather than how to apply them, is what matters most. Granted that political scientists need to "get together" with statisticians and mathe-

[7] May Brodbeck, "Models, Meaning, and Theories," in L. Gross (ed.), *op. cit.*, p. 385. Italics mine.

[8] Some of the more useful works dealing with statistics and probability include: Richard von Mises, *Probability, Statistics, and Truth,* (3d ed.; Macmillan, 1957); Bertrand Russell, *Human Knowledge; Its Scope and Limits* (Allen and Unwin, 1948), esp. Part V; Ernest Nagel, *Principles of the Theory of Probability,* IEUS, Vol. I, No. 6 (University of Chicago Press, 1939); William Kneale, *Probability and Induction* (Oxford University Press, 1949); A. Kaplan, *op. cit.*, Part VI; James C. Charlesworth (ed.), *Mathematics and the Social Sciences* (The American Academy of Political and Social Science, 1963).

maticians, and that seems a matter of prime importance when we consider the role that factor theories are likely to play in the discipline (statistics provides one of the best foundations available for the treatment of factor theories), but the answer is not to make the political scientist a third-rate statistician.

The statistician, like the mathematician, is concerned with the formal or logical aspects of statistics; as part of his training he learns how to perform statistical operations and how to develop further techniques should they be needed. He does not learn how to apply them unless he enrolls in some branch of applied statistics, and when that occurs the training does not usually include a discussion of the foundations and the meaning of the assumptions on which the calculations rest. When statistical techniques are employed in any discipline, the statistician functions as a "service unit," and not as a director of operations; he can no more validate a particular application of statistics than an adding machine can validate the use of addition in a particular case. The key role in applied statistics devolves on the subject-matter expert—the person who is able to say whether or not the concepts in the statistical calculus are satisfied. The statistician can only guarantee the accuracy of the calculations; their meaning, if any, requires interpretation by someone who knows the data.

To take an example, even a near-perfect correlation between two variables can be totally meaningless. There is always the possibility of accidental or spurious correlations. We might, for example, obtain a "statistically significant" correlation between the number of fish caught in a given year and the amount of foreign assistance voted by the Congress in that year. Clearly this provides no evidence whatever of any causal relationships between the two events; statistical correlations are never anything more than evidence for the existence of such relations, to be overruled by empirical evidence when it is available. The point is that the meaning of "statistically significant" is formal, and it refers to nothing more than the existence of certain proportional relationships between two sets of numbers. The numbers need not refer to causally related phenomena. Mastery of statistics, in brief, implies nothing whatever about knowledge of subject matter; when there is a conflict, it is always the latter that holds.

A final point relating to the use of statistical techniques in political science is that the data must be amenable to combinations, that is, they must be additive measurements for the calculus is fundamentally arithmetical. In view of the limited scope of this type of measurement in the study of human behavior, the data being manipulated statistically needs to be examined carefully, and inferences from the data must remain within the limits set by the original measurements.

When all this has been said, however, statistics remains an important tool in political explanations, partly at least because the general statements used in political science tend to be probabilistic rather than universal in form. Statistics can be an important source of general statements, for what is called statistical inference, a procedure for generalizing about whole populations from the characteristics of suitably selected samples, can produce generalizations of considerable use and value. Other techniques, like stratification and cross-referencing, provide a useful means of studying the interrelationship of variables in a given situation when the data can be measured. So long as they are applied knowingly and not by rote, they are useful and even essential for the systematic study of politics. The greatest danger in the use of statistics, as Kaplan has noted, is that it is easy to forget that "statistical techniques are tools of thought, and not substitutes for thought."

Mathematical theory of games

One of the more interesting mathematical structures to appear in the social sciences in recent years is the theory of games developed by John von Neumann and Oskar Morgenstern, chiefly for use in economics. In its variant forms—game theory, decision theory, utility theory—it has been adapted widely in economics, military affairs, and certain kinds of political situations. Like all mathematical structures, game theory is formal and logical; it has no relevance to the real world until and unless its axioms are fitted to the facts. But the situation which the theory envisions resembles many aspects of real life, and since it exposes the underlying logic of behavior under the stipulated circumstances, it seems to offer real insights into the structure of rational human behavior. The early form of the theory, for example, treated situations in which two antagonists pursued antithetical and mutually exclusive goals according to a given set of rules where one antagonist's gain equalled the other person's loss (zero-sum game). Since that time, various other forms of game theory have been worked out in which one player's losses do not equal another player's gains, and in which the game is not limited to two players. The calculations involved are complex, understandably, but the applications are correspondingly wider. We shall deal only with the two-person, zero-sum game, the simplest form of the structure, but other variants may well prove more useful in political science in the future.[9]

[9] There are a number of good books on the theory of games. J. D. Williams' *The Compleat Strategyst* (McGraw–Hill, 1954) is the simplest and clearest introduction to the two-person, zero-sum game available, but it does not deal with recent developments in the theory. R. Duncan Luce and Howard Raiffa's *Games and Decisions* (John Wiley, 1957) is excellent, and Anatol Rapaport's *Fights, Games, and Debates* (University of Michigan Press, 1960) is very good indeed. Richard C. Snyder's *Game Theory and the Analysis of Political Behavior* (Free Press of Glencoe, 1961) is good, as is Thomas C. Schelling's *The Strategy of Conflict* (Oxford University Press, 1963). William H. Riker's *The Theory of Political Coalitions* (Yale University Press, 1962) is excellent. Numerous articles on the subject have appeared in *Behavioral Science, The Journal of Conflict Resolution, World Politics,* etc. Schelling's book includes the application of non-zero-sum games that employ threats and promises; uses the theory for analysis of empirical situations in a very knowledgeable manner. Riker's model of political coalition calls attention to some very interesting properties of competition under stipulated circumstances.

It is important to be clear at the outset about what the theory of games purports to do and what it cannot do. Game theory has nothing whatever to say about the way in which people *do* behave in real life, or about the way in which they *ought* to behave. What it can do is state the way people would behave if three conditions are satisfied:

1) If the person can always decide, in every situation, which outcome is preferred among the available alternatives, and at what price or risk it is preferred.

2) If the person can use all of the information available to him and calculate the actual outcomes of a situation that is determinate and the expected outcomes in situations involving risk.

3) If the rules governing the sequence of permissible actions, and their range, are fixed and explicit.[10]

Whether or not those conditions are satisfied in given circumstances is a matter that cannot be determined from the theory; it is an empirical question to be answered by the subject-matter specialist.

The essentials of the two-person, zero-sum game are quite simple. Two players pursue antithetical goals according to a specified set of rules; various outcomes of the conduct of play are possible. The amount of information available to each player may be partial or complete; for example, in chess information is complete whereas in poker information is partial. The number of outcomes must be finite, and each outcome must have stipulated consequences for each player. The object of the game may be stated in various ways. A common example is the so-called "minmax" solution in which a course of action is sought which will produce a maximum gain at minimum risk. Other solutions may prefer to increase risk but maximize gain or decrease risk still further and minimize gain.

Game theory offers a means for making "rational" choices

[10] Partly quoted and partly paraphrased from Anatol Rapaport, "Mathematical Models," in L. Gross (ed.), *op. cit.*, p. 369.

among alternatives by evaluating the consequences of each alternative and assigning it a weight. Obviously, the weighing of alternatives cannot be performed by any logical structure; that is a matter for human judgment. And the

theory cannot function until the alternatives have been evaluated, for the theory allows for choices only after the evaluation has been made in numerical terms. This done, the game theory offers a logical technique for selecting strategies that will achieve stipulated results. In this, it resembles very much the construction of the role of reason in ethics put forward by Stephen Toulmin; reason can help us select the correct action for achieving a goal once the goal has been fixed.[11] The theory of games seemed for a time to offer social scientists a magnificent opportunity to place decision making on a rational foundation, but as Luce and Raiffa point out, "Initially, there was a naive bandwagon feeling that game theory solved innumerable problems of sociology and economics, or that at the least it made their solution a practical matter of a few years work. This has not turned out to be the case." Yet the situation envisaged

in the theory resembles very closely the position of a trader in a competitive economy, or a national state in a hostile and competitive world. It is useful to inquire into the reasons why these great expectations were not realized.

The crux of the difficulty has been the need to evaluate alternatives and specify a numerical coefficient for the amount of gain or loss to be had from each alternative. Once this has been done, the theory will perform its work quite rigorously, even in very complicated situations. Unfortunately, the theory says nothing about the manner in which evaluations are to be made, and no logical structure can infer evaluations from factual evidence. If every person has a pattern of preferences that is consistent, and if each order of preference can be assigned a numerical utility

[11] Stephen Toulmin, *The Place of Reason in Ethics* (Cambridge University Press, 1960).

function, then the rational player will select the outcomes with the greatest utility functions and choose the strategy that will lead to them—a tautological assertion, but very useful.

In practice, the utility function has proved difficult to define with the needed precision. Luce and Raiffa, writing in 1957, asserted that if it was theoretically possible it had, nevertheless, proved impracticable even in ideal experimental situations. Others are more sanguine but no one is prepared to assert that the task is possible outside the framework of a very simple game (which did not stop political scientists from trying to stipulate utility functions for very complex situations like foreign relations, however). Some sense of balance is needed here, surely, to prevent attempts to do the impossible or, more frequently, inhibit claims that the impossible has been performed. Most of the arguments in politics can be construed as arguments over utilities. They are not, as we might think, concerned with the best means of attaining a maximum utility but are concerned with the problem of trying to decide whether or not a particular outcome is desirable. Since the heyday of American Progressivism, the virtues of the expert in government have been extolled by a considerable and influential group in society, not least the university professors themselves. Yet there are no experts on values, only experts on the achievement of stipulated values. Granted that the expert can assume the existing value system and choose alternatives that maintain it; but that is a poor base for democratic politics.

On the positive side, game theory in its various guises does offer a valuable formal procedure for exploring the complications and ramifications of the various alternatives fully and accurately; in this sense it performs like any other logical system. When the values to be achieved by decision makers can be stipulated, as in military affairs or certain aspects of economics, game theory may be very useful so long as its function is not confused. That is, wherever the function of policy is to achieve agreed outcomes under given circumstances as swiftly and efficiently as resources permit, the application of game theory may be useful. It can, for example, help locate rocket sites, allocate supplies and materials, and so on. But politics seems not to produce the conditions in which game theory can be applied. Political decisions tend to hinge upon the selection of values, and a logical structure that presumes the values already selected is not very helpful in the selection. One of the principal dangers attendant upon the use of game theory is that it may encourage the user to assume a rational, stable, value structure where in fact none exists.

TECHNIQUES FOR EXPLORATION

It is always easy, too easy perhaps, to chide the members of a profession for omissions, but a number of promising avenues for approaching the study of politics have not yet been explored very thoroughly. It can be assumed, I think, that political science will tend to follow other kinds of academic inquiry into increasing rationalization and formalization in the next few decades. We can expect increased methodological sophistication, a wider application of logic in the broad sense of the term, and increased reliance upon statistical and other mathematical systems. In these circumstances, much more attention will have to be given to the linguistic and semantic foundations of inquiry, the use of experiments, and the utilization of modern electronic apparatus as an aid to the exploration of inference.

Linguistic analysis

There is little justification today for the muddled terminology and poor syntax that appear so frequently in discussions of political phenomena. A systematic attack on the nomenclature is long overdue, and if it would not provide any solutions to political problems, it would have the merit of clarifying the actual problems being investigated. Already, a few attempts to make use of linguistic analysis with political materials have been published, but the need for a systematic, large-scale attack on the problem still remains. The aim, of course, is clarification of meaning, elimination of ambiguities, and precise determination of the content and logical form of terms and propositions. Analysis of this sort solves no problems and provides no explanations, of course; hence it cannot be construed as an end in itself. But its contribution to a sound discipline are beyond measure and few academic disciplines are more in need of its cauterizing touch than political science.[12]

Experimentation

The experiment is another technique seldom used in political science, largely, no doubt, because the materials are difficult to control. Although it would be difficult to achieve the level of precision in experimentation that physical science has reached, there is no reason why fruitful experiments cannot be carried out in a much looser framework, and in any case it is wise not to overestimate the degree of precision that science actually achieves in the laboratory. Careful planning of experimental design, which is the crucial part of any experiment anyhow, could extend the use of experiments very considerably, and if the outcome proves less precise than we might wish, it could still provide a useful foundation for the development and validation of theory. A great many groups and organizations already in existence could be used for experimental purposes, and some of the work done by psychologists with small groups has already produced information of considerable value

[12] Three of the best efforts to attack political problems through the medium of linguistic analysis are T. D. Weldon's *The Vocabulary of Politics* (Penguin, 1953), Robert A. Dahl, *A Preface to Democratic Theory* (University of Chicago Press, 1953), and Thomas L. Thorsen's *Logic of Democracy* (Holt, Rinehart, and Winston, 1962).

about human behavior in stipulated circumstances. The use of experimental situations to test postulational theories and models appears as a particularly appropriate use of the technique. Any field investigation is, in fact, a loose form of experiment, and deliberately contrived investigations of this sort, using "natural" laboratories, seem far more useful than isolated or unsystematic investigations not impelled by theory.[13]

Use of computers

Finally, political scientists ought to begin exploring the potential of the modern electronic computer as rapidly as possible. Once the naïve conception of the computer as a glorified adding machine and statistical sorter is replaced by the concept of a powerful logical apparatus capable of investigating almost any imaginable property of a specified system, we can cease using computers as simple statistical devices and begin developing their real potential. The computer, bluntly, can handle any problem that can be stated in clear, precise English; it can examine the properties of any social theory that can be framed in words, however elaborate it may be. There is almost no limit to the uses that can be made of the machine beyond our imaginations.

For example, it is possible to program an idealized "political man," building into the program the characteristics determined by empirical studies, then examining the logical consequences of these assumptions in any stipulated set of circumstances. How is a person with a particular kind of past experience, particular beliefs, particular values, likely to respond to a given external environment? Questions of

[13] Sidney Verba, *Small Groups and Political Behavior* (Princeton University Press, 1961) is worth careful study. The fine article by Richard C. Snyder, "Experimental Techniques and Political Analysis; Some Reflections in the Context of Concern Over Behavioral Approaches," in James C. Charlesworth (ed.), *The Limits of Behavioralism in Political Science* (American Academy of Social and Political Science, 1963), is also worth reading.

this kind are well within the capacity of the computer. One could create a number of "persons" within the computer, each with particular characteristic behavior patterns, and examine the consequences of their interactions under different conditions. One can simulate a bureaucracy and learn something about its operation, examine the interaction of office and personality, and so on through an endless list. Nor does the political scientist have to learn how to program the machine expertly. The hardest part of the task is working out the initial data and rules of operation that must be fed into the machine. Computers, in other words, must be fed the data and theories of operation they use in their computations. They will then examine and elaborate the consequences of the theory with a speed and accuracy no human can match. It is even possible to program a computer so that it will develop its own rules of operation as it goes along by extrapolating from its own past experience. The computer, in short, is an incredibly versatile instrument, and it ought to be adapted to the study of politics in significant and sophisticated ways, and not merely employed as a glorified calculator.[14]

THE LIMITS OF FORMALISM IN POLITICAL SCIENCE

No discussion of the uses of formal logical and mathematical structures in political science can avoid reference to the limits that must be observed in their use. The tendency for contemporary political study to seek formal specifications of its operations wherever possible is laudable. But it can be misleading, at least to the extent that it suggests

[14] See *Proceedings of a Harvard Symposium on Digital Computers and Their Applications* (Harvard University Press, 1962); Harold Guetzkow (ed.), *Simulation in Social Science: Readings* (Prentice-Hall, 1962); Edward A. Feigenbaum and Julian Feldman (eds.), *Computers and Thought* (McGraw-Hill, 1963); W. Sluckin, *Minds and Machines* (Penguin, 1954). Feigenbaum and Feldman contains a thorough bibliography of work being done with computers.

that formal apparatus can solve any of the really fundamental problems in politics, or implies that other disciplines have achieved more than political science *because* they have formalized their procedures as fully as possible. Formal logical systems have no intrinsic value for man; they are only tools, and tools are always limited by the materials to which they are applied. It is a profound error to believe that all questions can be answered logically, or to attribute to logic conclusions reached by other means. We should neither expect more from logical apparatus than it can perform nor seek to apply logic to kinds of problems where it cannot offer a solution.

Logic and choice

The prime limit on the usefulness of logic is that it is incapable of making choices. A logical system can choose, of course, if the rules for making the choice have been spelled out in the axioms, but in that case the person who selects the axioms actually makes the choice. The question "Is A more important than B?" can only be answered by a logical system if some rule is available for making the decision; no logical system can derive the rule from factual considerations. The limitation sounds mild until we realize that any inquiry takes in broad areas where the rules for making choices cannot be stated formally and absolutely.

Inquiry aims at the explanation of particular phenomena through generalization and theorizing. But which phenomena are worth explanation? The answer to that question is an act of judgment and no formal criteria can be specified that relieve the investigator of the task of selecting. As inquiry proceeds, the investigator must continue to exercise his judgment, selecting what is relevant and discarding what is irrelevant, and thus establishing the boundaries of his study. Again, no set of formal rules can set these limits; they are acts of evaluation and judgment. The point is not trivial though it may be commonplace. An unbounded sys-

tem has no meaning, and a system whose bounds are too constricted is open to criticism on the grounds that relevant evidence has been ignored. The grounds on which relevance is established are empirical and not logical; the judgment is not a logical choice but a matter of judgment. The most complex logical structure available to man is only capable of self-reproduction; deductive systems cannot produce more than the content of their own premises. The rules for ingesting data into the system are, therefore, incomplete until the logical system is complete, and to ask a logical system to postulate its own boundaries is logically equivalent to asking Euclidian geometry to establish its own postulates. Only man, so far as we know, can go beyond his postulates but the procedures by which this extension of knowledge is accomplished are not presently known. Presumably what occurs is a blending of past experience and training with new information to produce relationships and conceptions not hitherto considered, but no formal system can specify or predict the outcome.

The frame of reference

To continue, every attempt at explanation takes place within a framework of assumptions that define a particular field or outlook, and the field that is selected as a framework will obviously influence the nature of the explanation rather considerably. The selection of a "universe of discourse," then, is an important part of inquiry. But here too we find that judgment, and not logic, is at work; the procedure cannot be formalized. A simple example will illustrate the point. Let us seek an explanation of two simple facts: first, that a stick placed vertical to the earth's surface at one point casts no shadow at noon of a given day; second, another vertical stick located 1,000 miles to the north of the first casts a shadow about 14½ degrees from the vertical at the same time. Two assumptions are needed to explain the two facts, but two quite different pairs of assumptions explain the facts equally well, other things being equal. If we assume that (1) the earth is round, and (2) the sun is distant, we account for the data by assuming that the sun's rays are parallel at both points on the earth's surface, and conclude that the earth's surface must be curved. A simple calculation will then provide a rough figure for the circumference of the earth, for 14½ degrees is roughly one twenty-fifth of the total circumference of a circle, and if this corresponds to a distance of 1,000 miles, the total circumference must be about 25,000 miles. Of course, we know from other data that this is the "correct" set of assumptions to use, but it is easy to forget that this is not a logical consequence of the facts. For the data can also be explained by using quite a different pair of assumptions. If, for example, (1) the earth is flat, and (2) the sun is very close to the earth, then the sun's rays are not parallel at both points and when they parallel the stick at one point, they cast a shadow at the other. Again, the facts are fully explained, but in this case the data provide a means of measuring the distance between the earth and the sun. Both explanations are formally consistent with the facts and neither can be preferred on logical grounds. The reason we select the first and reject the second is that we have other knowledge which invalidates the latter. In a new discipline, or one that is relatively undeveloped, the additional information needed to make the choice may not be available—a useful warning against overreliance upon formal relationships.

Generalization

A third major form of activity that cannot be formalized is the making of generalizations. Despite the best efforts of a great many highly competent scholars, the "problem of induction," the justification of propositions that move from the particular to the general, remains unsolved. There simply is no logic of induction, no formal rule or rules that can move us from specific facts to general statements, although J. S. Mill's attempt to specify rules in his *System of Logic* is at times useful. We cannot say why Tycho Brahe collected facts by the thousand without being able to generalize about the heavens while Kepler, using Brahe's data, originated the famous and fruitful laws that bear his name. The essential part of explanation lies beyond the power of logic; it is performed uniquely, if not mysteriously, by human beings.

Enough has been said, perhaps, to indicate the kinds of limits on formalization that must be respected. This ought not to lead to the repudiation of every effort to produce formal rules for guiding inquiry, but it does indicate the need to go beyond formal rules in the conduct of inquiry into politics. Certain kinds of intellectual work required for adequate explanation cannot be specified in logical terms. This is not necessarily an impediment to the development of explanations, for we do select data for explanation, we do adopt explanatory frameworks for our explanations, and we do produce useful generalizations about the subject matter and agree on their validity. The things that political scientists say make sense, usually, to other trained political scientists even if they cannot be justified by any formal mechanism.

Implications

There is an important lesson here, and if it sounds trivial it is nevertheless worth repeating. The only possible basis for a sound performance in political science is a thorough knowledge of the subject matter, of the standards of criticism and evaluation that have been developed by others who struggled with the same intractable material. This may sound like methodological conservatism of the worst sort but it is really only a recognition of necessity—we need tools for dealing with questions that cannot be answered with logic. Without a knowledge of the basic materials, the most highly skilled logician available is quite helpless when he seeks to apply his training. An understanding and appreciation of the methodological problems involved in the study of human behavior is an essential part of the equipment of any competent scholar; formal competence conditions what is done and rescues us from haphazardness. But when this much is granted, there remain serious gaps in the structure that must be filled by ingenuity, insight, intelligence, or intuition. Each scholar must contribute in some sense as a unique individual and not merely as a cog in an elaborate formal mechanism, and who would have it otherwise?

Political science, in other words, has little reason to look forward to any methodological millenium when some "master technique" will finally be developed that will solve all of its problems. It is clear, for example, that the basic techniques employed in the sciences have only a limited applicability to politics and their use in no case guarantees the quality of the results. Every academic discipline has its own integrity to preserve, its own phenomena for explanation; they shape the discipline inexorably. Technical proficiency, as every musician knows, is no substitute for musicianship; formal proficiency in logic or mathematics is not a substitute for a thorough knowledge of politics. No technician can dictate to the subject matter, and to lose oneself in the study of technique is to become a technician and not a political scientist.

There is, perhaps, a fuller sense of the meaning of "technique" that avoids this narrow implication, the sense in which it refers to the capacity to perform competently in a given field. Here is a goal worth pursuing, surely, and it ought to be just as possible to learn politics as any other subject, to acquire standards for making judgments or decisions as scholarship demands. What is important to note here is that this kind of technical proficiency cannot be measured in terms of mastery of rote operations; it involves, necessarily, the capacity to deal intelligently with unique problems. Self-conscious awareness of what is being done is

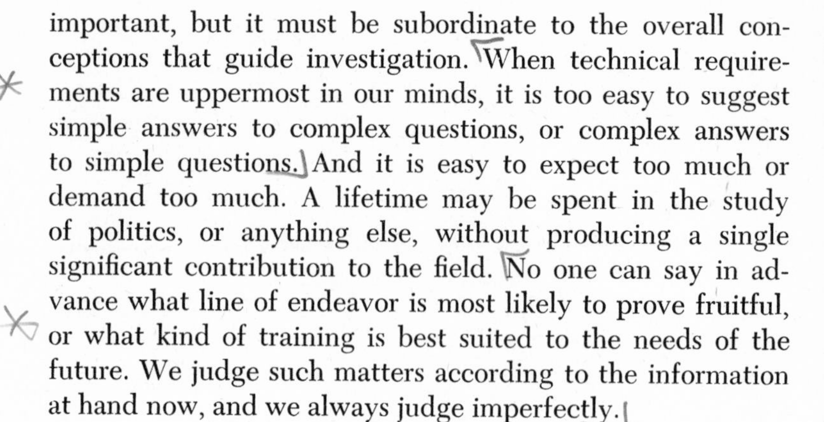

important, but it must be subordinate to the overall conceptions that guide investigation. When technical requirements are uppermost in our minds, it is too easy to suggest simple answers to complex questions, or complex answers to simple questions. And it is easy to expect too much or demand too much. A lifetime may be spent in the study of politics, or anything else, without producing a single significant contribution to the field. No one can say in advance what line of endeavor is most likely to prove fruitful, or what kind of training is best suited to the needs of the future. We judge such matters according to the information at hand now, and we always judge imperfectly.

CHAPTER EIGHT

VALUES

THE study of politics proceeds at a number of different levels simultaneously, for there are various conceptions of the task from which the student may choose. Thus far, we have been concerned with the kinds of activities involved in the explanation of political phenomena, in the formulation of theoretical structures that relate observable phenomena in a meaningful fashion—what may be referred to as political theory in the strict sense, or perhaps philosophy of political science. In the physical sciences, this is the sum total of the inquiry; there is nothing further to be done when the explanation is complete. Criticism, in the sense that it can be applied to social phenomena, could have no object in science. Yet some strict empiricists have insisted that this is also a necessary and sufficient definition of political science. That view seems inadequate.

The fact is that what we call values or ethics impinge upon politics in a number of direct unmistakable ways. For one thing, political decisions *are* value judgments, in most cases at least, and this alone is sufficient to add another dimension to the study of politics. Explanatory systems that seek to relate political phenomena cannot avoid reference to human values and the means chosen for their achievement. One may study amoeba for a lifetime and yet not feel called upon to criticize their way of behavior; political activities cry out for criticism. The belief that political science can be carried out wholly in descriptive terms, that no political scientist can, qua political scientist, criticize political activities, seems too restrictive. What political scientists do is in some degree conditioned by what political scientists *can* do; the nature of politics, not the nature of natural phenomena, determines the nature of political science.

The difficulty with this point of view, as is often noted, is that it sanctions all sorts of special pleading in the name of political science, for the standards of criticism have not been established. That is, criticism of ethics and values cannot be carried out in logical–empirical terms, and some persons deny the possibility of establishing any standards. Yet that seems not an adequate reason for ignoring the normative; rather it suggests that some effort should be made to provide the foundations for responsible normative criticism. The logician's inability to relate factual propositions and normative argument does not mean that there are no relations or connections whatever between facts and values. To the contrary, they are very intimately related. Values are assertions about facts, and factual evaluations of consequences have an enormous influence on value judgments. That is the reason why scientific data, and scientific standards of inquiry, have an important part to play in discussions of values and value judgments.

SCIENCE, POLITICS AND VALUES

It may seem odd to assert that science, or the scientific attitude, which was largely responsible for the near demise of normative philosophy in this century, may provide a means for dealing with philosophy of values, but that appears to be the case. The initial impact of scientific philosophy on moral theory or philosophy was harsh; from G. E.

Moore's *Principia Ethica* through the works of Ross and Ewing, A. J. Ayer, C. L. Stevenson, Stephen Toulmin and other followers of the English schools, traditional moral philosophy has been badly treated. By and large, there has been an inordinate concentration on the linguistic and logical aspects of ethical usage and not too much attention to the actual content of value propositions. Much of that criticism should prove useful when moral philosophy turns once again to the consideration of matters of substance—as it surely must do. However, the point here is to indicate the manner by which the substance of ethical criticism will be influenced by the sciences, not to discuss the methodology of ethics. The treatment is necessarily fragmentary and incomplete, for the task would require a full volume of its own. It is, however, possible to indicate some of the ways in which the spirit of scientific inquiry, and the hard data of scientific enterprise, can be useful in the pursuit of values.

The task of normative philosophy is to criticize and evaluate social and individual behavior, to give "good reasons," as Stephen Toulmin would have it, for or against particular modes of human behavior, though Toulmin's good reasons are perhaps too formal and restrictive. Some contemporary ethical theorists deny that this is possible, of course, though on different grounds, depending on the theory of ethics they accept. A. J. Ayer, in the first edition of *Language, Truth, and Logic,* at least, argued on analytic grounds that ethical statements are mere pseudo-statements. Others assert that ethical judgments are mere ejaculations; still others claim that ethical judgments are emotional responses with no basis in fact or logic. No one, significantly enough, denies altogether that ethical judgments are made, or that they have meaning. The argument is really confined to the logical properties of ethical propositions and the reasons used to support them—proof in the usual sense of the term being out of the question.

The construction of ethical or value judgments that will

be employed here, though not completely defined, runs as follows. Ethical judgments are primarily emotional responses, generated out of the human capacity to react imaginatively to situations, real or projected in the imagination, involving other human beings. There is involved, as C. L. Stevenson has pointed out, an evaluation of alternatives, a projection of consequences of choice that depends in some degree on factual data, open to change or correction on factual grounds. The emotional reaction may be primitive, but it is socially and intellectually conditioned; education plays an important part in value judgments. Further, as we acquire more knowledge, our capacity to trace the projected consequences of alternative courses of action improves. A good part of the argument over values depends in some measure on differences in the factual interpretation of the consequences of particular choices, not on the actual values.

Science impinges upon this construction at two vital points. First of all, the spirit of scientific inquiry, the honest, objective, and unbiased approach to the subject, is as much at home in normative criticism as in any other part of intellectual inquiry. In fact, it is in some ways even more important in ethics than in physics, for in the latter the results of thinking are usually open to criticism by others; in certain aspects of the process of making value judgments or normative criticisms, only the individual himself can say with certainty whether the public utterance accords with the subjective state. Second, science offers a means of broadening and strengthening the grounds on which criticism rests. That is, every normative judgment rests on a factual base and science can contribute heavily to the quality of the base. Before a proposal to sterilize the feeble-minded can be evaluated, for example, the consequences of the policy need to be explored as fully as the existing state of knowledge permits, and in this factual exploration science can help enormously.

NORMATIVE POLITICAL PHILOSOPHY

What I am proposing, then, as a significant part of the field of political science, is a normative political philosophy, basing its mode of thought on the criteria of science so far as it can, and taking its content from the corpus of scientific knowledge where that is possible. The method employed for this purpose has been described very well in Professor Michael Oakeshott's introduction to Hobbes' *Leviathan:*

> Political philosophy may be understood to be what occurs when this movement of reflection (on political life) takes a certain direction and achieves a certain level, its characteristic being the relation of political life, and the values and purposes pertaining to it, to the entire conception of the work that belongs to a civilization. That is to say, at all other levels of reflection on political life, we have before us the single world of political activity, and what we are interested in is the internal coherence of that world; but in political philosophy, we have in our minds that world and another world, and our endeavor is to explore the coherence of the two worlds together.[1]

The two worlds will not be complete, obviously, and the comparisons will be partial, but the general conception of a comparison of what is and what might be, or even what is and what is thought to be, seems to capture the essential core of what is involved in the criticism of individual and social values. In general terms, it begins with a statement of the human predicament and produces normative criticism as a solution to that predicament. It is the function of political science to state the terms of the political world man has built and the goal of the political philosopher to criticize that world in terms of another "world" that is an intellectual construct. Science can help establish the necessary properties of that world as against the contingent, and this is important since necessity is beyond criticism, and it can

[1] Thomas Hobbes, *Leviathan,* Michael Oakeshott (ed.) (Basil Blackwell, no date), p. ix.

contribute substantially to our total conception of what the human condition might be.

Normative criticism, or value criticism, can focus on two aspects of the total social process; both are essential. In the first case, criticism is directed against the consequences of adopting or maintaining a particular course of action or mode of behavior. These arguments will be relative to time and place, culture-centered, perhaps, and tentative. In the second case, criticism is directed, not against the behavior and its consequences, but against the line of reasoning, and the quality of reasoning by which a conclusion is reached. In this context, criticism is relative to the standards of reasoning that men have achieved at a given time, and the culture in which the argument is framed is irrelevant. The parallel here is to the standards of scientific argument, which are entirely unaffected by cultural factors; for example, there is only one physics, not an "Eastern" and a "Western" physics. This bifurcation of the grounds on which moral criticism can be based is essential, for it exposes an area in moral discussions that might otherwise remain hidden from view and it opens a way to reducing the importance of cultural relativism. Two moral arguments may lead to quite different conclusions in two different cultures, yet both can be considered "moral" if the quality of the reasoning is sound. After all, we can expect cultural distinctions to decline with time, if recent experience is any guide, and in the very long run their influence should be minimal. And even in the short run, concentration upon the mode of reasoning as well as the consequences of policy or behavior tends to reduce differences in values within a given culture (bearing in mind the fact that every large national state today is an amalgam of cultures and not a single culture). Consider the following illustrations:

1. A man arrives at a decision regarding the best behavior pattern to follow in a given situation quite honestly

and sincerely. His past experience is limited, therefore he omits consideration of certain aspects of the problem that others feel are decisive. Here the reasoning may be above reproach but the conclusion is open to attack because it is inadequately grounded. It is necessary to do one's best, but it is also the case that one's best may not be good enough.

2. A value is asserted dishonestly, for example, without conviction or belief. Again, the separation of reasoning from consequences is useful for the value may be admirable but the person asserting the value is not. The reasoning is as important as the conclusion, in value judgments as in explanation. The case of the "white lie," told to avoid unnecessary and useless pain or hardship, is covered by an extension of the same principle.

3. When values are asserted as a conditioned reflex, where they are consequences of indoctrination rather than judgment, the separation of value from reasoning again provides a basis for judging the ethical actor separately from the actions he performs or proposes that is most useful. In this case, there is no ethical content whatever to the action, unless it had been reasoned prior to being established as a habitual action.

Although this approach to value judgments may sound hopelessly idealistic, it is important to bear in mind that the purpose of the criteria is not to provide a basis for condemning a particular person for immorality. We are searching for grounds on which values, and the arguments on their behalf, can be criticized philosophically. The separation of the quality of the intellectual activity leading to the value judgment from the consequences of applying the value judgment to a given society exposes a facet of the total structure that makes for more effective and meaningful criticism. To omit either, or consider them together, would omit something from the criticism that ought to be included. Granted that a full examination of any particular case may require the work of several scholars, or even several generations, the nature of the critical function demands at least this much.

Further, there is implied in the argument that one fundamental aspect of value judgment can be controlled only by the person, for no man can really know the relation between asserted values and reasoning except in his own case. Perhaps for this reason, social philosophy has tended to concentrate on the social effects of given actions or policies rather than on the quality of thought that generates them. Here Kant seems more reasonable, and science more instructive. Criticism of reasoning is commonplace in science, as in philosophy. Indeed, "normative" criticism in science is largely confined to discussion of the quality of reasoning, the honesty, objectivity, and absence of bias in the reasoner. And it is at least possible that political philosophy could employ the same standards of thought. In matters of this sort, there must be some degree of mutual trust; when sincerity is in doubt, discussion ends, for there are no objective criteria to which final recourse can be had. To accept a trust, however, implies a responsibility to live up to the standards implied. Happily, the standards can be universalized. Honesty and truthfulness, self-conscious integrity of thought, freedom from bias, so far as is humanly possible; these are the common standards for mankind—not subject to cultural variation or national determination. There seems no good reason why the standard of reasoning employed in normative discussion could not be agreed. It would have to to be self-policing, but that is true of any academic undertaking anyhow.

The content of a value system, the actual rules of behavior proposed as a human standard, is much more amenable to cultural influence than the quality of the reasoning which leads the critic to support it. To put the point in another framework, the human predicament is differently defined by different cultures, and with good reason, for the predicament in which a particular man finds himself does depend very much on the culture in which he lives and the position he occupies in that culture. Again, it seems possible that by making use of scientific evidence it might be possible to standardize the conception of the human predicament in some measure, and bring it into line with the best evidence currently available to man. Indeed, using the standard already established, philosophers have a positive responsibility to do precisely this. The concept is central to ethical reasoning, it provides the base on which man seeks to explain himself to himself and to others, to relate himself and his aspirations to the world in which he finds himself. This elaborate and incomplete set of intellectual constructions is the prime source of taste and judgment, social goals, and personal ethics. It points the direction in which man searches for satisfaction and meaning in his own life and in his social environment. The task, in these terms, is not to seek to define man and his predicament *de novo* but to amend, alter, clarify, and redefine our conception of the human predicament so that it is compatible with the conception of man and the universe that science presently suggests. This would hardly provide a solution to all of the problems of ethics, of course, but it could very much narrow the gap between different ethical systems, suggest the points at which disagreement is genuine and fundamental, and eliminate inconsistencies—a task very much worth performing.

In the remainder of the chapter, I shall try to illustrate the consequences of making such amendments in terms of the Judaic–Christian tradition that is presently the dominant influence on the value systems accepted in the Western world. Some of the consequences are trivial, of course, though they are included for the sake of completeness. Others, however, strike at the very heart of the tradition and entail a major revision in our thinking about man and his values. In practice, scientific evidence suggests that the unfortunate dualism—which dominated philosophic speculation long before Descartes began to write—needs to be replaced by a simpler, unified construction. This suggestion is neither original nor surprising, perhaps, but the reasons on which it is based give it added significance.

SCIENCE AND VALUES: AN EXAMPLE

The Western conception of the human predicament, which is shared by most of the peoples who live around the borders of the North Atlantic, began to take shape in ancient Greece and in the Middle East in the first millenium B.C. Hellenic, Hebraic, Christian, and Roman thought mingled freely in the first centuries after the Roman Empire was established to produce the philosophic foundations that have dominated Western thought in the fields of philosophy, law, government, education, religion, and ethics. Until Renaissance and Reformation, the tradition was unchallenged, and in one sense the development of twentieth century philosophy can be viewed as an attempt to deal with those challenges—with Marxist determinism, with the statism implicit in Hegel and others, with the impact of Freud, and with advances in science. The slow rate of change that marked society down to modern times can be attributed to a number of factors, not least the dominant influence of Christianity and the Christian Church. There was, for example, no science worthy of the name for more than 1,500 years, and it is no accident that the period of Christian dominance over Western thought coincides with the nadir of scientific enterprise, and indeed with a period that was profoundly antiscientific in its outlook.

Since the sixteenth century, and perhaps slightly earlier, a second tradition appeared in Western thought, parallel to and often opposed by the older philosophic outlook. The rejuvenation of the physical sciences was followed by a period of intensive activity on a limited front, producing, in due course, an immense flood of new knowledge and new theoretical structures. Although those responsible for the rebirth of science were reluctant to admit the fact, the development of science generated a rift between the scientific outlook and the dominant philosophy that widened steadily. Here is the prime source of the "ethical dilemma" that so much concerns philosophers at present. The Enlightenment turned men to the study of their social and political institutions, using now the tools suggested by the sciences and not the philosophers. We need only look to eighteenth century France to see the extent to which social thinkers were influenced by the sciences and the consequences of that influence. Here were new grounds for separating the older tradition and the modern temper.

The two traditions

The fact is that contemporary Western thought comprises two major strands that are fundamentally incompatible, and the failure to rationalize them, understandable and perhaps inevitable, coupled with an unwillingness to abandon either of them, accounts for much of the confusion in contemporary discussions of value. The clash of the two systems of thought—the one older, theologically-oriented, and "traditional" and the other modern, scientific, empirical, logical, and antimetaphysical—was avoided, for the most part, by the use of a crude but highly effective device; that is, the conflict was simply ignored. This dualism in our tradition, perhaps more than any other single factor, has inhibited effective discussion of values in this century. The intellectual credentials of modern philosophy cannot be discredited; the emotional attachment to traditional philosophy will not be abandoned. Since reconciliation seems impossible, perhaps because of the extent of the vested interests involved, the result is a stalemate. In such stark terms, the position stands overstated; some persons have evaded the horns of the dilemma by choosing one horn. But as a generalization about the whole broad stream of modern thought, it contains the essentials of a most valuable proposition.

Consider the course of Western philosophy since Newton's day. The prestige of science has increased steadily, and the scientific outlook, however inaccurately interpreted, has become the accepted standard of legitimate intellectual enterprise. Yet, with a few notable exceptions, philosophers have sought either to retain a tradition in social, political, and ethical discourse that is fundamentally incompatible with the scientific outlook or they have abandoned philosophy altogether and concentrated their attention on method and technique, avoiding matters of substance. There has developed no middle ground on which the basic issues of thought—the fundamental terms of the human predicament—can be trashed out. For lack of criticism, contradictions pass without comment, sacred cows graze undisturbed in our intellectual pastures, and untenable propositions continue to be held in the face of all evidence. The influence of traditional philosophy is greatest in precisely those areas that define and shape the structure of our value system, for it is this region of human thought that was abandoned to tradition by the philosophic offspring of modern science. The result is a kind of philosophic schizophrenia in social values that is incurable so long as the basic contradictions remain untouched. Intellectual life remains compartmentalized, one segment guided by the precepts of a philosophic tradition whose guiding principles were laid down in another age and the other proceeds to inquire into the consequences of scientific advance in every area except the normative. We often deplore the fact that politics is still carried on in terms adapted from the needs of the seventeenth century; how much more significant is the use of standards of normative judgment that date to the very inception of Western civilization. The scientific outlook is a powerful force in the modern classroom, laboratory, or business, but it is usually left behind with the other paraphernalia of the vocation when the individual returns home to family and society and sets about enculturating his children.

This dualism needs to be abandoned. The separation on which it depends is artificial. Its consequences are wholly undesirable. Vocational, personal, and social judgments do not relate to three separate and distinct aspects of human life. They are generated by the same substructure of assumptions and beliefs about man, society, and the universe as any other intellectual construction. If the accumulated wisdom of science is a necessary guide and limit in one sphere of human thought, as it seems to be, then it should perform the same function in all others. Thinking that is qualitatively superior in science is also qualitatively superior in other areas of human thought.

Sources of conflict

How did Western man arrive at this impasse? It would be pleasant, perhaps, to ascribe our troubles to some fundamental error in the thought of the ancients, carried forward heedlessly through countless generations, but history does not permit that solace. To the contrary, the ancient Greeks took for granted the unity of all human knowledge, and they intermingled science, ethics, mathematics, philosophy, and politics in a manner that is somewhat bewildering to the modern mind—too accustomed, no doubt, to compartmentalization. The educated Greek of the classic era used his knowledge indiscriminately and often to very good effect. That is not to say that the Greeks were not frequently in error, nor that they did not fall into particularism and dogmatism. But, in other cases, the Greek thinker did his best with the material at hand, seeking a balanced outlook in which ideas were consonant and each bit of knowledge had its place. That best was at times remarkably good. The Greek conception of philosophy aimed at making life meaningful and this forced a reconciliation of man and universe, science and philosophy, ethics and politics. Any information was relevant, and if the quality of the data was poor by current standards, the attitude was admirable. The lucidity, undogmatic outlook, and endless inquisitiveness of the better Greek thinkers is still a model worth emulation.

When this order of Greek thought expired, philosophy and science dissolved a long-standing merger, leaving philosophy to marry religious mysticism and science to wander alone in a morass of technical ineptitude and contempt for observation—a direct inheritance from the Socratics. Not until modern times did the speculative temper reappear, and even today there is an unfortunate tendency for the philosopher interested in the sciences to play the impresario to the scientist's virtuosity, ignoring the task of reconciling the new ways of science and the philosophic tradition. How much was lost to Western thought when the Greeks foundered cannot be assessed quantitatively, perhaps, but the decline in quality is striking. The influence of the Sophists had turned the Greeks to self-examination by the fifth century B.C., and if a naïve and at times vulgar anthropomorphism sometimes appears, this can be pardoned as a reasonable peculiarity of an infant enterprise. The speed with which the initial limitations were transcended is a clear indication of the genius for speculation that was fermenting. In some writers, a concept of the human predicament that is surprisingly "modern" appeared very early—a speculative, tentative, informed, and critical outlook. Plato, after all, stands outside the main stream of Greek thought; Platonism was a temporary bend in the stream that returns to its previous course in the works of Aristotle. The achievements of later Greek science, as in the work of Aristarchus of Samos, were remarkably good considering the state of technology. Freed by political tragedy from the suffocating influence of classic Greek statism, Greek thought turned to individualism and became skeptical, logical, empirical, and critical of entrenched dogma; it sought to make man a free and responsible creature, living in an explicable universe—a "natural" part of that universe—subject to natural laws of development, free to forge his own goals and the means of attaining them. Relativistic, man-centered speculation dominated post-Aristotelian thought, though its achievements were overshadowed by the immense prestige of the older schools. When this tradition died, the world was not to see its equal in the West for more than fifteen centuries. I have perhaps overstated the case, but the general validity of the historical pattern is beyond dispute.

Obviously, Greek thought did not simply disappear from the earth when Rome assumed control of the Mediterranean; much was carried over into Roman thought where it merged with elements of Hebrew thinking through the work of men like Philo Judaeus, and with some few concepts taken from Roman experience to form the main stream of medieval philosophy. Unfortunately, as it now seems, it was not the lucid and critical thought of Greek science and empirical philosophy that survived, but the Platonic aberration. The supremacy of Christianity in the fifth century spelled the supremacy of Plato over Aristotle and the Hellenistics, of Orphism over skeptical rationalism. It was an intellectual catastrophe of unparalleled dimensions. The philosophy to which we are heir is rooted in the history of the early Hebrews and the mystic idealism of the divine Plato. It is an odd heritage indeed for a scientific-minded community. Fundamentally, it is Oriental, mystical, idealistic, opposed to empiricism, observation, individualism, and skepticism alike.

Medieval synthesis

The qualities of the tradition are perhaps best seen in normal medieval thought—the channel by which it reached the modern age. Medieval philosophy combined in a single structure a conception of man and the universe and a set of fixed relations between the two that lay beyond man's power to amend. The purpose of human existence was fixed; moral philosophy was subordinated to the attainment of that purpose. In modern idiom, Christianity offered man a "package deal" and the convert needs must take the whole package. Security and purpose, an understanding of the scheme of things, however sorry, were to be had at a price. Today, the price seems excessive, for what man gained in security and status he bought with the prerogative that the Greeks had prized most highly—freedom to determine his own goals and pursue them by means of his own choosing. Speculation was stifled and philosophy was channeled into a single, essentially nonproductive groove, particularly in regard to human social affairs and individual values. The exigencies of current politics may have led those who directed the new religion to concede political and social authoritarianism as a price for toleration, but when the Church acquired political authority and social power, still more authoritarianism followed as a necessary condition for the maintenance of that authority and power. The end of man was defined in absolutes and enforced by an authority which only the very few could contest. Even in the field of ethics there was an absolute loss, notwithstanding the fact that the Christian ethic doubtless mitigated some of the harshness of medieval barbarism; things may be done for the wrong reasons. The viable form of the Christian ethic proved to be the *Lex Talionis* of the Old Testament, rephrased as the doctrine of "doing unto others." The truly unique moral precept in early Christian thought, "turning the other cheek," proved more than ordinary men and women could enforce in their everyday affairs. It remained for the Reformation to produce the ultimate in the repression of human thought—the cruel and pitiless doctrine of predestination that emerged from the sixteenth century savagery of Calvin's Geneva—but the works of man had by then been condemned to insignificance by the ordering of religious-secular affairs bestowed on the Christian tradition by the enormously influential St. Augustine.

Western thought thus entered its modern phase with a concept of the human predicament that in effect denied that the predicament was, or could be, real, let alone amenable to human direction and control. Life was conceived as a purposeful sequence leading to a fixed goal in which man had little to do but obey. Human affairs were necessarily ordered according to the precepts of secular and religious authority, ordained by higher authority. The physical life of man was subordinated to a spiritual goal. The world of the senses was decried as a puzzle for fools, any attempt to pierce the veil shrouding the operation of the universe was an impiety. The final measure of things, the ultimate rationale of human conduct, was divorced from all human needs and aspirations save faith; it rested on a mystique.

The other-worldliness and indefinability of the medieval conception of the human predicament was a source of strength so long as men remained ignorant; in the contemporary world, it is a fatal weakness. It enabled man to ignore the conflict between scientific principles and philosophic principles for centuries, yet is is peculiarly amenable and vulnerable to objective criticism. The fact that science and religion continue to share the same bed is an indication of the extent to which a dual standard has been accepted by Western man. The rule of contradiction must first be waived.

The present situation

The modern rationalization of science and faith accrued gradually, largely, one suspects, because of the peculiar circumstances in which modern science arose. The early moderns—like Copernicus, Vesalius, or Galileo—worked in an intellectual atmosphere in which tradition reigned supreme and unchallenged, perhaps unchallengeable; the superiority of the spiritual was taken for granted. The scientists were, for the most part, religious men who were not at all interested in challenging accepted dogma even if it had been possible to do so; witness the timidity with which they approached publication. Bruno was perhaps an exception, and Bruno paid the price. As the slow trickle of scientific information began to appear, the conflict with received doctrines was passed over or denied. When this was no longer possible, the scientist, with or without pressure from authority, simply separated his working principles from the beliefs that governed his daily life and continued as before. The belief grew, doubtless in all sincerity, that men must deal with two separate, different, and equally valid orders of information. The notion survives in the mistaken argument that science has nothing to say about religion; what science has to say has an enormous impact on our beliefs about religion if it is taken seriously. Early modern scientists, however, did not face this dilemma. Science had little influence on philosophy, education, or ethics; these areas remained under the firm control of church and state; nothing in the position of the scientist forced him to face the dichotomy in his own thinking and the philosophers were little disposed to the attempt.

The "neutral" position of science with relation to human values and other philosophic considerations was made possible by a genuine, and for the scientist tenable, separation of life and work. Physical science is concerned with matters so far removed from philosophy and social values, superficially at least, that the scientist can easily ignore the relationship. The social scientist, on the other hand, cannot avoid making a decision about the matter for the intimate conjunction of the structure and function of human society and the value system on which it rests do not permit dualism. Private affairs and professional speculation merge in a single entity and a conflict of principles is not easily reconciled. In the first lavish outpouring of the Enlightenment, this dualism was attacked with a will and traditional philosophy was, in some areas at least, submerged in a rising tide of scientism. The older tradition survived the initial outburst, perhaps as much by virtue of the intemperance and ill-considered extremism of the attackers as by reason of any intrinsic merit in its arguments.

The problem remains untouched in essentials. The student of politics begins his training with a construction of the human predicament that would be perfectly comprehensible to the classic Greeks or to the medieval scholar. Yet in virtually every other respect, the modern scholar has at his command a mountain of information that removes him as far from the Greeks as they in their turn were removed from their stone-age ancestors. The tools needed to refurbish our foundations are available, and the task ought not to be delayed by emotional attachments, sentiment, or dogmatic adherence to dubious traditions. Science, it is said, has no tradition; it has only a present and a future. An excellent credo for political science.

What must be done, then, seems clear. The task now is to indicate the general outlines of the new construction of man's predicament that emerges when the enterprise is carried out. The basic principles can be established fairly clearly, though the specific applications of these principles may prove somewhat complex. What follows should not be considered more than a tentative initial step in the direction of a viable construct, and only the principal features of the structure are considered. Their importance for the specification and defense of human values will, I believe, be evident.

A RECONSTRUCTION

A scientific philosophy of politics, first of all, will be tentative, relativistic, and partial, eschewing elaborate system building (not empirical theoretical explanations, of course) intended to encompass the whole of humanity's past, present, and future. There is no room in science for the absolute, exclusive, and inflexible; men must learn to live with uncertainty and insecurity in a world that is only partially explicable. The attempt to comprehend the inscrutable or fathom the unknowable is doomed to failure; essentially, they are meaningless. Man must explain what he senses, rely upon his own products, and relate his goals to his capacities. The responsibility for the future, as for the present, is his and his alone. The measure of man is man, or more accurately, man's conception of himself; there can be no other standard.

This construction of the human predicament may be construed as a calamity or as a golden opportunity, depending upon the premises from which we begin. The traditionalist can argue that it is impossible for man to live a full life under these conditions, as it was once argued that morality is absolutely contingent on religious belief. Yet if man's future depends on himself, the search for social and ethical principles, for modes of argument that carry conviction for other men, is validated. When such questions are left for human decisions, the effort to decide leads to the kind of intellectual activity that seems wholly appropriate to man as we know him and wholly consonant with scientific inquiry. Who is to say that man must fail when failure cannot be defined? Man's search for goals may be endless but it is not purposeless; it simply finds its purpose in the moment, not in some final consummation. To argue that this is beyond human capacity is by implication a calumny on the species and an unwarranted derogation of human capacity, not justified by the evidence.

Metaphysics

A scientific political philosophy will be empirical and rational, in broad terms, and not metaphysical. In practice, this amounts to a denial of the supernatural and the extra-perceptive until such time as perceptive evidence justifies their acceptance. There is no need to deny subjectivity or to stultify the arts and all forms of literary expression. Indeed, there is no need to postulate a universe without order, but we must understand that the order is imposed by man and not intrinsic in the structure. Teleological doctrines can be abandoned. The universe may be stable and orderly but there is no sign of the Hegelian spirit, no prime mover, no Marxian inevitability. The universe is as it is, and it functions as it does because of its organization; all such matters are to be defined in terms of human perception. There can be no purpose beyond man's power to understand; what could it mean? In particular, the false analogy between the universe and man-made machines—like watches—should be avoided. Machines are characteristically orderly structures and designed to fulfill some purpose, hence an understanding of the machine does involve reference to that "purpose." Living as we do in a world of man-made things, orderly arrangement is a sign of human intelligence at work and if the analogy is inviting it is, nonetheless, untenable. Watches are made with a concept of telling time in mind; their essence precedes their existence, to follow Sartre, and the parts are fashioned to contribute to the predetermined whole. But nature begins with component parts that are not intended to fulfill some grand design; the grand designs are random aggregations or accumulations of primary elements and there is no need for purpose in the explanation of the scheme. Because oxidation and osmosis are essential to human life is no justification for the assertion that they exist to make human life possible.

Further, man is unable to assign greater importance to one portion of the universe than another, except in relation to his own wishes and desires, and there is no reason to suppose that man himself occupies any special status except in his own value schema. In relation to what is already known, man is trivial and may not even be unique, for it is statistically likely that conditions similar to those on earth recur many times in the whole universe. Man lives on a minor planet, orbiting around a very ordinary main-sequence star, located rather stodgily in the middle regions of a moderately large galaxy that is only one of millions already identified through optical telescopes. The life span of mankind, taken collectively, is finite and trivial. The star that provides the energy that makes life possible is doomed by its own processes; eventually it will lose the capacity to generate energy from its own contents and leave the earth either burned to a crisp or floating in space—barren, cold, and lifeless. The earth is a deathtrap and the possibility of escape, given the human life span and the immense distances involved, seems slight. Measured against the known universe, man is a puny thing indeed.

Teleology

The life of man that science discloses seems to enjoin the introduction of the concept of purpose. Processes run their course, the entropy of the system moves to maximum, and life, which apparently originated in the accidental concatenations of raw materials typified in the earth's primordial slime, will end. The universe will neither rejoice nor be sad; concern, like suffering, is a human quality. So far as the system is concerned, man can only say that it exists. He may, if he chooses, seek to decipher its operation in terms of his own invention and to make use of that knowledge to alter the system to suit his own desires or needs. That is a matter entirely for human decision. The operation of the system may result in the destruction of mankind or it may work to his benefit, and if we, as men, can feel compassion on the one hand or joy on the other, that does not alter the processes one whit. Conceptions like goals or ends, hopes or desires, optimism or despair, are relevant only to human life, so far as we know. Man is only being reasonable when he makes himself the center of his own universe and the standard for measuring the value of his own constructions. It is futile and primitive to rage or despair in the fact of facts, though it is also human to do so; it can only succeed in making life miserable. Man can only accept what he is able to learn and build his future hopes upon his learning, seeking to make life intrinsically meaningful in terms that carry conviction for other men. Doubtless this leads to some modified form of hedonism, but that is not a criticism. The prime task of philosophy, in this context, is to seek to define a satisfactory mode of life within the realm of the known and the possible. Deliverance is out of the question.

Clearly, we have made of man something far removed from the "image of the creator" envisioned in medieval philosophy. That simply cannot be helped. Man is a part of the universe, neither more or less important than any other part to anyone but himself. He is a living organism, a physicochemical system, to be investigated by the methods of physics and chemistry. He is also a psychic phenomenon capable of very complex interrelationships with the living and nonliving elements of his environment. He lives in close association with others of his kind and this aspect of human life makes politics, and normative philosophy, possible and necessary. From the strictly biological point of view, man is an integrated and orderly system, self-sustaining and self-regulating. But, as Herrick says:

> There is no evidence that these lawfully ordered processes are in any way influenced by extraneous, unnatural agencies.[2]

The chief source of confusion in the past has been the extent to which the universe appears as an orderly and well-regulated dynamic system. Yet this too is explicable in purely scientific terms:

[2] C. Judson Herrick, *The Evolution of Human Nature* (University of Texas Press, 1956), p. 42. Similarly, Ralph S. Lillie, *General Biology and Philosophy of Organism* (University of Chicago Press, 1945), especially pp. 30–31.

> What the course of evolution presents to us is essentially a picture of the method by which complex efficiently operating beings, such as are found in living things, do indeed arise without a contriver, without a pattern or guide. The method is . . . to move in all directions until some direction is found in which progress is possible. The method is to provide structures of every possible type, most of them so imperfect and inefficient that they disappear, but, among the rest, some that continue to exist, some that are efficient. These then serve as the foundation from which another great set of experiments are launched.[3]

Man, the most complex of all living things, thus emerges as the outcome of random associations and chance variations, interacting with an environment determined by natural processes.

Justification

If that seems unlikely, we need only examine the instrument used for the process. Man is the outcome of endless variations on a single theme, and the unity of the theme supplies the key to understanding the process. Life moves physically in an unbroken chain, an endless transmission of basic material from one generation to another. All that is needed to alter the end link in the chain is a random variation in an earlier linkage; that is supplied by genetic theory. Various elements in the human environment can induce such changes (radiation, for example); some prove viable and others do not. The failures are lost, the rest remain awaiting further changes. It is the element of continuity, the actual physical transmission of living material that makes possible the wondrous complexity of man. All that is needed is a single cell, originating in a living organism, separating from its source, and able to grow and differentiate, then reproduce. At the level of the single cell, modern genetics is believable.[4]

[3] H. S. Jennings, *The Universe and Life* (Yale University Press, 1933), pp. 64–65.

[4] E. N. Willmer, *Cytology and Evolution* (Academic Press, 1960); Carl

The changes that evolution requires are minute, physicochemical, and unpredictable. A living cell is an awesome affair for which the human imagination can scarcely contrive adequate adjectives. In a small space, less than a thousandth of an inch across, nature has produced an information and control center that is the finest example known of the rule of parsimony. The controlling mechanism is built into the chromosomes, a set of giant molecules, each a combination of other substances, systematically ordered. The most significant element in the structure is a material called DNA (deoxyribose nucleic acid) which is constructed of a sugar, four chemical bases, and phosphoric acid, arranged in a long spiral staircase to form a chromosome. There are hundreds or thousands of turns in the staircase, and countless individual elements in the combination. The patterns that can be created in a single molecule by varying construction, spacing, order, etc., are astronomical, and each variation produces a slightly different organism. The parts interact with each other, and with the whole, and the total structure is in some measure affected by the environment. The system is finite, theoretically capable of analysis, and logically quite capable of storing the information needed to direct human development.

The "mystery of life" that the poet has sung about for ages may disappear in this kaleidoscope of parts and pieces, but man's sense of amazement at himself need not follow. From a simple beginning, or perhaps from many parallel beginnings in the primeval ooze, the whole range of living things developed through what is essentially a single process. Sexual reproduction, which increases the possibility of variation enormously by combining cells from two dif-

---

P. Swanson, *The Cell* (Prentice-Hall, 1960); Bruce Wallace and Theodosius Dobzhansky, *Radiation, Genes, and Man* (Holt, 1959); David C. Ride, *Heredity and Human Nature* (Vantage Press, 1959); Dorothea Rudnick (ed.), *Cell, Organism, Milieu* (Ronald Press, 1959); and James A. Peters (ed.), *Classic Papers in Genetics* (Prentice-Hall, 1954), among others.

ferent lifelines, hastens the process. It is estimated, for example, that a single pair of human parents may produce any one of 20^{24} different genetic combinations in their offspring, each in some respects unique.[5] Indeed, the extent to which individual humans are genetically and morphologically unique is really surprising. Without entering once again into the pointless controversy over nature and nurture, the implications of this uniqueness are quite interesting. The brain is in every case physically and psychically different from all others, and the sensory apparatus differs widely in efficiency and sensitivity from one case to another. There are gross variations in irritability, capacity to respond emotionally, nutritional needs, metabolism, and so on. All this adds up to a wholly satisfactory (for the individualist) conception of men who live unique lives, who live in unique psychic worlds, who can, imperfectly perhaps, share what they choose to share. Here is a true "mystery" of life to be explored, and perhaps to be gloried in.

Reprise

The human predicament that emerges in the scientific prism is in many respects blurred and indistinct, and there are endless questions for further exploration and discussion. The main outlines seem clear. Conscious man, an organism with wide perceptive powers, able to respond to others, to think, to create, to give joy and sorrow to others and to himself, is the beginning. The system is "open" and capable of endless creative alteration in response to self-stimulation and external environment. Even if we grant man a desire to reduce himself to a set of axioms and the laws of logic, it is beyond his power to succeed. We are, each of us, immense reservoirs of untapped potential, and no man can say

[5] John L. Fuller and W. Robert Thompson, *Behavior Genetics* (John Wiley, 1960), p. 15. This excellent book offers some very interesting information about the relationship between genetic structure and human behavior.

with any certainty what man in general, or man in particular, may do or become. There is enough in man, honestly faced, to satisfy the desires of anyone who does not seek to become a god among men.

Does the scientific view of man as an organism endowed with a fantastic logical control apparatus imply a deterministic world in which man is not "free"? If by "free will" or "free choice" is meant that man can in some manner transcend the limits imposed by his own structure and experience, then there is no free choice for man; that would be impossible by definition. But that is not really the right question, and perhaps it is not a question at all. Man is not a cold and quiescent system fixed for all time; he is a dynamic structure able to enlarge his own experience, build and tear down what has been experienced. Behavior produces an ever-changing pattern of experience, and experience directs choice. Two points stand out: first, the machinery may be similar for all men, but the content of the machinery is dynamic and expanding; second, there is not one man but many men, and their interrelationships, particularly through the complex symbolism of language, introduce a major stimulus to expansion of experience. Man's ability to think, and to interact with others, produces a range of possibilities that is not even theoretically determinable. The universe may be deterministic, in the sense that experience determines behavior, but so long as past experience does not determine future knowledge, and it does not, then behavior in the future is contingent on the future and not on the present, and in that sense remains, and must remain, indeterminate.

The universe as it stands imposes certain basic demands on mankind, but few of its demands can be construed as necessities. In modern times, the needs of brute survival are already solved, and we hold in our hands the machinery needed to spread the benefits of civilization to all men. The imperatives that drive men beyond brute satisfaction are manufactured by men, not derived from the nature of the universe. The need for goals is obvious, and the search for adequate goals, and standards for determining their adequacy, justifies philosophy. The search must begin with man, who is both author and subject of his purposes. Men, as Professor Oakeshott has said, ". . . sail a boundless and bottomless sea; there is neither harbour for shelter nor floor for anchorage, neither starting place nor appointed destination." Perhaps we can agree with Oakeshott that the nature of the enterprise is to remain afloat and that the best guide to a seaman is found in the tradition of sailors; perhaps we may feel that ports should be charted, even though they prove to be mist on the horizon. In either case, the rules of sailing are human contrivances, and the course must be set by human hands. Certain rules are doubtless necessary to ensure survival and others to make life aboard ship bearable. But the means available for solving such problems are varied and there is no deterministic force to guide men along the right path; only experience, painful or happy, can serve as a guide. The peculiar combination of an absolute need to act, and a minimum of guiding principles for action, is an essential quality of the human predicament. Men must seek to combine the factors that make them men, and the factors that make them social creatures, in a manner that will make life satisfying. It is a formidable task.

Science alone cannot solve such problems. What it can do is eliminate some of the restrictions that might otherwise complicate the task and, through technology, place in human hands the tools that make physical control over the environment a reasonable goal. It can set man free to explore where he will, and encourage him to widen his outlook and broaden his experience. No line of speculation can be condemned on scientific grounds as hopeless, blasphemous, or irreverent. No generation can bind its successors to sterile discussion of stipulated questions so long as the spirit of scientific inquiry is maintained. And in the absence of external authority directing human affairs, science can aid man in his exertions. This need not lead to the primitive anarchy of Hobbes's state of nature, or to some utopian heaven in which everything is for the best. The basic problems of political life are timeless and insoluble, each generation must attack them self-consciously and vigorously, using the best means at hand. Man can do no more, and no less.

BIBLIOGRAPHICAL NOTE

General works: Luther J. Binkley, *Contemporary Ethical Theories* (Citadel Press, 1961); C. D. Broad, *Five Types of Ethical Theory* (Littlefield, Adams, 1959); William K. Frankena, *Ethics* (Prentice–Hall, 1963); Harry K. Girvetz (ed.), *Contemporary Moral Issues* (Wadsworth, 1963); Georgia Harkness, *The Sources of Western Morality* (Charles Scribners Sons, 1954); John Hospers, *Human Conduct: An Introduction to the Problems of Ethics* (Harcourt, Brace, and World, 1961); A. I. Melden, *Ethical Theories* (Prentice–Hall, 1955); P. Nowell-Smith, *Ethics* (Penguin, 1954); D. M. MacKinnon, *A Study in Ethical Theory* (Collier, 1961); Stephen C. Pepper, *Ethics* (Appleton-Century-Crofts, 1960); Wilfred Sellars and John Hospers (eds.), *Readings in Ethical Theory* (Appleton-Century-Crofts, 1952).

More specialized works: A. J. Ayer, *Language, Truth, and Logic* (Dover Books, no date, first published in 1935); F. H. Bradley, *Ethical Studies* (Liberal Arts Press, 1951); E. M. Adams, *Ethical Naturalism and the Modern World View* (University of North Carolina Press, 1960); E. F. Carritt, *Ethical and Political Thinking* (Oxford University Press, 1947) and *Morals and Politics* (Oxford University Press, 1935); John Dewey, *Theory of Valuation*, IEUS, Vol. II, No. 4 (University of Chicago Press, 1939); John Dewey and James H. Tufts, *Ethics* (Henry Holt, 1936); Abraham Edel, *Method in Ethical Theory* (Bobbs-Merrill, 1963); A. C. Ewing, *The Definition of Good* (Routledge and Kegan Paul, 1947) and *Second Thoughts in Moral Philosophy* (Routledge and Kegan Paul, 1947); R. M. Hare, *Freedom and Reason* (Oxford University Press, 1963) and *The Language of Morals* (Oxford University Press, 1964);

David Hume, *An Inquiry Concerning the Principles of Morals* (Liberal Arts Press, 1957); Henry Hazlitt, *The Foundations of Morality* (Van Nostrand, 1964); Immanuel Kant, *Lectures on Ethics* (Harper, 1963); Henry Margenau, *Ethics and Science* (Van Nostrand, 1964); Bernard Mayo, *Ethics and the Moral Life* (Macmillan, 1958); A. I. Melden, *Rights and Right Conduct* (Basil Blackwell, 1959); G. E. Moore, *Principia Ethica* (Cambridge University Press, 1960); Arthur N. Prior, *Logic and the Basis of Ethics* (Oxford University Press, 1949); D. Daiches Raphael, *Moral Judgment* (Allen and Unwin, 1955); Bertrand Russell, *Human Society in Ethics and Politics* (Simon and Schuster, 1955); Moritz Schlick, *Problems of Ethics,* trans. Davin Rynin (Dover, 1962); Benedict Spinoza, *Ethics* (Hafner, 1949); W. T. Stace, *The Concept of Morals* (Macmillan, 1962); Charles L. Stevenson, *Ethics and Language* (Yale University Press, 1944) and *Facts and Values* (Yale University Press, 1963); Stephen Toulmin, *The Place of Reason in Ethics* (Cambridge University Press, 1960); C. H. Waddington, *The Ethical Animal* (Allen and Unwin, 1960); T. D. Weldon, *States and Morals* (John Murray, 1946); Sidney Zink, *The Concepts of Ethics* (St. Martin's Press, 1962).

From among these books, I believe that A. J. Ayer, G. E. Moore, Stephen Toulmin, C. L. Stevenson, Hume, Spinoza, Prior, and Waddington were most useful. Abraham Edel's work on method is invaluable, as is Prior's short study of logic and ethics. Toulmin's work is stimulating, but he uses a conception of reason that is isomorphic to logic, and this limits the value of his conclusion. Stevenson's separation of the factual and ethical components in values is classic. Waddington's book, and the recent work by Margenau, are most germane to what is done here because both men approach ethics from the scientist's point of view.

CHAPTER NINE

CONCLUSIONS

THE physical sciences and the philosophy of science are mines of information for the political scientist who takes the time to explore them. Both methodologically and substantially, science has much to offer the student of politics. The patterns of explanation, methods, techniques, and procedures, as well as the general attitude or approach to the subject matter, can all be used, with suitable safeguards, in political studies. And the information that science has accumulated has considerable value for the student of human behavior, particularly as it affects the framework in which political phenomena are evaluated and appraised. A brief review of the principal findings of the study, and some of the inferences that may be drawn from them, may serve to round out the discussion and perhaps clarify some of its objects.

The first point to be made, and it cannot be repeated too often, is that political scientists cannot abdicate their own discipline in the name of science, or any other discipline. The problems of politics have their own intrinsic interest, and they can be studied, however imperfectly. It would be pointless to tighten the methodological standards of the discipline at the expense of meaningful content; it would be unreasonable to become scientists at a price of ceasing to be political scientists. It is both desirable and necessary that some political scientists concentrate on methodological questions while others search for new data, classify, construct theories, and carry out the other functions of explanation; and it is essential that some attention be given to reasoned criticism of political values. So long as no one insists that one particular aspect of political study is both a necessary and a sufficient definition of the enterprise, only good can come from the division of labor. No phase of the discipline is logically prior or intrinsically superior to the others. The nature of political science is determined by the nature of politics, and not the converse.

It is also clear that political science is not, and is not likely to become, a science in the same sense as physics or chemistry, or even biology. The point is trite, but it sets a limit to ambition and clarifies the methodological task. Politics may aspire to follow the sciences where it can, but within limits set by its own needs, materials, and aspirations. Science and politics differ in certain fundamental ways, and if the differences can in principle be eliminated, they are presently beyond our power to control. The gulf that separates the two areas is not so wide as some might think, of course, but neither is it so narrow that it can easily be bridged. The common goal is adequate explanation, but the meaning of the term depends on the subject matter to which it is applied, and it is for political scientists to decide what constitutes an adequate goal, or a suitable explanation, for political science.

In general, then, emulation of scientists is highly desirable wherever it is possible. Moderate empiricism, sound analytic techniques, careful attention to terminology, self-conscious attention to logical inference, quantification, and the use of scientific data, are all strongly commended to the attention of political scientists. Judicious application of scientific criteria in these areas would do much to improve the quality of the work in politics. But the accomplishments of science ought not to be exaggerated, lest we expect too much of ourselves, and of the scientists. In science, as in any other study, much is left by the wayside, and formal procedures extend only so far, leaving much that is inexplicable. Method and technique tend to fail at precisely the point where the difficulty is greatest, leaving adequate scope for individual effort.

In this context, particular importance should be attached to the informal, and perhaps intangible, aspects of scientific inquiry. The attitude of mind that characterizes the physical scientist at his best is especially worthy of emulation. The attitude is not, perhaps, so well defined as scientific technique or formal logic, but it is far more meaningful and useful than any alleged "scientific method." The apparatus of science, it should be remembered, is a consequence of the attitude of mind, and not the converse. The flexibility of outlook, freedom from dogma, eclecticism, skepticism, imagination, speculativeness, relativistic attitude of mind, and intellectual boldness and daring found in the great scientists are wholly admirable. Science is truly an abbatoir for sacred cows, while in politics the pastures are full of them, including many strayed from the economic and religious herds. The merciless application of a scientific sledgehammer to some vulnerable portion of the anatomy of these beasts would be a great service to humanity. Men have made political and social fetishes out of all sorts of logical absurdities and the need for a crusty iconoclasm toward conceptual framework, procedural rules, and inherited body of knowledge alike could hardly be greater. The scientific outlook would be a useful remedy for the subjectivity, emotionalism, and imprecision that characterizes so much of the political literature. When every proposition must stand on its own feet and cannot be justified by some *ad hominem* presumption that defines status in terms of person, the discipline might rid itself of its intellectual barnacles and perhaps some of its intellectual leeches as well.

Science is acutely conscious of the ongoing quality of its life. Each new generation produces new problems, and new solutions to old problems. Viewpoints change, if not for the better, at least for the greater satisfaction of those who hold them. One of the peculiarities of political society is that the voice of authority is usually the voice of a generation past its prime. One need not advocate forcible suppression of the aged, or the rather harsh solution to the problem adopted by the Eskimo, but there is a genuine need to examine new proposals on their merits rather than in terms of how well they accord with the beliefs of generations soon to expire. Many of the techniques and methods, the points of view, and even the personnel employed in political science have passed their prime and are no longer useful. Past performance, whether a concept or person, is no guarantee of current usefulness, as every baseball manager knows and the editor of every learned journal ought to know but often does not. The need to eliminate what is no longer useful and what may be an impediment, is often as great as the need to add new things.

The elimination of the mystical, the metaphysical, the meaningless, and the maximization of the use of empirical data in political theory is well within the range of possibility. *Homo mensura,* man is the measure of all things—so said Protagoras some 2,500 years ago—and so it still remains. The search for purpose and value begins with man himself, in the here and now. Of course, history has its function in the inquiry, for if history teaches us nothing it may, nevertheless, illuminate the route by which man arrived at his present state—codify his experiences, as it were. This may appear to elevate expediency into a fundamental principle of politics, and there is a sense in which this is truly the case, but the implied censure is not justified. Any discipline that rejects metaphysical teleology can only seek to calculate the outcome of particular modes of behavior as fully as knowledge permits, realizing that its calculations are necessarily incomplete, and choose from among them what appears at the moment as the most desirable outcome—"desirable" being defined by the accepted value system. Man must, in this sense, determine what is "expedient" in the light of the present. But that need not mean the end of reasoned judgment; man is simply forced to act under conditions where reasoned judgment is incomplete. So is science, but the consequences are less readily apparent.

Finally, it seems clear that political scientists could make much wider use of the data of the physical sciences than is presently the case. The lack of facilities for interdisciplinary study is deplorable, and the degree candidate seldom has time or opportunity to gain any real competence outside the narrow perimeter of his special interest. Nor is there a journal or association that can encourage this line of development. Whether or not it would be possible to organize a course of study that would lead to the kind of nonspecialized expertise in subjects related to political science is hard to say—it would be a formidable undertaking. But every academic institution could examine its own facilities with an eye to broadening the science background of social science majors, not simply by offering them watered-down survey courses in general science subjects, but by producing specialized courses that would concentrate on questions of interest to social science majors; for example, neurology and physiology, genetics, behavior genetics, major theories in physics and cosmology, and so on. Ideally, the social scientist should learn about the work being done in science at the highest levels, but that is probably administratively, hence, academically, impossible.

Having underlined, perhaps to the point of tediousness, what political science can learn from the sciences, it is time to turn about and look at some of the less desirable consequences of modern science—at some things to be avoided or minimized. For science reaches far deeper into the intellectual structure of the times than matters of methodology, epistemology, and method; its influence transcends the pedagogic questions we have been discussing. Science, surely, tends to generate its own standards of legitimacy and its own attitudes of mind, and if some of them are admirable, others can become mere prejudices. Immense prestige means power, and power implies the capacity to do harm as well as good, not in the trite sense that atomic weapons can cause immense physical damage but in the more fundamental sense in which it is possible for science to alter the basic structure of human thought and action, inhibiting some lines of behavior and encouraging others, on grounds that may seem irrelevant to the inhibitions and encouragements from the political scientist's point of view. Indeed, science may do such things in ignorance, or in the belief that it is benefiting mankind; such are the consequences of power. Science, when all is said and done, is only a human construction, a tool to be criticized like any other instrument—on social grounds as well as scientific grounds—whether or not the criticism is acceptable to the scientist. Man is entitled to object to a world in which science reigns supreme on grounds that are fundamentally unscientific and have his objections heard with respect. Science, in other words, can very easily become a sacred cow, and perhaps the most dangerous specimen of that bovine family ever to appear on earth.

Some of the common misconstructions of science seem to tend in this direction. Consider the belief that there are only two possible approaches to inquiry—the scientific, and the antiscientific. This conception is understandable, but it is erroneous and can be dangerous. There is ample room for a nonscientific outlook, in political science and elsewhere, and if an antiscientific attitude is foolish, an unscientific attitude is not. There are good reasons for human behavior that are beyond scientific justification, and an excessive predilection for science can too easily lead to the view that anything that is not scientific should be ignored.

Yet science has nothing to say about values, qua science, or about a great many other things that matter enormously in politics, and in human life generally—values, esthetics, the passions and purposes that infuse men's lives and give them meaning. Bentham's conclusion that pushpin is as good as poetry may be logically sound—given his premises—and scientifically acceptable, but it is emotionally and intellectually arid and not worthy of serious regard. No logical examination can duplicate the esthetic satisfaction to be obtained from great art. And if social theorists are at times curiously evasive on this point, the political scientist is still entitled to give serious attention to the "human" properties of his subject matter. Accuracy at the price of grace, style, and wit might be an expensive luxury. The scientifically inclined are prone, like other men, to take themselves too seriously at times, confusing dry and pedantic prose with accuracy and failing to realize the value of style. At times they lack taste.

More serious still, it appears that the influence of current trends in science is to separate still further, through specialization, the general reader and the expert. C. P. Snow's comments on the subject were widely read, duly lamented, and forgotten. The trend has appeared already in social science. Formidable mathematical structures are needed to understand the work being done at the frontiers (horrid phrase) of economics. The average treatise in behavioral science seems to require doctoral-level competence in statistics. Sociologists like Talcott Parsons produce formal systems that require endless and perhaps, wasted, hours of deciphering before their meaning, or lack of it, becomes clear. One hesitates, in this day and age, to assert that a discipline ought to stay in touch with reality, or to follow the Ford Foundation into support for "practical" research, yet it should be said that it is hard to see how the manipulation of abstract and formal models, or complex syntactical aggregates, is related to the accumulation of knowledge.

In fact, they seem only another contribution to methodology. All theory should explain observable fact, and a theory that cannot be explained in ordinary language is prima facie open to suspicion, particularly in political science. Immensely complicated statistical tables are quite meaningless until they are interpreted, and those who take the time to compile them should do us the courtesy of telling us what, if anything, they mean. Perhaps it is significant that the great theorists of the past—scientific, economic, or political—have been eminently readable. Einstein's own popular explanation of his theory remains the best available; Keynes was a magnificent stylist, and a pleasure to read; Schrödinger and Heisenberg, or Max Born, write beautifully and what they are saying is readily understood. What possible excuse is there for unintelligible jargon in political science? Perhaps Hume and Russell should be required reading for everyone? There may be no logical grounds for asserting communicability as an ideal, yet common sense recommends it and the principle of parsimony adds its support. Too often, overcomplexity seems, on close examination, only a camouflage for ineptness.

Science has its own little snobberies and, taken seriously, they can be a serious impediment to original work. After all, to be scientific means, in strict terms, to be intolerant and prejudiced—from the poet's point of view, at least. The general public happens to approve of the set of prejudices that science deploys, perhaps because it need not live with them, but prejudices they remain. What is to be said, for example, of the disapproving frowns conferred by the science-minded on those who fail to work along approved lines? The charge that one is "academically unsound" is all too often no more than the assertion that the canons of scientific "detachment" have been ignored—even when they are not applicable to the enterprise. The example of C. Wright Mills springs to mind, or Bertrand Russell, or Veblen; sound or not, such writers are worth reading. Must we all play Pangloss to the establishment? Are we to view scientific murder with scientific detachment? Survey what Churchill somewhere called "the immense sum of human misery" without a twinge of sympathy? Because science cannot condemn genocide, is the political scientist to remain neutral on the subject? Surely, in political science perhaps more than elsewhere, there are stupidities to be exposed, icons to be shattered, injustices to be damned, evils to be remedied, waste to be deplored, and myths to be exploded? If the academician repudiates all responsibility in such matters, especially in areas where his competence extends far beyond that of the man in the street, or the man in Congress, where on earth can responsibility lie? Knowledge always carries responsibility. One cannot stand aside and allow a child to harm itself out of ignorance when the means of preventing the mishap are at hand. This is not a scientific question, but a human problem, and it must be answered.

Science inhibits the speculative temper, oddly enough, for it is a fact that in an age where science reigns supreme we have reached the nadir of social and philosophical speculation. As Daniel Bell notes in the *End of Ideology,* men have failed to indulge very heavily in criticism or speculation in recent decades; others have noted the decline of speculative philosophy and sociology. The reason that suggests itself is that excessive caution, enjoined by some knowledge of scientific standards of validity, has so raised the standards of acceptable argument that no one is prepared to argue until his position no longer requires argument. One can as easily be exposed to ridicule through speculation as through personal peculiarities of dress or behavior, these days at least, yet speculation has its values, ill informed and partial though it may be. Political science is not responsible for charting the future course of mankind, and it is only pompous and pretentious to act as if this were the case. Mistaken arguments and speculative errors have been a fruitful source of new knowledge in every field, not least the sciences. That a proposition is speculative means that it should be handled with care, not discarded without a glance. The merits of a proposition, not its origins, parentage, or logical classification, are our prime concern.

In broad terms, the influence of science is generally conservative and limiting, its general strategy has been to analyze, restrict, classify, and confine. Yet the exceptional scientist has never been bound by any rules of this sort. And for political science, conservatism could be a profound error in tactics, in teaching as well as research and theorizing. Problems are solved by direct attack, and not by limiting beforehand the approach to be used against them. Rigid insistence on accepted patterns of analysis may be valuable training, but it is only training; it may not be the best way to work with real problems. Academic inquiry is not a Marine Corps drill. Some room must be left for the flights of fancy of the young and erratic, and the not so young; there is a place for disputatiousness and for the "maverick." Let them not be stifled in the name of science, or in any other name.

When we have been asked of a particular assertion whether it is clear, unambiguous, and logically related to other propositions, we have not yet exhausted its possibilities, and in political science we may not yet have come to its real significance. There are emotional connotations to consider, for emotions play a vital role in human development, and strong emotional response or commitment is often a precursor of accomplishment—Freud or Marx will serve nicely as examples. Sometimes it appears that the twentieth century ought rightly to be labeled the century of emotional apathy; the curious, detached attitude of the young at the mid-century mark can readily be observed. The "bored" generation is with us, it seems. The great ethical systems of the past have lost some of their appeal and religion has moved from formalism and ritual to narrowing the gap between the religious life and the everyday occurrence—and not in the early Christian sense either. The great political systems have proved inadequate. Democracy, divorced from an eighteenth century conception of liberty to which it was never really akin, has become almost a meaningless symbol. Democratic socialism seems to have failed in Europe and communism has been inundated in a welter of international antagonisms. Mankind is left with a sterile and menacing nationalism as a basis for social cohesion. Science is not, of course, responsible for this condition, and science can have no solution to it. Yet if dogmatic ideology and rabid partisanship are both to be replaced, someone must formulate the replacement. That does not mean that political scientists ought to rush out and throw themselves into the mainstream of current politics to sink or swim. In fact, that is neither wise nor desirable, as a general principle; it inhibits the very freedom of thought and action that academic life is intended to promote and needs to survive. But political science can be aware of the urgent problems of the day, and express its feeling firmly so long as the position is self-consciously taken and honestly defended. If politics could be reduced to a laboratory science, which happily it cannot, what a frightful bore it would become.

Political science must, then, maintain some willingness to search for values in a world that appears as our own creation, and for means of supporting those values against all comers. The essential factor is criticism, whether it appears as invective, satire, or even sheer rudeness. The appalling lack of satire in contemporary life has often been noted; it is no accident. Profound and biting criticism begins with values strongly held and they are lacking. Yet men respond overwhelmingly when genuine satire appears, and therein lies the best hope for the future. One of the best programs to appear on British television in years, and one of the most popular, was a vicious and biting satire on contemporary life; transferred to the United States it was an instantaneous success. It was transformed immediately from satire into entertainment.

It is possible, of course, that men have been misled by the constant harping upon the "ethical dilemma" that is so much a part of contemporary writing. It is, after all, only a logician's dilemma, and they are not ordinary folk. Man can, after all, live without science or technology, logicians or political scientists. Their absence may shorten the life span, render life itself risky, squalid, and brutal, but the human potential remains so long as the species survives unimpaired. The absence of values, on the other hand, makes society impossible and culture meaningless. A man who lives his life without the benefit of modern science may be pitied, but he cannot be scorned; the man whose life is untouched by love or appreciation of beauty, by the power of art or the joys and splendors of friendship, unappreciative of the splendors of human achievement, he is indeed less than a man. We need to keep our perspective in these matters.

Yet values alone are not enough—that is the trouble with dogma. Men need values they can defend, without apology, and without resorting to some puerile nonsense like "I like it and therefore it is good for me." Here is task enough for social philosophers in any age. We need to learn more about what values are possible, how they are argued, where they are derived, and what functions they perform. No man who has learned to value music and art can believe that all other men, given an opportunity to make these things a part of their lives, could fail to love and respect them too. He may be wrong, of course, but the evidence is not convincing. There will be differences in taste, but taste is not thereby eliminated.

If social values are argued, widely and fiercely and honestly, we will have done our best. The laws of society are only values imposed on human behavior; social institutions are devices for enforcing other values upon us; social mores are values that particular groups accept. The consequences of value judgments cannot be inferred from the procedures by which they are chosen, nor can they be validated by reference to the constitutional code in which they happen to find root. Values must be studied as values, not scientifically, and yet scientifically. Life without values has no meaning, and science can contribute only indirectly. Here, in the last analysis, is the chief reason why the omnipotence of science in human life is impossible—and undesirable.

INDEX OF NAMES

INDEX OF SUBJECTS

This book has been set in 11 point Caledonia, leaded 2 points, and 10 point Caledonia, leaded 1 point. Chapter numbers are in 10 point News Gothic Condensed Bold caps; chapter titles are in 18 point News Gothic Condensed caps. The size of the type page is 24 by 41½ picas.